HIGH ROAD TO COMMAND

HIGH ROAD
TO COMMAND

* * * *

The Diaries of
Major-General Sir Edmund Ironside
1920–1922

EDITED BY

LORD IRONSIDE

LEO COOPER · LONDON

First published in Great Britain 1972 by
LEO COOPER LTD
196 Shaftesbury Avenue
London WC1

Copyright © 1972 Lord Ironside

ISBN 0 85052 077 0

Printed in Great Britain by
Billing & Sons Limited
Guildford and London

CONTENTS

MAPS

ILLUSTRATIONS

Introduction

This book tells of my father's adventures as a Major-General on his tours of duty across Europe and the Middle East and on to Persia between 1920 and 1922. It is a sequel to *Archangel 1918-19* in which he describes his campaign in North Russia.

At the time the people of the defeated empires and nations were learning to adjust to new leaders and to the new frontiers given to them by the Allies. The major problem facing the Supreme Allied Council in its reconstruction of the European States was not so much reparations or division of soil and spoil as containment of the new menace of Bolshevism. The Council was already involved in the internal politics of Russia through the military landings at Archangel and Murmansk, but the nature and extent of the menace and the determination of the Bolshevik leaders was not fully recognized, and in any case the collective will of the Allies was not strong enough to inspire another costly and cohesive effort. The policy was to ignore and forget.

Faced with urgent economies at home, public opinion in Britain was strongly opposed to continued expenditure on military forces stationed abroad. But British interests were at stake and if these were to be protected hurried withdrawal was impossible. The struggle lingered on, and while enthusiasm for the fight dwindled away our forces overseas became less and less well equipped to deal effectively with armed attack by rebel formations.

At home my father felt frustrated and impatient, but abroad he found the opportunity for that independent fighting command on which he thrived. He had achieved the enviable position of being the youngest Major-General in the Army, had received a knighthood at the age of thirty-nine and was generally acknowledged as being an outstanding commander. Unfortunately there were more major-generals than jobs for them, and those without an appointment had to stay at home on half-pay while they waited in forced semi-retirement for up to two years or more for the list to move. Because of my father's age he had been told that he could conceivably wait as much as four years before being offered anything and regulations did not allow officers on half-pay to accept other employment if they wished to remain eligible for further appointment. He was determined not to idle his time away and continued with his foreign language studies, and through his many friends kept in touch with events. So wide was his reputation that he had many sympathizers and supporters in high places, and it is difficult to imagine now, in spite of the swollen major-general's list, that he would have been allowed to retire voluntarily, or even forced to do so, without first being offered some active appointment in order to retain his services for the Army.

As it turned out, temporary appointments kept him actively employed until he was offered in 1922 what was probably regarded as the greatest prize of all for a major-general, the Command of the Staff College, an appointment which lasted for four years.

The story of these temporary appointments was almost completed in August, 1959, the month before he died. Fortunately I was able to piece together the manuscript, when I went through his papers, and I decided that as soon as I had the time I would complete the story as he had planned and offer it for publication myself. Because of the completeness of the original text very little alteration has been necessary. But where I have thought it desirable to make changes or additions I have done these with full reference to my father's diaries. This task has of course been made easier by having discussed the layout of the book many times with him and knowing the background.

The first episode recounts a Foreign Office mission to Hungary to supervise the withdrawal of Roumanian troops. The presence of an imposing British General who could speak Magyar was calculated to speed up the operation and give effective backing to the Allied Council's directives. Backed with personal authority from Lord Curzon and Admiral Horthy, the Regent of Hungary, he travelled through devastated Europe unarmed, in uniform, with two cars, an ADC and two drivers without difficulty. On the return trip a day was spent at the French battlefields, studying the Passchendaele Ridge from the German point of view with the, countryside still devastated beyond recognition, even though three years had passed since the famous attack. This was the scene of the successful exploit by the 4th Canadian Division which was so close to his heart, and I feel that his description of the Passchendaele attack is inadequate without some account of his life with that Division from its foundation in England to the Vimy Ridge attack immediately before Passchendaele. I have therefore included this, drawing on the résumé of the war which appears in his diaries.

The second episode took him East again, this time to Anatolia, where Greek faced Turk after the break-up of the Turkish Empire and where the Supreme Allied Council were faced with the prospect of having the Treaty of Sèvres thrown back in their faces through failure to present a united stand on its enforcement. Hardly was the ink dry on the paper before the Greeks had persuaded the Allies that with military backing their forces would move into Smyrna, and by their presence establish their rights within the newly-defined frontiers. The Allied Council grasped at this opportunity to extricate themselves from their predicament and backed the Greeks, however unpalatable this might have appeared to the defeated Turks. The fact that my father travelled openly in uniform on the Orient Express to Constantinople through the disputed areas without being molested by either Greek or Turk shows how confused the situation was at the time. Clearly everybody along the route was aware of the arrival of a British General and were therefore in no doubt that some military action was intended. The fact that there was no reaction could be put down to many things—war weariness, lack of leadership and economic depression.

Having arrived at Constantinople he took command of the Ismid force and was given the task of clearing the Ismid Peninsula so that it could be handed over to a Greek Commander. The handover came sooner than expected and with it a new appointment in Mesopotamia, which eventually turned out to be Command of the Forces in North Persia. This episode was perhaps the most significant when one looks at the importance of the development of the Persian oilfields by British companies and the survival of the present Pahlevi dynasty of Shahs on the fringe of the Middle East hot spots. But within a few months withdrawal of the forces was planned and the job came to an end. Then out of the blue came special instructions to go to Baghdad and on to the Cairo Conference, convened by Winston Churchill, who as Colonial Secretary had been given a special responsibility for Middle East affairs. It was at this conference that Churchill offered my father the command of the Levies in Iraq, to be followed by general command in Iraq until the RAF were ready to take over security duties. Nothing came of this project as my father was injured in an aeroplane crash on the way to Iraq to take up his command and there followed a long sea trip home in a hospital ship and convalescence which is described in the last episode. Fate, it seemed, had abruptly intervened to provide the circumstances in which my father was chosen to be Commandant of the Staff College. If he had not been in England at that time would he have still been selected? Winston Churchill assured him that it would have made no difference, but those on the spot get the best opportunities.

During his cruise with the Fleet, at the invitation of Admiral Sir Charles Madden, my father was able to see the Royal Navy at work, and so when he arrived at Camberley he knew that he was more than well equipped to make a success of his first permanent appointment as a Major-General.

All these episodes are characterized by the strong influence that he exerted on those with whom he came into contact. His reputation as an energetic commander preceded him wherever he went and his name was widely known throughout military and political circles.

His presence was felt by all under his command and he was constantly on the move to see his subordinates, sometimes travelling hundreds of miles under difficult and often extreme conditions. Everybody was kept on the go and there was no time for idleness. Morale was consequently high, and he later reflected that his experiences were the best of training for the very high command to which he aspired and which he later achieved.

I

MISSION TO HUNGARY

13 March to 16 May, 1920

Twenty-four hours after signing a one-year lease on the Old Mill Cottage at High Wycombe, one of the late Lord Redesdale's houses, my father accepted the Presidency of the Military Mission to Hungary and, as he recalls in his diary, this was his first dealing with the Foreign Office, Lord Curzon being Foreign Secretary at the time. Ten days of battling with them and other government departments followed in order to acquire passports, visas, instructions, cars, drivers, spare parts, uniforms and money for the trip. He wrote, 'It has been difficult to get anything out of the Foreign Office. They are the very masters of procrastination and compromise. Apparently Curzon lives in a world of his own and has never tried to delegate authority. Consequently even the smallest things have to be referred to him and, as his health is none too good and he is often away, it can be imagined how things are held up.'

The journey to Hungary took fifteen days, starting on 13 March, 1920, and arriving in Budapest on 27 March. His route took him through Boulogne, Paris, Langres, Belfort, Basle, Zurich, Buchs, Innsbruck, Salzburg and Vienna.

CHAPTER I

Journey to Budapest

On my return to England in November, 1919, after the campaign in Archangel, I was lucky enough to be promoted a Major-General for service in the field. Life should, therefore, have been bright enough, but just on account of my quick promotion I found myself on half-pay with nothing to do. My position had been politely explained to me by the Military Secretary at the War Office. Owing to the war the list of major-generals had become so swollen that I could not expect any permanent appointment for many months. Some generals had already been waiting on half-pay for more than a year, and as my name stood at the very bottom of the list I might well have to wait longer than that. For me the months of waiting on half-pay might be lengthened into years. He added, however, that odd jobs did occasionally turn up, and I should be considered for them.

My wife and I had succeeded in finding a small furnished house at High Wycombe in Buckinghamshire. It was the first home we had ever made together where we could at least set out our few possessions and enjoy them. We had our small daughter to amuse us and enough money to pay our way if we lived quietly. There was a small kitchen-garden in which I could work, and there were the daily papers to read. But as each day passed it was borne in on me more forcibly what an expensive thing leisure could be in life. It was no good my friends telling me that I needed a rest, after the strenuous life I had been leading for the last five and a half years. I did not need a rest. I was very fit in both mind and body, but I was haunted with the thought that I might have to spend the best years of my life in idleness. I wanted to work, but our antiquated regulations would not allow me to do so.

I could already speak most European tongues, but so far I had never tackled Italian. I could read the language well enough, but I had literally never heard it spoken, so I made up my mind to study it thoroughly. After a search I found a language mistress at Wycombe Abbey, the great school for girls which lay near us. For a month we made good progress, though my methods of learning a language flustered the poor young woman considerably. I had no use for boring sentences designed to illustrate some rule of grammar, and composed of words for which I could never have the slightest use. My method was this. I used to take the first six thoughts which came into my head each morning and find the colloquial equivalents for them. Being my own thoughts they contained the words I should want in conversation, and which were more easily fixed in my brain. I can well remember the first thought I gave her. It ran like this 'Damn it all! I won't be able to stick this half-pay much longer!' It contained under a dozen words and yet we could form a dozen more thoughts from it. She had to refer many of my thoughts to friends in London, so that I got the translations colloquially perfect and not pedantic in form. She told me pathetically that she found teaching me difficult, as my thoughts were not usually those which she encountered in her school life.

At the end of February we had to stop. I was summoned to the War Office for an interview. The General Staff were in trouble over the state of military affairs in Eastern Europe, and wanted to know whether I would accept a mission there under the Foreign Office in Hungary. I would receive the full pay and allowances of my rank and the mission would last for at least three months. I accepted with alacrity. I had always been fascinated by the history of the Magyar people, and as a subaltern I had spent three months in their country learning the language. My interest in the story of this sturdy race, so unlike any other in Europe, had been aroused by the fact that my Saxon ancestors had spent most of their early days in Hungary. After the murder of King Edmund Ironside in 1016 his two infant sons, Edmund and Edward, were sent over to King Canute's relations in

Denmark, so that they might be quietly done away with. But there appeared to be no one ready to carry out this wanton murder, and the children were sent to the care of King Stephen of Hungary. At his Court they were treated as members of a royal family, and when they grew to manhood both of them married Magyar princesses. Edmund, the elder son, died young without issue. Edward, the younger, who married Agatha, a niece of King Stephen, was granted the Castle of Rákvár in the Baranya as a residence. Here they brought up their family of three children, Margaret, Christina and Edgar.

In 1057 Edward was summoned to England by King Edward the Confessor, to whom no children had been born, with a view to his taking his rightful place as heir to the throne of England. He duly arrived with his family at the port of London, but before he could present himself to the King he was suddenly taken ill of some mysterious disease and died within a few days. Princess Agatha with her three children were received at the English Court, remaining there until the death of Edward the Confessor in 1066.

It will be remembered that with the Norman invasion threatening England, it was Earl Harold who was elected King and not the direct heir to the throne, the boy Edgar then probably aged twelve. After the defeat and death of Harold at Hastings, the Princess Agatha embarked in a ship with her family, with the purpose of regaining her homeland through the Baltic. Their ship met with strong easterly gales and was driven past the narrow entrance of the Skager Rack until it found refuge in the Firth of Forth. With great difficulty the royal passengers were taken ashore at a place now called St Margaret's Hope, on the northern shore of the Firth. News of the plight of the Saxon family reached Dunfermline where King Malcolm Canmore held his Court. Within a matter of minutes the King was mounted and galloping to the scene of the landing, only a few miles away. There was a happy sequel to this meeting, for in 1068 the Scottish King married Margaret, the elder daughter of Edward the Atheling and granddaughter of King Edmund Ironside.

This union of the royal families of Scotland and Saxon England

B

brought much benefit to Scotland. For a quarter of a century Queen Margaret ruled beside her warrior husband, bringing religion and kindlier living to his turbulent people. And when she died shortly after King Malcolm was killed in 1093, three of her sons and two of her grandsons succeeded to the throne, reverencing and maintaining much of her way of life. For a period of 117 years the influence of Queen Margaret of Scotland remained to guide the people into which she had married. The boy Edgar grew to manhood in Scotland, taking part in many of the Scottish raids into England. Twice he reached as far as Durham, and on one of these occasions he was crowned King of England by a Bishop of England. He never proved a great military leader and in his middle age he made peace with the Norman Kings of England, receiving from them the grant of an estate in Normandy which he held for a couple of years. He was then deprived of it as a consequence of a quarrel between King William Rufus and a former owner. He died at a great age, probably when he was well over eighty, in the year 1139, during the reign of his nephew King David. It is from this Edgar the Atheling that the Scottish family of Ironside is reputed to be descended.

On 1 March I was called to the Foreign Office to see Lord Hardinge. The reason for my proposed visit to Hungary was this. The Roumanians had been behaving badly. When Bela Kun set up his Communist régime in Budapest, they had invaded Hungary without informing the Allied Council in Paris of their intention to do so. They maintained that the outbreak of Communism in Hungary was not only a menace to themselves but also to the whole of Europe. Their troops were the only ones available for dealing with the situation, which was so grave that not a moment could be lost in dealing with it. They had there-fore acted immediately. The Allied Council recognized that there had been a good deal of truth in what the Roumanians had said, but now the danger was past. Bela Kun had fled the country and Admiral Horthy, the Regent of Hungary, had now organized sufficient forces with which to maintain his government. The Roumanians were, however, showing no desire to leave the territory they had invaded and withdraw behind their own frontiers. Reports had it that they were levying toll on all Hungarian agricultural farm machinery, and that as a consequence of their depredations there was now a grave danger of famine in Eastern Europe. My task was to go out under the auspices of the Allied Council to hasten the withdrawal of the Roumanians.* The mission was to consist of myself and one staff officer, and as the quickest and safest way of reaching Hungary I was to motor out there. Two cars had already been set aside for me with two lately demobilized RAF drivers to act as chauffeurs. I was to leave England as quickly as I could, the choice of route across Europe being left to me. It sounded a most engaging trip and I was all anxiety to get started.

As I walked back from the War Office to my club I began to wonder whether it would not be much better to go by train to Budapest. At the corner of Pall Mall I turned into the office of Messrs Thomas Cook & Co. to investigate. I was told that express trains were running regularly twice a week from Paris to Vienna. From there, ordinary trains were running regularly to Budapest. To make doubly sure I wired to Frank Lindley, the British Minister in Vienna, who had been our Minister during my command at Archangel, asking him to verify the trains. I also asked him whether cars could be hired or bought at moderate prices in Austria or Hungary. His immediate answer was to the effect that trains were running well and that, owing to lack of petrol, cars were laid up everywhere. The currencies of Austria and Hungary were now so depreciated that cars could be bought or hired at low prices. He advised me not to motor out to Budapest.

Armed with this information I returned to the Foreign Office with a new project. Lord Hardinge had gone off to join his chief in Paris, and I could not gain access to anyone who was prepared to take action on his own. The young gentlemen in charge of the arrangements of my mission refused to contemplate any new plan. They even insisted that I was wrong about the trains and their departures from Paris to Vienna. In any case the two cars were waiting for me at the Army Depot in Earl's Court. They were new cars. Their registration and engine numbers had

*See Appendix, p.240.

already been forwarded to Paris, where Lord Curzon himself would sign the the International Passes, so that I should have no trouble at any of the frontiers. Politely but firmly I was told that I had been misinformed about cars in Austria. To clinch the matter, these young men naively told me that the cars which they were providing for me were costing the Foreign Office nothing, since they were being transferred from the War Office as a book transaction for £600 each. It was obvious that they were in great fear of their chief. I argued no more, as I did not wish a report to be made to Paris that I was a cantankerous and contentious General. My trip might well be cancelled by an angry chief. All officials at the Foreign Office were desperately hard worked, and reasoned that however bad the cars were I should somehow get to Budapest.

Having a wholesome suspicion of thrown-up army cars, I ran up to Earl's Court to inspect those which had been set aside for me. They were indeed two new 18 hp Rover–Sunbeams which had been delivered by the makers more than a year ago and laid up ever since. This was bad enough, for they would need a lengthy overhaul before they would be fit for a long journey on indifferent roads. Then to my horror I saw that they had oil sidelamps and acetylene headlamps. Their miserable lighting system was enough to preclude them from being used at night, for where would one be able to procure carbide in an exhausted Europe? I searched the depot for cars like the Cadillacs we had used in the 4th Canadian Division in France, but anything with an electric lighting system had been snapped up long ago. The final blow came when the two demobilized RAF drivers were produced. They proved to be recruits of a few months' service who had never been out of England. I returned to the Foreign Office to have one more try at changing the plan to buying cars in Austria, but in vain. The young gentlemen were entrenched with a note from their chief that the plan was not to be changed. And then they produced what they thought must be a *bonne-bouche* to keep me quiet. I was introduced to the staff officer who was to come with me to Hungary. He was a full colonel in the Indian Army, who required a few more months of service to produce him his full pension. I remembered him coming to

Ambala in India in 1906 to take over a regiment of cavalry, when I was still a subaltern. He must have been at least twenty-five years older than I was. I thought it was bad enough to have two recruits as motor-drivers, but a full colonel as a staff officer was too much. I asked him whether he could speak French, to which he replied that he could not, but that he spoke several Indian languages. That gave me a chance to say that I did not think he would be suitable. The only bright spot in the whole business was that I had been given permission to take my ex-Russian servant with me. He at least was used to travelling anywhere in any conditions.

I had had enough of the Foreign Office, but when I had to apply to the War Office I found them even more difficult to deal with. In accordance with the Army Council's order my mission had to proceed to Budapest in khaki uniform. As I came under the DMI for administration I went in to see him, an old friend, Major-General Bill Thwaites. Together we went off happily enough to see the QMG, expecting that we should be given a simple note to the nearest depot, ordering the men to be clothed in khaki. It did not prove as easy as this, for the QMG demanded that the men must be properly enlisted before they could be clothed. The two RAF men refused at once to do this. They had just been demobilized and had drawn their clothing money and spent it. We went off to see the Adjutant-General. He was also very kind, but ruled that the men must be enlisted for long service in the Army. Backwards and forwards we went, getting more and more angry every time we interviewed the two great men. It was no good. I took Bill Thwaites back with me to lunch at my club, and there half-way through our meal I bethought me of an Imprest Account with the Foreign Office. This time I had drawn trumps. Within a couple of hours I had been given an order on the Paymaster-General for the opening of an Imprest Account for £500. I drew a cheque on this and with the men hied off to Messrs Moss Bros in Covent Garden, where the two drivers were turned into RASC men and my servant into a Gunner. All for the sum of £15, with a blanket for each.

When the pseudo-RASC drivers presented themselves to draw

the cars they were asked for their papers. Of course they had none. I had to go and draw them myself, cursing everybody who had anything to do with the mission.

Time dragged on and I got no nearer a start. On 8 March I was ordered to pay a visit to the Prime Minister of Greater Roumania, Dr Vaida Voevode. He had escaped from the Peace Conference in Paris for a short rest, and was lodged in a suite at the Ritz. I spent two hours there with him. He was a short, dark-complexioned man of fifty, speaking fluent but execrable French. He told me that for many years he had been the leader of the Roumanian Party in Transylvania under the Magyars, and then treated me to a tirade against his former masters. How brutal they were. No minority dared to raise a word to ask for the smallest liberty or remission of taxes. He laid stress upon the fact that his country was now the most important state in the Balkans. They had just saved Europe from Bolshevism, and ought to be treated with more respect than was being accorded to them. The one desire of his country was to obey the orders of the Allied Council, but the evacuation of the food depots, which had been set up in Hungary for the use of their forces, had been delayed by deep snow in the mountains behind them. To my remark that there were now no mountains inside new Hungary which could prevent them from withdrawing to their own frontier, he merely shrugged his shoulders. I would understand, he said, that he was no military man and had to go by what his military advisers told him. When I told him that it had been generally reported that many Hungarian farm machines were being commandeered and transferred to Roumania, he vehemently denied the accusation. If anything was being taken away, it could only be what the Germans had stolen when they invaded Roumania. As soon as I reached the scene of action I would see how his country was being maligned. Everybody told lies about Roumania, but now at last the Roumanian people had come into their own, and they expected to be treated as were other important European States. Ringing for a secretary, he dictated a letter to General Averescu, the Roumanian Commander-in-Chief in Hungary, directing him to afford me every facility for going wherever I wished.

On the 11th the mission papers arrived. The staff officer who was to come with me, Lord Edward Hay, a Captain in the Scots Guards, had been given them as he passed through Paris on his way home from Palestine. They had been buried under a sheaf of more important documents awaiting the signature of the Prime Minister and the Foreign Minister. It seemed almost incredible that the Foreign Minister had to sign the papers for such a tiny mission as mine.

That afternoon we set off on our journey. Disaster soon overtook us, for the driver of my car managed to get his gears jammed on Chatham Hill, on our way to Folkestone. The car stopped immediately and we had to stay the night at the police station in Chatham. The next morning a gang of men dismantled the gearbox and released the gear. It was thus not till midday on the 13th that we disembarked at Boulogne, and midnight on the 14th that we limped into Paris. The cars were suffering from every conceivable ill—slipping clutches, bad petrol pressure and a collapse of the lights. The tyres were rotten and we had puncture after puncture. A very ignominious start. I cursed the young men in the Foreign Office for being so obstinate.

After writing my name in the Embassy book I went round to pay my respects to the Military Attaché, General Sackville-West, commonly known as 'Titwillow' to his friends. I had never met him but was anxious to do so, as I had been runner-up to him in his appointment. Besides being Military Attaché he was also British representative on Marshal Foch's staff. As a youngster I had always been keen to be a military attaché in Paris, Berlin or Moscow, and had steadily prepared myself linguistically for these posts. I had failed to get Paris and soon I should be too senior to hold such a post. All the panache seemed to have disappeared from them, and Sackville-West appeared to be glued to his office together with a large number of assistants. Perhaps I had made myself too bright a picture of the life of an attaché, judging from the days when the famous Gunner, Jimmie Grierson, had served in Berlin and Petrograd.

My arrival was not looked upon with great favour. I was told curtly that all the arrangements for the withdrawal of the Roumanian Army from Hungary were in the hands of the

French Marshal, and no one else had the right to question his orders. All was going well in Hungary. I was advised not to waste my time in going to Budapest, for I should find nothing to do there. 'Titwillow' then asked me casually to let him have a look at my orders and credentials, so that they could be registered in his books. It was obvious that there had been some form of rumpus between the British member of the Allied Council and Marshal Foch. I did not wish to be mixed up in any such squabble, nor to have my journey cancelled to Budapest, so I told him that my orders were personal to myself and I could not disclose them to anyone. I had certainly no licence to throw up my task and return to England. I proposed to continue my journey the next morning. I took care not to disclose the route which I proposed to take across Europe.

In the attaché's office I was given the news that there had been a *putsch* in Berlin, organized by a man called Kapp. No one had any idea what had been the effect of this rising, so I made up my mind to go through Switzerland and over the Vorarlberg Pass, if it were open.

It was a painfully limping journey that we made through Nangis–Troyes–Langres–Besançon–Belfort to Basle. The only good thing I found was that through the demobilization of the French Army a large number of good motor mechanics had been distributed amongst the wayside garages. With their help our wretched cars were running moderately well by the time we reached the Swiss frontier. I had plenty of time to talk to all and sundry. France was indeed full of troubles. The cost of living was rising steadily and the currency was falling in value even more rapidly. Everyone was complaining that the repairs in the devastated areas were proceeding very slowly, what with officials dashing about in high-powered cars and plans being made by one department of state, only to be cancelled by another. Very little maintenance was being carried out and everywhere there was a great lack of paint. As usual, it was the women who were bearing the strain the best and I had few complaints from them. In all the cafés the food and cooking were excellent. Main roads were just a procession of large pot-holes, while side roads were impassable to light cars. Our cars stood up badly to the evil conditions.

Langres was crowded with buyers at the auctions of the United States motor transport. Prices were ruling very high owing to the horde of speculators who were operating, hoping to resell to needy smallholders at what are universally known as 'easy terms'. No rooms were to be found, so we spent the night on the floor of one of the cafés, in an atmosphere of stale liquor and tobacco. In the morning we washed and shaved at the communal pump. On our return to the café the women had cleaned the place up in some marvellous way. The smell had gone and they served our breakfast on a spotless tablecloth. We were glad to pay them a good *pourboire*.

At Belfort the General of the District came down to pay us a friendly visit. We were all in the local garage mending punctures and I caught sight of him standing at the door watching us. My mind went back at once to Marshal Foch. Had the old man caught up with us and should I be hauled back to Paris? All was well. The General had heard from the gendarmerie at the old Town Gate that a British General had gone through and was staying the night in the town. He had come down to pay us his compliments. He looked at me keenly without saying a word as I stood before him in my shirt-sleeves with a tyre tube in my hands, very dirty and dishevelled. Then he asked me how it was that I had been promoted a General of Division at so young an age. When I told him that I had served through the whole of the Boer War from 1899 to 1902, he would not believe me. But when I told him that I was not long back from Archangel and was on my way to Hungary, he brightened up considerably. He knew all about me as his son had served under me in North Russia. He told me that he was soon retiring for good and proposed to go to his little house in Tours to lead a life of ease. As he said good-bye to me he put his hand on my shoulder and wished me a quick journey to Budapest, adding somewhat sadly, 'Au revoir, mon général. Bonne chance avec les bolshéviques. Pour moi c'est fini la guerre. Mais vous, vous êtes jeune encore. Mais vous en aurez bientôt assez.' He stood there pulling his grizzled moustache as he watched us get into the car. Then as we drove off he drew himself up to salute us stiffly.

At the Swiss frontier there were hundreds of French workmen

passing into Switzerland. They must have been all well known to the *douaniers* who searched none of them. When we came to cross they asked me where I was bound for, and made no attempt to search us when I told them I was going to Hungary. Two of them whistled and smiled at us. We were all very hungry and I made straight for the Hotel of the Three Kings, which I knew well. Both inside and out everything there was spotlessly clean. Such a contrast to poor battered France with her lack of paint and general dowdiness. We had now got down to a routine, Kostia taking charge of the two drivers, who like so many young Britons abroad were too shy to look after themselves. Kostia, on the other hand, was always ready to take on anything. Edward Hay and I were soon settled down to a wonderful *déjeuner* at a table overlooking the river. The room was filled with refugees of many nationalities, despite the high prices which were being charged. When they saw our khaki uniforms they drew over to our table to ply us with questions as to what was going on in Europe. Had the Roumanians left Hungary, and what damage had they done? Had the Kapp *Putsch* thrown the Allies out of Germany? There was even a family which had been evacuated from Archangel while I was in command. I turned them over to Kostia, but to his own surprise he was getting a little rusty in his native language. They wanted me to get them a ticket from Genoa or Trieste to Vladivostok, and for nothing of course. They had spent nearly all their money. How truly Russian it was to spend so much at an expensive hotel. I wondered what the Swiss did with them when they had lost it all.

Close behind us there was sitting an elderly man dressed in an English tweed coat, with breeches and well fitting leggings. He wore a short goatee beard just going grey. When the crowd round us had cleared he came over and introduced himself. He was Count Géza Andrassy, a big Magyar landowner. He spoke English as well as I did. He told me he had managed to escape from the Communists, who had arrested him at his estate. Two of his old servants had helped him out of a back window and supplied him with a horse. It had taken him two days and two nights to get over the frontier into Yugoslavia, and from thence he had reached Switzerland through Italy. He wanted me to get him into the small state of Liechtenstein, where his daughter was married to the young prince. He was certainly not at the end of his resources, for he took a small chamois-leather bag out of his pocket and spilled its contents on the tablecloth before us. There glittered a handful of precious stones of all colours and sizes. He had entered Switzerland without papers, but said he could get some in Liechtenstein when once he got there. I had to refuse him a seat in one of our cars for fear of being stopped at a frontier.

For the night we moved on to the palatial hotel at Zurich, where we found more Hungarian refugees. All of them wanted to know when they could go home, and how much devastation the hated Roumanians had caused. They asked me what Britain was doing about all the wrongs which Hungary had suffered. It was pathetic to see the faith they still had in us. Few of them seemed to remember that they had been fighting against us for four years. Nearly all offered the excuse that they had been forced to do this because their King was also the Emperor of Austria.

Petrol was very short in Switzerland, and there was a horde of unemployed chauffeurs outside the main door of the hotel, ready to take any kind of work, but they were not allowed to cross the Swiss frontier into any neighbouring country. They told me that the Vorarlberg Pass was still closed, and would not be open for another month, but that I would find no difficulty in getting a truck attached to any train going from Buchs to Innsbruck, from whence onwards the road to Vienna would be open.

The road going down into Buchs was the only difficult piece we encountered throughout our trip. Luckily one of the drivers remembered that he had seen chains in the boots of both cars, and these were fitted before we tackled the descent. The forest trees came right down to the road on either side, so that the sun never penetrated to its surface at any hour of the day. At the worst point, a stretch of about a half mile, we slid down in bottom gear without any control over the vehicles, narrowly missing a couple of cars which had stalled in the middle of the road going up. At the station we met with the only unpleasantness we encountered, in the form of a young German-Swiss stationmaster, who was still suffering from the effects of seeing the German Reich defeated. The sight of British khaki made him turn rude and obstructive at once. It was only after I had telephoned to the Chief of the Railway Department in Berne that he was brought to his senses. Then a truck was attached to the first of the Kinderzüge which passed Buchs, taking back German children after a fortnight's holiday in Switzerland.

On the train I had decided to remain in the truck while traversing the tunnel, but on the advice of the guard we all climbed into the last coach for the journey through the tunnel. Even in the corridor of this we were almost asphyxiated by the fumes.

From Innsbruck to Salzburg snow was still lying on the ground and in the ditches, but the heavy farm wagons had beaten a clear track throughout. When crossing the narrow strip of Bavarian territory, over which the main road ran for several miles, we were not searched for any contraband, but we had an amusing contretemps with the old Bavarian landwehr corporal in charge of the first post. He looked at the magnificent passport signed by Lord Curzon with a certain disgust, being unable to read the grandiloquent terms in which his Lordship enjoined all and sundry to help Major-General Sir Edmund Ironside in his mission to Hungary. He asked us why we had not joined some touring club in England, for then all would have been simple. I told him that the only club to which we belonged was the Army Club. This beat him, but he signed our pass as he muttered, 'Ach so! Nun geht's! Hier in Bayern gibt's keine Klubs in der Armee!' He gave us permission to proceed if I would take a man on each of the cars and pay for their return the same day. After much searching I found a two-shilling piece in my pocket, and on being assured that this was worth any number of marks or kroner he accepted it for the return ticket. When we reached the Austrian frontier again I offered each of the landsturmers a bundle of Austrian notes, but each refused to accept them. I might have been offering them a snake. I then bethought me of the remainder of the luncheon which we had had made up for us at Buchs station restaurant. This they accepted eagerly, with a packet of ten Players added to it.

At Salzburg we put up at the deserted Oesterreichischer Hof, where I had to begin counting in depreciated kroner. I had bought 8,000 of them in Paris for £1, but now I found that they had depreciated to 12,000. It was my first experience of a badly depreciated currency, and I found it difficult to remember that the imposing looking 50-kroner notes were worth only one penny instead of fifty shillings. The cost of my whole party at the most expensive hotel had sunk to a few pence per day. I bought my first bottle of vintage Tokaj for the pleasing price of three pence. I had another surprise, for as I was putting our two old crocks away in a lock-up garage, I caught sight of two great Mercedes touring cars in a neighbouring garage. One was blue and the other red, and both of them nearly new. And I was told that the owner would take a cheque on London for £75 each. My mouth watered as I looked at their great engines and big fat tyres, their electric lighting and the general look of efficiency for rough work. I was sadly tempted to buy them both on the spot, or at least one. I had spent nearly £100 on repairs to our old things and would have to spend another large sum before they ever got home. I went away and had a drink to think things over. Our cars were now running as well as they ever would. But I pictured the faces of the young men when they were given a large bill for Customs duty to pay, when we reached Dover on our return. It was a glorious chance which I could not take.

On 24 March we drove into Vienna too late in the evening for us to think of troubling the Embassy, so I decided to aim for one of my old haunts, Sacher's Hotel. We had only the oil sidelamps on our cars and the city had no lighting of any kind. In the blackness and silence I missed my way and drew up to consider what we had better do. Not a soul appeared in the street from whom we might ask the way. Not a single clock broke the deathly silence with its chime. None of them were now wound up. We might have been in a city of the dead. For over half an hour we sat in the car whispering in a jerky way to fill in the time. Then away down one of the long streets there appeared a couple of pin-points, which appeared to be getting larger. Within another twenty minutes there arrived a two-horse tram, which began to disgorge some fifty tired men and women all loaded with heavy bundles of wood. I went over and talked to them. They had been out all day collecting firewood in the neighbouring forests, and this was to be sold before dawn. They never knew how much they were going to get for their bundles, for the currency was falling so rapidly that the price might be smaller before they could go and buy their daily bread in the shops. Everyone was praying for the coming of spring to put an end to their misery. I found that Sacher's was only just round the corner. We had not had anything to eat since early morning, but still we were better off than the wretched people with the faggots of wood.

When we drew up before Sacher's great oak door we saw that all the windows were tightly closed. No one came to answer our ringings of the bell, but by dint of all shouting together and hammering on the door we at last heard footsteps coming down the passage inside. We heard the bolts being drawn and then the door was slowly opened on its chain, till we could see the wrinkled face of an old woman appraising us with a very sour look. She seemed to be smoking a cigar and for a moment or two she blew out some wisps of smoke. Taking the cigar out of her mouth she asked us what we wanted, making a public scene outside her door. I told her that I was a British General who wanted a bed and some dinner as quick as possible, as we were all very hungry. Within a moment the door was opened and we were hauled inside, while two porters took the cars and the men round to the garages at the back. We were led to the dining-room and seated at a corner table. The room was fairly full of what the Viennese used to call *Schiebers* and we should now call 'Spivs', but they only threw us a casual glance as we came in, and then went on with their heated arguments over the currency and the price of food. They weren't hungry like the poor gatherers of wood outside.

When I had time to look round I espied a tall man in khaki sitting at another corner table. He had a long string of medal ribbons on his jacket, and on his sleeves were the many black braided rings of an admiral. He could only be British, so I went across and introduced myself to him. He proved to be Sir Ernest Troubridge, then serving as the Chief of the International Commission for Danube shipping. He at once came over to our table and stopped there yarning for a couple of hours. His head-quarters were in Paris, but he spent most of his summers moving up and down the Danube, inspecting the British gunboats and the traffic along the whole river. It was no mean job policing and running the Customs of the seven states using the great waterway of Eastern Europe.

In the morning I called on Frank Lindley, who was most insistent that I should stay with him and see something of the city. I had to refuse as I had been so much delayed in my journey out, and moreover I felt that there was nothing I could see but misery and distress, where I had once known such gaiety and good-fellowship. I had to go up to the Imperial Stables, where the British Mission kept their cars, in order to get mine filled up with petrol and oil. There I saw one of the great cream-coloured stallions belonging to the famous Reitschule, harnessed to a dust-cart which was clearing away the ever-mounting heaps of garbage in the streets. A visible sign of the evil straits into which the imperial city had fallen. There were long queues waiting outside the food shops, the people standing dejectedly there without the energy to talk to each other. They were all miserably clothed and underfed. The only other shops open were those which dealt in perfumes and scented soaps, and these one could smell from several streets off. I saw no one patronizing them. I came away with a heavy heart. The breaking up of the Austro-Hungarian Empire had left Vienna like a head without a body on which to live.

At Raab on the Hungarian frontier I was met by a guard-of-honour. As soon as my car with its Union Jack on its bonnet was seen on the outskirts of the town we were surrounded by cheering soldiers. With half a dozen on the running-boards we were conducted to the Town Hall, where I managed to get out of my car and walk over to a guard-of-honour which awaited me. After the salute I walked round their ranks with the wrinkled old NCO in charge. They were all real hard-bitten old soldiers with leather-like faces from long exposure to the sun, dressed in khaki of every hue, and all wearing the German type of steel helmet. Before I dismissed them I delivered a few words in my long-unused Magyar, thanking them for having paid me the honour of saluting me and wishing them well. This was greeted with loud shouts of 'Ejen! Ejen!' from the crowd of tattered soldiers round me. They all wore great turkey feathers in their bonnets, which gave them a Viking look about them. I was much touched by an old corporal coming up to present me with a particularly fine specimen for my cap. I was greeted with renewed 'Ejens' when I fixed it on.

Driving into Hungary was like entering the East. The road from Raab to Budapest might indeed have been a stretch of the mighty highway which runs from Delhi to Peshawar. There were the same water-buffaloes pulling farm wagons, their naked skins shining in the sun and their tongues hanging out of their mouths, all dripping with saliva as if they were dying of thirst. The very wheels of the wagons creaked as they do all over India. Wedding parties were passing down the road to a celebration in a neighbouring village. Herds of pigs and geese were being guarded along the grassy sides of the road by boys and girls in khaki jackets much too big for them, and the usual soldier's bonnet on their heads. They used long switches to control their charges, enjoying themselves immensely as they ran joyously shouting at every party they encountered. One decently dressed couple were walking down the road with their boots slung by their laces round their necks. It was doubtless to save shoe-leather, now so precious after the war. Between them they were carrying an enormous gander slung in a blanket. The bird regarded all the passers-by with the greatest interest. A little further on we saw three mounted herdsmen of the Alföld lolling in their saddles, one even having a leg thrown over the pommel as if he were riding side-saddle. They were guarding a batch of fifty fillies grazing on a patch of grass. Both they and their guards raised their heads every now and then to see who was passing by. The guards saluted us by raising the short stocks of their whips to their broad-brimmed hats they wore. But at the slightest sign of unrest amongst the fillies they were ready to deal with the culprits. A shout, a crack of their long whip-lashes or a sudden move to a flank at a gallop, was enough to bring all into order again.

At each village we were serenaded by a Tsigane band, which made us come to a halt until we had heard at least one tune. We had certainly been made to feel at home on our first day in Hungary. The Regent, Admiral Horthy, had sent me a pass which was to take me anywhere I wished to go in the country. I may say that I never had to use this pass. The sight of British khaki and the Union Jack was enough for the people to give us a spontaneous welcome.

CHAPTER II

Budapest

My first day in the capital was taken up with official visits. It had taken me twenty-four days to reach the Hungarian capital from the date that I received my orders at the Foreign Office. I ought to have done it very leisurely inside a week. He laughed as I apologized to the British Minister for having taken so long, but he assured me that the mere fact of a British General having been ordered to come out had hastened the withdrawal of the Roumanians. Now all was going well. I had arrived in time to see the last troops leaving Hungary. I was going to be asked to superintend this last operation. The French and Italian Commissioners, both senior generals of army rank, greeted me very kindly. They commiserated with me for having been brought out so far on a wild goose chase. They little knew how I was enjoying myself. Foreign generals never suffered from half-pay. They drew their full pay whether they were employed or not. Our Commissioner, a Gunner, who was only a Brigadier-General, got on very well with the two other Commissioners, Graziani and Monbelli, though he was so much below them in rank. And all three of them were loud in their praises of the Regent. There was no doubt that there was absolutely no reason for the Roumanians to have remained in Hungary so long. The excuses made by the Prime Minister, Dr Vaida Voevode, as to the depots they had set up in Hungary were just so much nonsense.

On the second day I was introduced to Admiral Horthy by the British Minister, who was good enough to leave me to a private interview with him after I had been presented. I do not think that I have ever met a man to whom I have taken a stronger or

c

more immediate liking that I did to the Regent. He was a man of slender build, a typical sailor of slightly over fifty years of age, speaking English almost without an accent. In whatever language he was speaking he never made extravagant gestures, but his keen dark eyes danced with light as he made his several points. His whole face lit up when I gave him a few words of greeting in my inferior Magyar. Our talk lasted for over two hours, in which he told me the story of the collapse and dismemberment of the Magyar State. It was a pathetic tale, but he told it calmly and without hate.

Admiral Horthy was born of an old Transylvanian Protestant family, which had migrated south to the estate of Kenderes in the middle of the Hungarian plain, after the defeat and disappearance of the Turks in 1687. He was born in 1868, the fifth of nine children, seven boys and two girls. In many ways I found him curiously like my old friend in South Africa, General Jan Smuts. Both had fought against us in war, and though both were extremely nationalistic, both had mixed with and made friends with many Britishers. In fact both had emerged from their fighting against us with a tolerably good opinion of us.

For nine hundred years the Magyars had held their heads high, resisting every attempt to destroy their way of life. During the last two hundred years, when the Hapsburgs were holding the Crown of Hungary with very doubtful right, they had been compelled to make one long fight to prevent themselves from being reduced to the status of the other minorities of the Austrian Empire. No Magyar could ever forget that it was the Austrian Emperor who had called in the Czar of Russia to help him to subdue them in the Revolt of 1848. Despite that desperate defeat they had been able to build themselves a strong Magyar State with economic frontiers, so that their country had become self-supporting. They had now been reduced to the state of a man who had suffered the amputation of both arms and both legs. He showed me a map of the Magyar State as it was before the 1914–18 War, with a shadow in the centre showing the size to which it had now been reduced. It had shrunk from an area of 263 thousand square kilometres to a mere 91 thousand. The whole economic structure of the state had been destroyed. Most of their

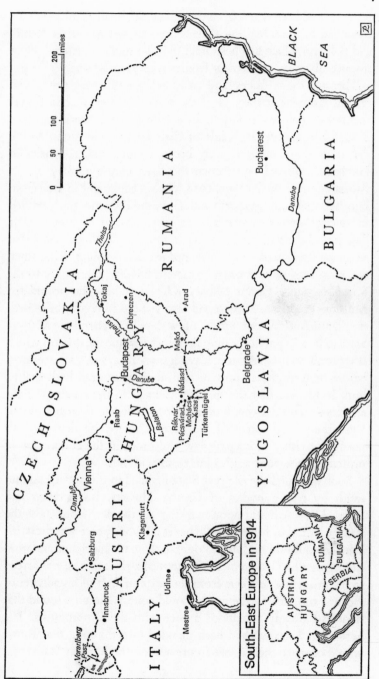

South-East Europe in 1914

factories had been taken from them, and the small number which remained to them had lost their sources of raw materials. Roads and railways which had been built to bring in these materials now stopped abruptly at the new frontiers, serving no one.

Through the weakness and incompetence of their rulers at the critical moment at the end of the war, the Magyars had found themselves helpless and without a friend in the world, to face dismemberment at the hands of their former minorities. As the defeat of the Central Powers became more certain, events in Hungary followed very much the same course as they did in Russia in 1917. In October, 1918, rioting broke out in Budapest, but their new and inexperienced King, the Emperor Karl, refused to sanction severe measures being taken against the rioters. The defences of the various fronts began to crumble. Soldiers deserted *en masse* and made for their homes. The young King then renounced his powers of government, handing them over to the Socialists under Count Mihály Károlyi, whom he nominated Minister-President. Károlyi had always been in favour of separation from Austria, and within a few days he declared the Magyar State to be a Republic, hoping thereby to escape the disaster which was certain to befall Austria. Having made no appeal to the country before he took this important step, indignation ran high against him. In his fear that the military element in the country might engineer a counter-revolution, he proceeded to disarm and disband the armed forces of the state. Thereby he destroyed all possibility either of keeping law and order in the country or of protecting it against aggression from without.

Soon he found the Magyar State invaded in the north, east and south by strong bodies of Czechs, Slovaks, Roumanians and Serbs. All were intent upon marking out the new frontiers to the states which they hoped would be set up when peace was declared. Károlyi could do nothing to oppose these invaders, and indignation against his Government rose to such a pitch that he was forced to try to form a new one from the extreme Left of his adherents. He was too late, for before he could consult them he found that they had already concluded a pact with the Communists. The Left-wing Socialists had been deluded into thinking that Russia would come to their rescue in preventing the Magyar State from being dismembered. Károlyi's Republic had been converted into a Communist State in a night. Like Kerensky in Russia, he ceased to struggle and disappeared from the scene.

It was at this moment that he, Admiral Horthy, had been approached by all the non-Communist leaders in the country. They asked him to accept the office of Regent of Hungary, an office which had been instituted by King Stephen. A Regent had always been appointed when the King was out of his realm or visiting the remoter districts on state affairs. In the hope of being able to rescue something from the chaos into which the Magyar State had fallen, he had accepted the great office which had been offered to him. He impressed upon me that he was neither dictator nor usurper, but a properly constituted Ruler of the State, until the moment should come when a king would be crowned in his place. He believed that the Magyars were monarchists at heart, and that one day they would ask for a king to reign over them, and it had to be remembered that the people still had the power of election in their hands. He himself would never take part in bringing back a Hapsburg to the throne against the will of the people. As he finished his story he rose and walked over to a window overlooking the Danube. He stood there for a moment in thought, and then turning to me he said these words, 'I am sure that my country will rise again despite all these troubles. Ours is a sad case. We beat the Russians. We beat the Italians. And we beat the Roumanians. And yet we have lost the war.'

Talking of the last Roumanian invasion, the Admrial freely admitted that this had contributed to the flight of Bela Kun. But he believed that he would have achieved the same results without having had to suffer the humiliation of the invasion and the damage which the invaders had caused.

In the evening I dined with the Károlyi family and some of their relations. The dinner was excellent and served with great ceremony. Almost as if there had never been a war followed by a revolution. The family certainly took their misfortunes most cavalierly. Only British had been invited, and in our honour only English was spoken throughout the meal. Most of the family spoke the language as fluently as if it had been their native tongue. On my right I had Géza Andrassy, the man I had met at Basle in the Hotel of the Three Kings. He had managed to get to his daughter in Liechtenstein, where he procured new papers, and was back in Budapest as soon as I was. He told me that his wife and son were in Czechoslovakia, considering whether they should change their nationality in order to save his estate in Slovakia. He had another estate in Transylvania, but that had already been taken over by Roumania. He was too old to change his nationality and after all who in their senses would want to be a Roumanian whatever the prize might be. It was at this dinner that I first heard the slogan, 'Nem! Nem! Soha!', which being interpreted meant 'No! No! Never!', alluding to the fact that they would never accept the mutilation of their precious land.

For the next day the Allied Commission had arranged for me to superintend the final withdrawal of the Roumanian Army at the little town of Makö. I was to inspect a cavalry regiment and issue the final order for it to leave. As I expected, it was very much a put-up job. The three Commissioners had signified that they would not come out, but that each of them was sending an officer to represent him. The plan was this. I and all the farmers and peasants of the area now being evacuated were to be taken out to Makö by train. To the train were to be attached two truckloads of Horthy's men, which were to be detached at a siding five miles short of the town. I was to dismiss the Roumanian cavalry at Makö at exactly midday, the zero hour for Horthy's men to leave their siding. There would thus be no chance of any trouble.

I had arranged to take a car with me so that I might be free to have a look round after the last Roumanian was reported to have gone, and after I had dismissed the other officers from attendance on me.

When I reached the station at Budapest I realized that we were to be given a show when we arrived at Makö. Two Tsigane bands were being loaded up, and there were more people arranging their seats on the top of the carriages than inside the compartments. Some fifty of Horthy's men were already in the trucks attached to the rear of the train. We started up to time and duly deposited the two trucks at the siding short of Makö.

At Makö station a large barouche awaited me with a pair of

horses and a coachman in Hungarian uniform. We drove straight to the little town square, where a Roumanian Dragoon Regiment was waiting to be inspected. The men were all young conscripts and looked remarkably well in their new light-blue uniforms. The horses were in very good condition, practically half of them with Hungarian brandings, showing that they had been commandeered in Hungary. I took ten minutes walking round the regiment with the colonel, and then told him he could go. He saluted me with his sword, gave an order and the regiment wheeled to its right by troops at a trot. Within very few minutes there was nothing to be seen of them but a cloud of dust towards the east.

Almost as if by magic the scene on the town square changed. From somewhere in the background there was hauled out a wooden platform, upon which the little Mayor and his officials mounted to deliver speech after speech to the cheers of the spectators. They expressed the feelings of the Magyar people. Joy at being delivered from the Roumanian foe. Disgust at seeing how much of their country had been taken from them. Anger at seeing farming machines and horses stolen from them under their eyes. A Szekler, one of the descendants of the old Magyar settlers in Transylvania, appeared in national dress on a gigantic stallion, which he had bedecked with red, white and green ribbons. He rode about amongst the crowd telling them that the Roumanians had stolen his house, his stock and all his worldly goods without a penny of compensation. Then the news that Horthy's men were coming caused a stampede to the edge of the town. Half an hour later I left the crowd dancing round a pole to the music of a Tsigane band.

After shaking hands with the officers of the Commission, who were going back with the train to Budapest, I got into my car and started due north to see what I could, keeping just inside the new Roumanian frontier as it was marked on the map. Roumanian gendarmes were going about with carbines slung over their shoulders, directing the marking out of the line on the ground. They were using long poles with Roumanian colours on them. I stopped every now and then to verify the line they were marking out. There were no Hungarian officials anywhere about, for

Admiral Horthy had issued the strictest orders that no Magyar was to go within two miles of the new frontier. The Roumanians were obviously curious as to what I was doing, for they took out their binoculars to have a look at the flag I was flying on the car. I then drew off towards the west to a large village I saw in the distance. I was met by a deputation wishing to report to me. All their old land was now over in Roumania, and they had none to cultivate. How were they to live? They had concealed all their seed-corn and they were ready to plant it now, if only I would say where it was to go. I could offer them no help. In another village I met a dapper little groom leading a great thoroughbred stallion up and down the village street, cheered by all the peasants round him. He proved to be an English groom who had been twenty years in Hungary—a Cockney who had not lost much of his accent. He told me that he and the horse had lain concealed for three weeks inside the centre of a hollowed-out haystack. All the time he had been terrified that the Roumanians would come and pull down his stack for fodder. During the last few days, when the Roumanian cavalry were passing through, he had been forced to hold the horse's nostrils almost continuously to prevent him from neighing. During his time in the stack he had been helped by two Magyar urchins who brought water for him and the horse, besides keeping 'Cave' for him. They had rigged up a cord which led into the centre of the stack and established an alphabet for transmitting simple messages by means of jerks. He produced the pair for my inspection, both highly delighted at having deluded the hated Roumanians. I gave them each a packet of Players which they started on at once, after offering one to their friend the groom. They inhaled them with the great gusto of confirmed smokers.

Another ten miles further on I began to see Roumanian stragglers in twos and threes, all mounted men riding across country and avoiding villages and roads. As soon as they saw us they broke into a gallop towards the east. A mile further on I came upon a Roumanian Major of the Supply Corps, having a heated argument with a bunch of Magyar railwaymen. The Major had half a dozen men with him, all with slung carbines, and he himself had an enormous revolver in a holster slung on his body. The Magyars were all armed with stout sticks. When we arrived both parties to the arguments drew over towards us to state their cases. According to the Magyars the Major had arrived with a dozen or so trucks, attached to an Hungarian locomotive, and claimed to have the points towards the main line opened for him. They declared that he was an hour too late and would not move the points. I walked over to the trucks, which the Major said were filled with necessities for the troops that night, only to find them packed with farm machinery—reapers, binders, ploughs and harrows—with the last four containing several large American tractors. The Major had been lying like a knave and I meant to show him no mercy, but the last thing I wanted was a frontier incident. Neither I nor Edward Hay had any arms, while the Major's party had at least seven rifles between them. And then I remembered Kostia, who never went out without his beloved automatic pistol which had been given to him in Russia. I gave him an order in Russian to disarm the Major, which he did at once by taking the revolver out of the holster and levelling it at the men and shouting in English to them to throw down their carbines. The Magyars were all for beating their enemies up, but I didn't want any murders to add to my troubles. I told them to clear out as fast as they could to the east, and the last I saw of them was the Major's fat legs in his long black boots as he lumbered heavily down the rough track, amidst the loud jeers of the Magyars.

We had made a good haul, which gave ample evidence of the looting which had been going on, but I was anxious to get more if I could before the light failed. I left Kostia behind in charge of the siding, with orders to have the fires drawn in the engine attached to the trucks, and to have the railway lines destroyed at the points. I gave him three carbines with which to arm some reliable men and left him to do what he could. The Magyars were all anxious to look after him, and I knew he wouldn't go hungry.

We had hardly done another ten miles before we ran into a convoy of fifteen Roumanian lorries, stuck in the mud, where floods had come across the road. Each lorry had a couple of men on it, but there was no officer present. I found their NCO arguing with a party of peasants, trying to prevail upon them to bring their beasts out and release him from the mud. This the Magyars were stoutly refusing to do. I had some half-dozen carbines in the car and with these we armed some old soldiers. Under my orders they soon hauled the Roumanians out of the lorries and sent them scuttling down the road. The haul was even more valuable than the last, for though the machines were smaller they were of the most modern sort, all the names of the Hungarian importers still to be read on them. I left an old NCO in charge with orders to take the carburettors off and hide them in a safe place. Though we motored on for another twenty minutes we found nothing fresh, and as it was getting dark we headed for the nearest village to seek a night's lodging. A local lawyer was called to us and immediately offered us his house. The priest was called in to supper with the result that we stayed up talking far into the next morning.

They told us that the setting up of a Communist Government in Budapest had come to them as a complete surprise. Bela Kun had been a Jew domiciled in Hungary, who had been taken prisoner by the Russians. In Moscow he had been educated—very willingly—in Communist theories and methods of starting revolutions. He was returned to Hungary and smuggled into the capital, where he had been working for some months against the weak Károlyi Government. They had at once organized a town guard in their village and had been able to arrest many of the Communists who had been sent to them from the capital. Hardly had they settled down when the reports came in of the Roumanian invasion. Against organized troops they could do nothing but offer passive resistance, which brought upon the peasants many a savage beating. Some were put in gaol, but as far as they knew there were no murders committed by the enemy. They described the wholesale commandering of machines, stock and horses. They both said that there had been no violating of their women.

The Priest was most interesting about the medley of races which there had always been in his parish. By cutting off what he called the outer ring of the Magyar State, the Allied Council seemed to have thought that they were going to do away once and for all with minorities. But it would soon be seen that they had created more minorities than there had ever been. Even after two-thirds of the state had been taken away, he still had as many as before. Some two million Magyars had been left in the territories which had been handed over to Slovakia, Roumania and Yugoslavia. He hoped that I would accompany him to a village in his parish, where he would show me what minorities really amounted to.

Next morning he drove out with us to inspect his specimen of a village. I found that it consisted of one long street, on opposite sides of which lived two different races. They had lived there in perfect peace for centuries. The gables of the houses were different. The gardens were different. Even the manner in which the firewood was packed was different. The two headmen were brought to see me and they were different in manner of face and clothing. One wore his hair long and the other had his close cropped. Both spoke Magyar and both called themselves Magyars. And yet the long-haired man was of Ruthenian stock, while the other was of Roumanian stock. Their church services were taken in Magyar, while the litany in one was read in Ruthenian, and in the other it was read in Roumanian. He had known periods when it had been necessary for a man to be sent to learn these languages so that the Litany could be read in the prescribed tongue.

On my way home I picked up Kostia at his siding, where there had been no further trouble from the Roumanians. The Magyars had given him a wonderful time, taking him as the outward and visible sign of their deliverance from the enemy. He was sitting in a comfortable chair on the railway line, surrounded by gifts which had been brought to him by the peasants. Ducks and geese, vegetables and white bread. He had also partaken of many glasses of a vin rosé which he had thought very good. I made him say a few words to them in English, telling them how glad he had been to help in their troubles.

On my return to Budapest I had a long discussion with the British Minister. We had collected ample evidence of the organized looting of precious farm machinery, and I could get little more in Hungary. I was quite sure, however, that I could get more evidence in Roumania, and I still had my pass given me by the Roumanian Prime Minister in London. The more I delayed the more chance there would be for the Roumanians to cover up their tracks. As I had not enough time to go and see the Regent, the Minister promised to give him all my news about the final evacuation.

CHAPTER III

Bucharest

I had never been in Roumania before and could not speak a word of the language, and I was also a little bit anxious as to my reception in the country. For by this time the military authorities must have learnt something of the instructions which had been given to me by the Allied Council. The first thing I wanted to do was to search the large railway sidings just inside the Roumanian frontier in the area of Arad. Having done this, I proposed to send my car back to Budapest and to catch the Bucharest express at the first convenient point. The Roumanians at Arad had agreed to my itinerary.

At the first Roumanian military post on the Arad road I found a guard-of-honour drawn up for me. Very different to the old and workmanlike guard which I had inspected at Raab. It was composed of young conscripts from a Dragoon Regiment, smartly turned out in light-blue, with slung carbines and very long sabres. The Captain of the Post presented to me the ADC who was to attend me while I was in Roumania, a young exquisite in well-cut breeches and long patent-leather boots. He sported an eye-glass. As he walked up to me to shake hands we were struck by the short mincing steps he took. This was explained later when we learnt that he was wearing 'height-improvers' in his boots. After he had delivered himself of the usual compliments he told me that a reception had been arranged for me at Arad, to be followed by a dinner given by the General. I scented some trouble, but when I told him that I wished to come into Arad by the road which ran parallel with the railway, he made no objection. All he asked me was that I should not arrive late for the reception or he would get into serious trouble. He spoke most excellent French.

We packed him into my disreputable car and made straight for the main siding, and there, as I had expected, I found all the evidence I needed. No attempt had yet been made to conceal what had been going on. The loaded trucks were there for all to see. In one single siding I counted 170 trucks loaded with farm machinery. They even had their eventual destinations in Roumania chalked upon them. I talked with the Roumanian guard on the siding, who luckily could speak Magyar, and from him I learnt that practically all the trucks were due to leave for their final stations that night. I had only just come in time. I also saw some thirty locomotives belonging to the Hungarian State Railways. Curiously enough I was not the only searcher going round the siding that night, for I came across a little French civilian sitting disconsolately wiping his brow. He had been sent from Paris to examine these so-called cemeteries of rolling-stock, which existed all over Europe. Thousands of French trucks had already been retrieved, but here in Eastern Europe he had met with no luck whatever. No sooner had a batch been collected than someone came in the night and took them away again. He was all alone and unable to speak any language other than French, with the result that no one took any notice of his papers, covered as they were by red seals and French writing. He told me that the Roumanians officials were the worst of any he had met. They laughed at his chapter of mishaps.

I drove into Arad just in time for the reception, which lasted half an hour, all the officers with their ladies being brought up to me, a parade which I found disconcerting. I spoke to all of them in French, but I could see that many of them had little facility in the language. All the officers were magnificently turned out in new light-blue tunics. Their wives were equally well dressed. After the ragged soldiers of Hungary, the army of Roumania looked as if it had been reclothed from general to private. The dinner brought many speeches which I did not in the least understand. It was soon over, thank goodness, but in a few moments we were trooping off to the local theatre to be introduced to a Roumanian comedy. Most of the audience were officers and men of the garrison, who had been given free tickets. They certainly laughed a lot and applauded the jokes in return.

I had no time to speak to the townspeople, who were largely Magyar. The handing over of this town had been one of the greatest outrages committed by the Allied Council, for Arad was almost a sacred town. There the Premier of Hungary, Count Louis Batthány, and thirteen generals of the Hungarian Army, were tried for treason after the Rebellion of 1848, and subsequently executed. Had it not been for the aid of the Czar of Russia, the Hapsburg King of Hungary could never have quelled the Rebellion. How different for the Magyars would their future have been if they had been able to throw off the Hapsburg yoke at that time.

The scene at Bucharest station reminded me of many I had watched at Delhi main station in India. A mixture of riches and poverty. Officials arguing with large families of peasants sitting waiting, with all their wordly goods done up in dirty linen bundles. They were ready to sit there for hours in order to catch their train. Immediately a train was announced, off went a chattering mob to make sure of getting a carriage. There were the same water-carriers and sweetmeat vendors shouting out their wares. The water-carriers did not carry a mussack, but used tin buckets with long spouts, and the drinkers all did the same as Indians do, they cupped their hands to receive the stream of water. Immaculate ladies with their officer-husbands promenaded idly in the station at Bucharest. That seemed the only difference between the Roumanian capital and Delhi.

At the hotel where rooms had been booked for us there prevailed a very different atmosphere to that at Budapest. British prestige was by no means high. The French manager declared that there had been no vacant rooms available when the order came from the Roumanian Chief of Staff, and that there were still none available. There he stood smiling crookedly at me, as if to say, 'There! That's for you!'. Our young and apparently innocuous ADC sprang to life by telephoning to the Chief of Police. Within a very few minutes he arrived in a large car and called for the manager. A list of rooms with the names of their occupants was handed to him. After a short inspection he marked off three rooms for us. The present occupants were ordered to vacate the rooms within an hour. The Chief of Police then turned and bowed to me, disappearing as quickly as he had arrived. The manager then approached me with a very different smile, explaining that Bucharest was living under a strict military dictatorship. No one had any civil rights. Out of sheer curiosity I asked to know the names of the people who had been thrown out of their rooms, but with a bow the manager explained that the Chief of Police had taken that evidence away with him.

The Military Attaché was away inspecting with the Ambassador, so I was entertained by the Chargé d'Affaires, a most amusing Irishman. He gave me a racy account of what was going on in the capital, with the dossiers of most of the notabilities in the country, high and low. From him I learnt for the first time of the summary dismissal of Dr Vaida Voevode from the Premiership. He had been replaced by General Averescu, the late Commander-in-Chief of the invading army in Hungary, who now headed a military dictatorship. In the Chargé d'Affaires' opinion this had saved Roumania from disaster. Dr Voevode tried to introduce too many democratic innovations before the people could understand what they meant. It seemed a sad start for the Greater Roumania which the old Premier had looked forward to with so much hope.

We spent the afternoon walking about the city looking at the shop windows and the passers-by. Business was very slack, the lei having sunk almost as low as the Austrian kroner. I looked in vain for a memento to take home. The narrow Calle Victoriei, the Bond Street of Bucharest, was thronged with high society taking a stroll or a drive in their cars. It was always said to be a fact that the police at either end of the street were wont to turn back all the ugly women, and that might well have been true, for we saw many very beautiful ones who had apparently passed muster. The manner in which the well-perfumed and made-up young officers ogled the ladies was not a pretty sight. I was told that there were hundreds of redundant officers, whom the Government was afraid to send back to civil life, in the certainty that they would never again fit into minor jobs. From the look of them I did not think that their fighting value was very high.

For the evening General Averescu and M. Take Jonescu had been invited to dine. The General was a very tall man with a small pointed beard just going grey. He certainly looked very distinguished in evening dress, with the Single Star of a Roumanian Order on his coat. I was told that he came of peasant stock and had risen to his high position through merit alone. He spoke the most excellent French whatever his origin had been. I found him very outspoken in his criticism of the Allied Council in general and Great Britain in particular. 'Why was it,' he said, 'that England always allied herself to her old enemies, instead of to the friends who had fought alongside her? Did she prefer Bolshevism to democratic rule?'. He thought that Roumania had received nothing but opprobrium for her recent intervention in Hungary. In actual fact her action had saved Europe from Bolshevism. Roumania had been and still was in a delicate position, as the nearest neighbour to Russia. How could she have allowed herself to remain sandwiched in between a Communist Russia and a Communist Hungary? Under such circumstances she could not have existed for long. The moment had not been opportune for the immediate launching of extensive liberal ideas, and so a military dictatorship had been forced upon the new Roumania against her will. The time would come for big ideas and reforms in due course, but not so long as the menace of Soviet Russia was hanging over Eastern Europe.

The General spoke very well and his ideas were clear, but I could not let some of his statements pass without challenge. I was well aware that the relations between Hungary and Roumania had always been difficult, but I thought it had been madness on the part of the Roumanians not to have done their best to keep on good terms with the neighbours who could best help them when they were in trouble with the Russians. Had they not been so precipitate in their advance into the Magyar State they would have realized that Bela Kun had no chance against the forces of the Regent. And then, to make things worse, the Roumanians had engaged in the wholesale commandeering of all the Hungarian farm implements they could find. Thereby they had increased the hatred of the Magyars against them. Averescu merely sat and shrugged his shoulders without denying my accusation. Then he changed his attitude, saying that looting may perhaps have been done, but never so bad as that which they had suffered under the

Germans. I reminded the General that the disappearance of the Austro-Hungarian Empire from Eastern Europe had weakened the West's position *vis-à-vis* Soviet Russia, and that it was therefore absolutely necessary for all the successor states, Roumania, Czechoslovakia and Yugoslavia, to join with Hungary against any aggression from Soviet Russia. M Take Jonescu was very much in agreement with what I said, while Averescu sat scowling in his seat.

After the guests had gone, in came Dr Vaida Voevode to my great surprise. Never have I seen a man so altered as he was in the short space of a couple of months. In London he had been full of the wonderful future which lay in front of the Roumanian race, which had been united at last. Now he was loud in his complaints of how the loyal Transylvanians were being treated. He, their old representative, had been thrown out of the Premiership while he was serving his country at the Peace Conference. How could a great state be built up under a military dictatorship? The Transylvanians felt as if they had jumped from one tyranny to another one which was worse than the first. How could Greater Roumania ever be consolidated when the Transylvanians were not represented in the Government? He thumped the table with his fist in his exasperation, repeating over and over again, 'But we shall beat them! We shall win in the end!'

I sat thinking of the weak crust of successor states which now faced Russia. The misshapen collection of four races which called itself Czechoslovakia, Poland, Roumania and another conglomerate state calling itself Yugoslavia. How could they resist the menacing infiltration of Russian Communism? How could they erect what the politicians of Western Europe called so naïvely a *cordon sanitaire* against the propaganda which was being directed at them?

On 3 April I had the honour of being invited to lunch with their Majesties the King and Queen of Roumania at the Controccni Palace. Besides the Chargé d'Affaires, myself and Edward Hay only two other guests had been invited, both obviously important American businessmen. We were all assembled in an ante-room and introduced to one another by an ADC in waiting. Then after an interval the side doors were opened to allow the King and

Queen with the Princess Elizabeth to come in. The King was simply dressed in a light-blue uniform with a single cross at his neck. I thought that he looked tired and ill. He spent a few minutes talking to me laughingly about my having been concerned with 'chasing the Roumanian Army out of Hungary'. He hoped that I had been impressed by his army and its behaviour, to which I replied that they were by far the best-dressed army in Europe since the war. This seemed to please him vastly, for he repeated it to the Queen who was talking to Edward Hay. At lunch I sat on the King's right, with the Princess on my right. I found her exactly like a young English girl, full of conversation about horses and dogs. When she came in she was accompanied by two spaniels, which sat looking at her with adoring eyes throughout the meal, waiting for a morsel from the table. Then just before the meal was over, two great borzois were allowed in. They too sat watching their mistress, but had the advantage over the spaniels that they could see what was going on upon the table. Discipline was strict, for none of the four received even the tiniest morsel.

The room was very Eastern with its small windows, the carpets magnificent, and in the various alcoves there hung painted ikons lighted by gilded hanging-lamps. The Queen was most gracious and animated, and it was always she who revived the conversation if she saw it lagging. Neither of the Americans were good conversationalists.

The party closed with an awkward incident. We had been invited out into a small formal garden, preparatory to taking our leave, when one of the Americans asked if he could take a snapshot of their Majesties, producing a small camera from his pocket at the same time. The King and Queen started to pose themselves, when they found that one of the Americans had taken post between them. The other took the snap, and in a wink they changed places and another snap was taken. It made me smile to myself when I thought of them tossing up for first time in the picture. It must have been heavy odds against a second picture being allowed.

My visit to Roumania had been a lightning one and I had only had a glimpse of the capital and its people. I should have dearly loved to go back to Budapest via Transylvania. The very name of the country attracted me. I had no reason for going there except sight-seeing, and at the moment that seemed out of place. The capital gave me an impression of insecurity. People were looking over their shoulders as if to see whether they were being followed. There were far too many policemen interfering with what was going on.

CHAPTER IV

Debreczen, Tokaj

On my way back from Bucharest I left the Simplon Express at Temesvar, where a light engine was to take me to the Hungarian frontier and my waiting car. The engine was not forthcoming and I had to wait four hours in the station restaurant, where I whiled away the time trying to decipher the advertisements which had been newly put up in Roumanian. A diffident little man who had been hanging about looking at me for some time at last summoned up enough courage to come up and speak to me. He was an Englishman who had lived in the town for fifteen years, earning a living by giving lessons in English to young Magyars. He had arrived in the country at the age of twenty, and now spoke with such a foreign accent that I could hardly believe that he had been born in England. He had a long story to tell me of how the Magyar population was being victimized. Many of his students, mere lads of seventeen, were being sentenced to long terms of imprisonment for the most trivial infringements of the language laws. He had now been informed that he would not be allowed to give lessons in English any more. He expected to be expelled from the country in a few days time. The poor little man said to me, plaintively, 'What have I done to them that they should take away my livelihood?' I could do nothing for him, but promised to report his case in Budapest. It was only another incident showing how difficult it was to deal with minority cases in the states of Eastern Europe.

Once more I made my report to the British Minister. I had begun to think seriously of making my preparations for going home, but the Minister told me that he had been invited by the

Regent to come to the ceremony of the swearing-in of the new recruits. He was unable to go and hoped that I would represent him there. It was to take place on 14 April. This suited me very well, for it would allow me to see a little more of the Magyars and their capital.

After spending a couple of days looking at the modern buildings and the magnificent bridges over the Danube, I arranged to visit the old Turkish fort which dominates the twin cities of Buda and Pesth, constituting the capital of the Magyar State. For nearly a hundred and fifty years it had been the headquarters of a Turkish Pashalyk, and in those days it must have been impregnable. A modern fort had been built upon the old one, but one could see the dungeons which lay deep down in rock below it. Now they were used for storing ammunition and military material. A young professor from the University, an officer who had served under the Regent, came with me to deal with the history of the place. We spent a lovely summer's afternoon lying on the ramparts, searching the Hungarian plain with our binoculars. There was nothing to impede our view in any direction. The little white villages, each with its cultivated area round it, showed up like pawns on a chessboard. A happy scene of peace and quiet, where one could pick out the long teams of oxen ploughing one behind the other. Far away to the south one could pick up the winding course of the great river. Only a hundred and fifty miles away lay that fatal battlefield of Mohács, where the Magyar nation lost its freedom to Suliman the Magnificent in 1526. Their King, Louis II, lost his life when withdrawing from the defeat, being drowned after a fall from his horse. It was not till 1687 that at the very same place Charles of Lorraine drove the Turks out of the country.

I asked the Professor how it was that the Magyars had emerged from their century and a half of servitude with so much of their old vigour. His answer was that they had been an organized nation, with a broad history of success behind them, hundreds of years before the first Mohács. They were unlike the unorganized tribes to the south and the east of them, which had also been overthrown by the Turks. The Magyars never ceased to harry their invaders, generation after generation, wherever they could find a weak spot in their armour. He told me also of the Szeklers of Transylvania who had helped to keep up the old Magyar spirit when times were bad. 'That is why we are so sad,' he said, 'to see this historic territory handed over to the Roumanians.' He told me that two million Magyars had been handed over with it to be a minority in the land where they had lived so long as masters. Pointing to the plain below us he said, 'All that was barren waste when the Turks left. It was we Magyars who built it up into a great state. Now that state has gone.'

I spent a day wandering about the shops, the most interesting of which were the second-hand ones mostly in the hands of the Jews. They were filled with furniture, carpets, glass and pictures, some of which had been sold by their owners after the war, but most had been stolen from them in the short Communist régime. The shopkeepers were always ready to strike a bargain for steady foreign currency, but I had neither the knowledge to choose anything worth having nor the means of getting it home if I did. In the end I bought a beautiful modern tea and coffee set from Hüttl's and succeeded in getting it home without mishap.

I dined once or twice in the popular restaurants, where for us with British currency the cost was ridiculously small. The best of dinners cost just three shillings and a bottle of Tokaj a mere shilling. I never tired of the Tsigane music. It had such a terrific spirit in it. One had only to hum or to whistle a tune for the leader to pick it up on his fiddle, and then the others followed after him immediately. My Magyar was improving, though I found that I had no longer the effrontery of my younger days, when I could make mistakes and not be ashamed of them.

The ceremony at Debreczen was to be a celebration of the liberation of the town from the Roumanians, combined with the oath administered to the recruits. I motored out early from Budapest with Kostia and took my breakfast on the side-walk of a café on the main square, from which I could watch the assembly of the country folk. They came in from the surrounding country in every conceivable kind of vehicle, drawn by horses, oxen and even water-buffaloes. All the people were in the highest spirits and were dressed in their best national finery. The women in white skirts and bodices of red and green velvet. A few of the older officers were in full Hussar uniforms with slung jackets. Every man who could find one, wore a large turkey feather in his head-dress, even those who were wearing busbies and plumes. The day began with three hundred officers marching down to the station to meet the Regent. He arrived dressed in his naval uniform and stood for a moment in the open door of a railway coach to receive the roars of 'Ejen! Ejen!' which greeted him. He was then escorted on foot to the centre of the town square, where a small platform had been erected. Here he stood alone to receive the addresses of the Mayor and Council. I watched him closely as he stood there looking at the people with a smile on his face. He made a striking picture, his clear-cut features giving an impression of quiet strength. He replied to the speeches of the civil authorities in a few simple words which all could understand.

The swearing-in then followed. The troops had been drawn up in a hollow square with their Colours in front of them, waving proudly in the warm breeze. A Colonel of Hussars stepped forward, turning to face the Regent in order to ask for his permission to read the oath. He then turned to face the troops which were called to attention after having doffed their head-dresses. Before reading the actual oath he made a short oration explaining what the oath meant. He told them that no Magyar must ever forget that his ancestors had maintained a proud record of service for close on a thousand years, from the time when their nation entered Europe. They were now going through troublous times, but they must stand united as their forefathers had done before them. If they did their duty before God all would come right in due time. The Colonel then read the oath, being followed sentence by sentence by the thousand recruits on parade. Their voices as they repeated the sacred words sounded strong and virile, showing that they understood the importance of the oath. I saw many an old soldier and even some of the older women-folk repeating the words like any young lad. The Colonel then saluted the Regent and took his place behind him on the platform.

I felt deeply moved by this ceremony. The clear voices and the obvious enthusiasm of the recruits could not fail to impress the onlooker. I as a Briton sympathized with them over the tragedy which had befallen them. When they raised their heads after the oath had been sworn they seemed to shake their shoulders, as if they had got rid of some great weight which had been pressing them down. They still remained Magyars. There was no call for vengeance.

The ceremony then passed to the Blessing of the Colours. The Ensigns came forward to lay their precious burdens on an improvised altar covered by an Oriental rug. The Roman Catholic Bishop was the first to come forward with uplifted hand. He looked magnificent in his high mitre and gorgeous robes as he spoke his prayer in Latin. He was succeeded by three military chaplains in uniform, a Lutheran, a Calvinist and a priest of the Orthodox Faith, all reciting their prayers in Magyar. There were tears in the Regent's eyes as I went up to him to shake him by the hand and offer him my warmest congratulations. He gave me a very firm grip of the hand as I turned to stand beside him to watch the march-past which followed the parade.

I felt that these Magyars had uttered an expression of faith as men who had been defeated, but whose spirit remained as indomitable as ever.

My time in Hungary was coming to an end, but I had made up my mind that there were two places I must go and see before I left the country. The first was to visit the castle in which my ancestors had been brought up during their exile in Hungary, and the other was the Tokaj district where the famous wine is produced. Tokaj lay not far to the north of Debreczen, so I decided to visit it first.

The little town lies on the right bank of the Theiss, nestling close under the slopes of the Tokaj Mountain, a miniature extinct volcano on the northern edge of the Hungarian Plain. I was told that the virtues of the wine made from the grapes grown in the vineyards of Tokaj come not only from the soil but also from the fact that they catch the first frosts of winter before those grown on the plain. This is the signal for the whole population to turn out to gather in the grapes. In the old days the best vintages were always sent to the imperial cellars in Vienna, but I was able to get hold of a couple of dozen bottles of the famous Essenz of 1895. These I was able to transport back to England without a casualty. I remember that the last two bottles were shared many years later with Mr Winston Churchill and Admiral of the Fleet Sir Charles Madden. The town was a quaint little place and the tiny inn, in which we stayed most of the time, was most homely and comfortable. The first sound I heard in the morning was the beat of a drum, and on looking out of my window I discovered a very old man in uniform making an announcement of a big sale of vintage wines. He was the town-crier.

On the second night of my stay in the town I was visited by a Magyar landowner, who had heard that I was staying at the inn. He stayed and had dinner with me, insisting upon choosing the wine we were to drink before, during and after the dinner. His house was further up the Theiss on the right bank and close to the present Hungarian frontier, and he gave me a warm invitation to visit him and hear his story of what had occurred after the war. He also had an interesting deputation of Ruthenians who were at the moment visiting him. They had come to try and make an arrangement for them to keep their stock in the plains. If they remained in the winter in the hills they would lose a large number which they could ill afford. He knew that I would like to hear their story.

His house was most comfortable and he was still a man of considerable means, though his estate had been almost halved in size. The new frontier with Czechoslovakia had been traced on a map, no one knew by whom, without the least attention to the economic situation or to the actual terrain. He had never been consulted, and the first he had heard about it was the arrival of a large party of Slovaks with hundreds of pickets flying their national colours. With these they began to mark out the new frontier on the ground. He could make no resistance and there were neither troops nor police who could intervene, though he reported what was happening to the capital. The line they marked ran almost directly through the middle of his property, ignoring farm-tracks, boundaries of fields, farm-buildings, watering-places and supplies of firewood. In fact the hundred and one things upon which good husbandry depends. He had been a large stock-breeder, and as such had divided his farm into two halves. The southern for winter grazing, as it lay in the plain, the northern for summer grazing, as it lay in the hills. He had now very little stock left, since his northern half had been taken in mid-summer, and with it went the stock summering up there. He had never received any compensation, either for the land or the stock which had been taken from him. His land and stock had been parcelled out to small Slovak farmers, and these were now with him, trying to arrange to run their stock on his southern half in the winter. It all seemed a hopeless muddle and as far as the Magyars were concerned an outrageous swindle.

He then produced a map of the monstrous new state of Czechoslovakia which had been set up on the demand of President Masaryk, so as to produce something which could be governed by the Czechs. It was over 700 miles long from west to east, and in places hardly seventy miles broad from north to south. In the west Czechs and Germans predominated, in the centre there were Slovaks, and finally at the extreme eastern end there had been stuck the little Ruthenian nation, much as one sticks a stamp on the right-hand corner of an envelope. Four separate people and four separate languages. Two people with separate cultures and two others with none.

I met the Ruthenian deputation the next morning. It consisted of the old leader and three of his contemporaries and three young men. They came to see me bare-headed, with long hair and long moustaches, but none with beards. One of the young men was clean-shaven. Their white linen shirts were embroidered with brightly coloured patterns, and over their shirts they wore short sheepskin jackets. Their dark trousers were stuffed into gaudily coloured stockings. Most of them were wearing sandals on their feet. Their story was a pathetic one. The land which their people had owned and occupied for centuries had been taken and allotted to new masters, and they had been transferred with the land as if they were serfs. No notice of this had been given to them. They could not understand how this order had been given. Who had the power to give it? They found themselves 600 miles from these new masters, who lived in a big city called Prag and who spoke a language they could not understand. Roads, railways and telegraph lines to Prag from their country did not exist, and no one answered the letters they sent to the Government there. All communications in the old Austro-Hungarian Empire ran from north to south, through Vienna and Budapest. The old headman in charge, a peasant of over seventy years, told me the story of their precarious position in the following words:

'You see, Excellency, we are a poor peasant people who have lived always in the Carpathians. Our life has always been ordered as follows. In winter we go out into the forests and cut down trees. These we slide over the snow down to the streams below. There we cut them up. With the larger logs we make rafts. On these rafts we load the smaller logs which are to be sold as firewood. We float our rafts down to the plains where live the Magyars, because God made the rivers to flow that way. There we sell all our logs, remaining for the season to work in the fields, taking home with us when the work is done either money or corn as wages. We then can live another winter in our mountains in comfort. Our present rulers will not allow us to go to Hungary any more. Why are they our masters? Why have they the right to say to us that we must do this or that? We are a free people. Do not these masters in Prag understand that our rivers do not flow to their towns? God did not make it so. We understood the Magyars, but we do not understand the Czechs. Please tell, Excellency, what we may do to be free again.'

As I motored back to the Hungarian capital over the great plain, I was once more struck by its similarity to the plains of India. All the same old wells were there, from the creaking Persian wheel with its earthen pots to the long pole with a weight at one end and a bucket at the other. There was the same great leathern bag, with a pair of water-buffaloes hauling at the other end of the rope as they walked down a steep incline, to bring up a load of water for the fields at a higher level. I thought at times that I could hear the same old chant of the Indian water-workers towards eventide. Then just before we ran into the capital we passed through the carefully tilled and watered fields of the Bulgarian settlement, which drives such a profitable market-garden trade with the two cities.

The Regent received me in the Imperial Palace which had just been evacuated by the British Mission. If my memory serves me well, he had established himself in a simple set of rooms, austerely furnished with a plain office desk and some ordinary straight-back chairs. The room was completely dominated by a picture of a Bengal tiger ready to spring, which was hung on the wall facing the door. I know that the Emperor was a famous shot, but I doubted if he had ever shot a tiger. The picture must have been presented to him by some Indian Prince whom he had entertained.

I found the Admiral in great form, keeping me entranced with his yarns about the British Navy in Malta, where he had played polo with the officers and enjoyed himself immensely. He told me that he hoped he had imbibed something of the finest navy in the world. He thanked me for what I had done for his country, and hoped that I would report what I had seen in the proper quarters in England. Hungary needed a friend in the world in her time of need. Would I remember that? She was now more than ever cut off from the rest of the world since she had lost all access to the sea. She was surrounded by the weak successor states, still jealous and frightened of what the Magyar State might do. As he put it, the Allied Council could hardly have built up a weaker barrier against Bolshevism if they had expressly tried to do so.

I thanked the Admiral for his kindness during my stay in Hungary. I should never forget the welcome which had been given me throughout the country. I was now going down to visit Rákvár in the Baranya, where my Saxon ancestors had been brought up. As soon as he heard this the Admiral sent for his ADC to bring me a time-table of the river steamers. My best way was to go straight to Mohács where there was a good pier for landing cars.

As I stood in Horthy's simple quarters in the Palace bidding him farewell, I wondered when and where we should meet again, if we ever did. Again he asked me to tell the British authorities that he was neither dictator nor usurper, but the legally elected Regent of Hungary. And then as our hands met he added, 'Tell them also that never, even if there should be an unanimous plebiscite in my favour, will I ever accept the royal crown.' He meant them to understand that he was seeking nothing for himself. He only thought of his people, just as Smuts had thought of the

Boer nation when he was called to Vereeniging for the armistice talks*.

We did not meet again for thirty-seven years, but during that long period we did manage to keep up a correspondence whenever it was possible for letters to pass between us. I watched his career as Regent with growing interest and admiration, just as I had watched that of Smuts as he came closer and closer to us, until at last he had accepted the rank of British Field-Marshal. The more I looked back on them the more did I see how similar they were in character. I knew that the guiding principle which Horthy had kept before him was to heal the anger which had possessed the Magyars after they had realized the clauses of the Treaty of Trianon, and to press for restitution of some of the land which had been taken from them by quiet negotiation. It was much the same principle which Smuts had kept before his eyes after the Boer War of 1899–1902 had come to an end.

Horthy had no easy time, and one of the years which brought most anxiety was that of 1921, when the young and inexperienced King Charles IV made two separate attempts to resume his position as King of Hungary. The details of how the Regent was able to persuade the young King to abandon his idea of resuming the governing of his country show clearly the mettle of which Admiral Horthy was fashioned.

* My father was the officer who rode out with Capt Jardine of the 5th Lancers to the Boer lines to find General Smuts and escort him back to Port Nolloth where he embarked for Cape Town to attend the Peace Conference.

CHAPTER V

Mohács, Rákvár

The trip down the Danube on the old river steamer reminded me of many I had made on Indian rivers. There was the same muddy, slow-flowing current in all its great breadth, winding between low reed-grown banks. It was almost as if I were looking at a jungle again. The weather was fine and warm and a mattress made a comfortable armchair on the deck. The old skipper of the steamer had been working on the Danube for fifty years and knew every twist and turn of its course. In the evening, when we had tied up at a small landing-place, I played several hands of the curious game called 'Skat'. The stakes were low, which was lucky for me, for I was not a class-player as he was.

My coming visit to Mohács had leaked out. I was met at the landing-stage by a body of notables, amongst whom was the old Priest who had been so kind to me when I started learning Magyar as a subaltern. He brought a great piece of news for me. In an old chest in the village church of Nádasd, there had been discovered a sketch of the Castle of Rákvár drawn about two centuries before by one of his predecessors. He was proposing to send it for safe-keeping to the Museum at Budapest, but promised to let me copy it before it went. It had been most beautifully drawn on parchment, now all yellow with age, though the fine writing was still legible. It settled without doubt the actual site of Rákvár, the place where the Saxon princes were brought up.

I was delayed in my efforts to trace the actual position of the two battles of Mohács through having to attend a feast in the Town Hall. Numerous speeches of welcome were delivered, to which I had to reply in my inferior Magyar, helped out by interjections in English and German. I drank a good deal of their most delightful rose-tinted wine and shook hands with a multitude of people. I was hard put to it to prevent them from forming a cavalcade to help in a reconnaissance of the battlefields. None of them could give me a clear account of what had happened, but they were all ready to take part in the search. The Danube must have shifted its course many times since the days of 1526, and there remained only a tradition that the Magyar Army had been drawn up on the open ground some three miles south of the town of Mohács. They were facing almost due south, with their left flank on the river and their right in the open, covered by their cavalry. In numbers they counted little more than 30,000 men.

Suliman the Great had reached Belgrade on 9 July with an army reputed to number 300,000 men with 300 guns. His most important corps—the Janissaries—were still coming up the Danube by boat on their voyage from the Black Sea. After collecting his army on the Drave he leisurely prepared to cross it at Essek, which lay 60 miles south of Mohács. It was thus not till 29 August that his advanced troops showed up on the Magyar front. They showed no signs of preparing for battle, and seemed to be laying out a camp near a small hill called the Türkenhügel. This sight was too much for the Magyars, anxiously watching the careless and objectless manoeuvring on their front. After great pressure had been brought upon him by his immediate subordinates King Louis ordered an immediate attack. The enemy light troops were driven from the field with little difficulty, but while the Hungarian cavalry were reforming after a charge, their advancing infantry were attacked on its exposed right flank by the whole strength of the Turkish host. The Hungarians were beaten back in disorder towards the river. Within an hour the fight was over. Over 20,000 Magyars were slain. King Louis was drowned after a fall from his horse, while attempting to escape across the swampy ground.

I lay for an hour on the top of the Türkenhügel trying to reconstruct the terrible scene. It was a miserable business that the fate of a great fighting nation should have been left in the hands of an incompetent leader with no military knowledge. He seemed to have no idea of the immense strength of the enemy who was advancing so slowly towards him. Little or no information had

1 The Inter-Allied Commission for the evacuation of the Roumanians from Hungary. The Roumanian officer is second from the right. On the extreme right is the Hungarian stationmaster.

2 General Ironside inspecting the Roumanian cavalry.

3 The freeing of Debreczen from the Roumanians. Admiral Horthy is seen talking to General Ironside.

4 Horse power! A Rover–Sunbeam in difficulty.

come in from Belgrade and the King took no steps to procure any himself. His command was one long tale of indecision. At first he decided to hold a line on the Drave, but abandoning that idea he made preparations to hold one on the Save, until he finally took up his position south of Mohács. Although 'the bloody sword' had been sent throughout the country to show how critical the situation was, there were dissensions amongst his own people. John Zapolya, the Voevode of Transylvania, advanced as far as the Theiss and there remained till the fatal battle was over. King Louis' own brother-in-law, Charles of Austria, made no single move to help him. Surely it was a moment when Louis should have withdrawn towards his backward allies and so bring them into the coming battle. If on the day of the battle he had ridden straight for the Türkenhügel, he would have seen with his naked eye the size of the forces which were advancing against him. Even then he would have had enough time to effect his withdrawal. As a result of his poor generalship the flower of the Magyar nation was destroyed, while the nation itself passed into bondage for a hundred and fifty years.

Unlike the Normans in Britain, the Turks had come with no idea of founding a new state. They cared nothing for the land which they had seized. They exacted all they could from the enemy they had defeated, destroying their way of living without attempting to set up a new and better one. They hardly mixed with the conquered people, and when they were at last defeated at the second Battle of Mohács in the year 1687, they disappeared from the scene like a blight dissipated by the sun. They left nothing behind them.

After supper I motored the seventeen miles to Pécsvárad where I had been told there was a good inn. There I found the old Priest with the guide who was to go with us the next day, an old herdsman of the name of István. He must have been nearer seventy than sixty, though he stood as straight as a ramrod. His face was burnt the colour of old brown leather, and from the vast wrinkles on it there peered at us two eyes of piercing blue. I treated him to a good *soupie* of the local brandy, which he swallowed in true ghillie fashion. When the Priest told him that I was a descendant of the people who used to live in the Castle, he at once asked whether I was going to build it up again. He had tended his herds on its slopes for fifty years and it would be nice to know that there was someone living there.

It was reputed that the estate of Nádasd had been one of King Stephen's hunting resorts, consisting of an expanse of fifty square miles of wooded hills, rising in places to 1,200 feet above the road which completely surrounded the area. On three sides two streams, the Wildwasser and the Alt, ran close to the circular road; where the Alt had its source, almost in the centre of the estate stood Rákvár on its 400 foot high conical hill.

In the morning we motored up to Nádasd, taking our lunch with us and picking up old István in the village. We turned left on the circular road, where the Alt had been canalized to supply the two mills Kömalom and Pitzermalom, and stopped half-way between them. It was the old man's first trip in a motor, and when I looked round to see how he was faring I saw him holding on like grim death with both hands. When we stopped he stepped out in a half-bewildered state, shaking his shoulders as if he had got rid of a heavy weight. After a minute he asked me to explain how the carriage ran without an animal to pull it. As we looked up towards the top of the hill there seemed to be no sign of a path, and the whole slope seemed to be covered with thick shrubs about three feet high. Even through my binoculars I could not see any opening in the wall of the Castle above. Then we were off in single file, first István followed by the Priest, then Kostia followed by myself in rear. István set a very hot pace, despite the fact that he was using his sickle all the way to cut a path for us. Half-way up I called for a breather and gave everyone a cigarette to smoke. The old Priest was almost as excited as I was, for in all his time at Nadasd he had never climbed the hill. The first ditch was at least ten yards wide and about ten feet deep, the second ditch a little bigger each way, with a wall on the inner side. Of the wall some five feet remained, though I judged that its original height must have been about twenty feet. Our guide had brought us to a small gap, obviously quite modern and probably made by the herdsmen. We stepped inside down to a level of two feet, only to find that the centre of the building was now overgrown by large oaks. It was not till we found a point of vantage on the ruined tower that we realized how large the building must have been in its prime. With its courtyard it must have been ninety yards long by thirty-three broad. At the north-east end stood the remains of two towers, and at the south-west end the single tower from which we were looking. The size of the enclosed space must have been necessitated by the need of a refuge for the family stock in case of danger. The south-east face of the hill was almost precipitous and there were no ditches, the outer wall of the building rising straight from the slope.

For an hour we sat on the ruins of the south-west tower, enjoying the sun and eating our most excellent lunch, washing it down with that wonderful vin rosé of which I had partaken at Mohács. We hazarded guesses as to what sort of a life the inmates of the castle had lived those eight hundred years ago. It seemed fantastic that so much of the castle walls had remained. I wanted to know what language the three Saxon children had been taught to speak. Was it the Magyar of their mother or the Saxon of their father which they used for ordinary conversation? The priest solved the question by saying that they would have used Magyar for conversation and Latin for writing or reading. As far as Saxon was concerned I think we may take it that very little Saxon was spoken, for the two infant boys could hardly have spoken a word when King Edmund was killed in 1016. When Agatha, with her husband and three children, arrived in England, I think we may take it that they all spoke Magyar exclusively, and that the two girls, Margaret and Christina, could read and write in Latin.

I could find no trace of a well or spring on the summit of the hill, but there must have been one of them, perhaps even both. The source of the Alt was certainly very near, and this may have been used for the stock. The priest assured me that there had never been any excavations at Rákvár, and I thought how interesting it would be to spend a month fossicking about with an expert digger to find traces of the people who had lived there. I was loth to come away from the place, for my mind had hardly taken in all the details which had passed before me. I stopped and looked towards the east and found that through an opening in the hills one could get a view right up to the Danube and beyond. It was a memorable day in my life.

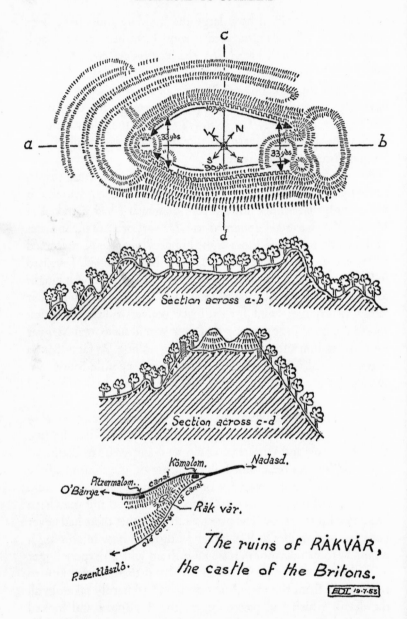

Section across a-b

Section across c-d

The ruins of RÁKVÁR,
the castle of the Britons.

On the way back we dropped István at Nadasd. I gave him a box of fifty Players cigarettes. His eyes nearly started out of his head when he realized what the little box I had given to him really contained. I would not let him break his box, so Kostia offered him one from his case. The old man produced a holder made of slate, for all the world like the pipes my Basutos used in the Kalahari. I have often wondered if there was some affinity between the Basutos and the Magyars. Did the Basutos come out of the centre of Asia? Had they marched from the north of Africa to the South?*

For our last evening we had a dinner for the old Priest in the inn, and a delightful one they gave us. I could have gone on listening to his tales of the Magyar peasants for hours. He knew them so well and loved them so well for their simplicity. What he now seemed to fear the most was a wave of emigration to the new world overseas. There were already many Magyars in America, living in their own communities and speaking their own language. Why should not the young men and women emigrate in order to avoid the hard times which must come to Hungary? He could not blame them, but still Hungary would need everyone of her sons if she were to survive in Europe as a nation.

When we started off next morning early, the old Priest placed both his hands on my head and solemnly blessed me.

* This goes back to the years 1902-04 when my father was on Special Service in German South-West Africa, living as a Boer trekker who had hired his services to the German Army Commader as a guide and transport leader.

CHAPTER VI

Journey Home

I had allowed myself two days in which to cover the 250 miles which lay between me and Klagenfurt, where I was to pick up Hay with the other car. But I had not reckoned on such bad road conditions. If I were a little late it did not matter much, for we had no fixed dates for our journey home through Italy and France. On our first day we could do only eighty-five miles, having to be pulled out of mud-holes in the centre of the road four times. Luckily there was no lack of help from the farmers and peasants with their animals. And the car suffered no damage. We were very tired when evening came, but we found a good inn and good hospitality within it. The second day went much better, especially when we struck the hard road to Marburg in Austrian territory. Finally, we drove into Klagenfurt just in time for dinner on 6 May. It was my birthday—my fortieth—but I had completely forgotten until Kostia reminded me of the fact.

Klagenfurt was one of the most beautiful places I have ever seen. The Austrians had made it one of their most popular holiday resorts, with fishing, sailing and very good bathing all the summer, and ski-ing and skating in winter. It hardly seemed possible that there could be any doubt as to the place being Austrian, but I was assured that there were many pockets of Yugoslavs in the country surrounding the town, which might well turn the scales against the Austrians. While I was there I was told of the sad case of an old Austrian Field-Marshal who was a Croat by birth. He could not go back to his own country, which had been handed over to Yugoslavia, and now lived in a hut near the lake. On an Austrian pension in depreciated kroner he and his wife and two daughters could hardly find enough money to supply one meal a day. I could not bring myself to go and visit him in his misery. As we had a large bundle of kroners in notes which would be of no further use to us, I sent it out to the old Field-Marshal with the compliments of a British visitor to the town.

The town was crowded with visitors in the way of Allied officers assembled for the Plebiscite which was to be held there shortly. I found myself bombarded with questions by the British contingent as to what was going on in Hungary. Their chief was a Lt-Colonel of Sappers who had been senior under-officer when I was a corporal at the 'shop'. He astounded me by asking what Horthy's White Terror had been like. I could hardly believe my ears, and yet his second-in-command, also a Sapper, backed him up by saying that he had some relations in Hungary and had heard a most horrifying story from them. Even though I told them what the Magyars had been suffering from Russian-sown Communism, and invasion by a Roumanian army, they would not believe me when I said that there had never been such a thing as a White Terror. I thought of Horthy and the English proverb about the dog with a bad name. Here was a bad name being given without a shred of evidence of any kind. I told them what I thought of Horthy.

My general plan for the journey home was to run down first to Mestre, so that all the party could spend a day in Venice. Then to motor straight across North Italy, making for the best crossing into France. Finally, to drive along the old battle-front so that I could spend a day at Verdun and another at Ypres.

Our first day to Udine was a trying one. The roads were crowded with lorries carrying stores to government depots for sale by auction. We drove all the time through thick white dust, despite the efforts of hordes of men engaged in flicking water on to the surface of the roads from any pool they could find at the side. They did this with long bamboo poles with a small leathern bag fixed at the end. In several places they had merely succeeded in making the road surfaces dangerously slippery. At the little hotel in Udine I saw for the first time an expert eating spaghetti. It was fascinating watching him winding the strings on a fork in the cup of his spoon. So neat was he that he never left himself with so much as a string hanging out of his mouth. We had four punctures coming down the mountains, but I managed to buy new Pirelli covers which fitted our wheels.

At Mestre we left both cars in a lock-up garage and the whole party went in to stay the night at the deserted Hotel Daniele. The two English drivers were quite incapable of looking after themselves, so I put them in charge of Kostia who always had a natural inquisitiveness which led him to enquire into everything he met with. We had plenty of money for them to enjoy themselves with, for the exchange was little better than the Austrian one. When he came back Kostia's only comment was to ask me what the natives did when winter came. Did they have sledges and good ponies like those in Russia? He would hardly believe me when I told him that Venice had no winter. We must have been the first visitors to the city since the war, for the guides descended upon us like vultures. They would not go away even when they were ordered to do so by the police, to whom I appealed. In desperation I tried my newly-acquired Italian to tell them that we did not want them. They merely bombarded us the more in every language they knew, in order to get our trade. We had to take refuge in a gondola which took us out of their sight.

Italy was in a bad humour. Everyone was grousing about the way their country had been treated after the war. All other countries on the winning side had made gains. Only Italy had got nothing. They seem to have completely forgotten that they could not find the men ready to go on fighting after the Armistice. They had themselves given up what they had asked for and been allotted to them in Anatolia. The people I talked to were firmly of opinion that the Allied Nations had clubbed together to see that the Italian currency remained low. The feeling in Italy was much worse than it was in France. There was a lot of talk about the value that would be gained under a Communist Government. British prestige in the country had fallen very low. All through our drive across the North of Italy we were made to feel uncomfortable. Food and drink was sold to us in surly silence.

Hundreds of lorries were moving about from town to town, filled with armed men ready to protect them from widespread strikes. Time and again we had to draw to the side of the road in order to prevent ourselves from being run down. For the first time I had to take off the Union Jacks from the front of our cars. I stopped at a bank to get a £5 note changed, and had an argument with the cashier who wished to give only half the proper exchange. In the end I refused to take what he offered and used French notes to carry me to the frontier.

My idea was to make for Turin where we would sleep the night, and then choose how we would move into France. We arrived at the *octroi* point outside the city, which certainly looked very deserted and empty of all traffic. I was told that there had been a Communist strike the day before, with a good deal of shooting. I was warned not to go into the city. I then rang up the headquarters of the Corps stationed in Turin and asked for permission to come in and see the General. I told the staff officer with whom I spoke that I was a British General in charge of an Allied Council Mission coming back from Hungary. After a good deal of talk a motor-cyclist was sent to the *octroi* to guide me in to see the General. At headquarters I found things as near chaos as they could be. Troops were out all over the country and there had been many clashes with strikers. I was turned over to the Chief Engineer to advise me on my road to France, as many of the telephone lines were down. I found him a very old and worried man. After consultation with one of his staff he told me that my best way was over Mt Cenis and that the road had been reported open. I was ushered out and sent down to the very dingy hotel, to which our cars had been sent. The hotel-keeper predicted a revolution and a siege of the city. He could supply no dinner, but directed me to a restaurant in a neighbouring street, and gave me a warning that it would be safer for me to clear out as early as I could the next morning. They were all very earnest, these people, but to me it appeared that they had all lost their heads.

I got my party up early and could issue only a couple of hard biscuits for the fifty miles we had to do to Susa. We were therefore all very hungry when we sat down to a hearty breakfast in the little hotel at Susa. It was really delicious with good coffee and a great basket of ripe black cherries, which cost just a few pennies. Even the two drivers, usually so very disdainful of foreign food, were satisfied. I was so sure of the report which the old Chief Engineer had given me that I made no further enquiries about the road, and though our two disreputable cars were surrounded by a crowd of sightseers, none of them asked where we were going. Perhaps they were as ignorant as the Chief Engineer. Anyway, they were good enough to wave their hands to us as we moved off. We had started sharp at 10 am, after filling up with oil and petrol and blowing up the tyres. The road looked good, though we encountered no traffic coming down, but passed that off as being too early for any cars coming from France. Most of the time we were in second gear and occasionally in third at the bends. The chains, which we had not used since our descent at Buchs, were working well. But both cars were boiling merrily, so that we had to halt to cool them and then fill up with iced water. We met more and more snow, until the track became a single one, and I began to curse the old engineer. We had met no one we could ask until a cart with a single horse appeared round a bend. The driver laughed at the idea of our going over the pass, but told us that a mile further up there was the last Italian Customs hut, and the men there would tell me the actual conditions on the pass. It was now nearly midday and we were all sure that the pass was closed, but we struggled on to the hut. Everyone inside was asleep and they none of them heard our loud yells. Then a head wearing a red nightcap appeared at a window and shouted to us to keep quiet. We got inside the hut and persuaded him to telephone to the French hut on the other side. It seemed almost ludicrous to us that these men did not have talks with each other at specified hours. In a few minutes we knew that the road was closed on the French side. There was nothing for it but to return to Susa and make a new plan.

In the same hotel where we had had such a good breakfast we now sat down to a belated lunch, and we all needed it badly, such was the effect of the mountain air. Lunching near us was a uniformed Italian Customs man, and to him I told the story of our mishap. He laughed heartily at what he called our innocence, but offered to put us through the Italian Customs at the Col de Genèvre, if we would give him a lift as far as that post. He proved to be an old soldier who had served in a Dragoon regiment in the war, full of grouses which always ended in a laugh at how the world went. He told me that there was Communism all over Italy, but the people who favoured a change to it did not know what Communism was. What Italy now required was a strong Government which would stand no nonsense. There were too many politicians playing for power, who were quite ready to make friends with the Communists, in order to get that power. None of these politicians realized what a risk there was in playing with fire. Democracy was not the thing for Italians in their present frame of mind.

He duly saw us through the Customs and by 6 pm we were at the French Customs post on the road to Briançon. The *douaniers* were living like troglodytes in a cave at the side of the road, their hut having been swept away by an avalanche together with all their papers. They made no trouble for us and passed all our motley collection of boxes and bundles without opening any of them. I rewarded them with my usual packet of Players. We talked a little about Verdun and Ypres and mud and filth. I told them some stories about the war in 1914 and they thought no more about contraband.

I was heartily glad to get out of Italy. The population was in a surly mood. They had expected much when they emerged from the war on the winning side, and were disgusted at the meagre reward which was meted out to them. Their position as a Mediterranean Power had been lowered rather than enhanced, for their enemies the Greeks and the Yugoslavs had gained much in territory and prestige. A great political struggle was evidently brewing in Italy, but I knew too little of the Italian people to be able to judge which way their thoughts were really moving.

All through my tour I had kept my accounts in a small notebook, changing my five-pound notes as I needed foreign currency, merely noting at what price I had bought it. In Austria, Hungary, Roumania and Italy the exchange had been so much in our favour that the expenses of my whole mission had amounted to very little. They were so many paradises for the poor traveller. But with the greatest care I had been left with packets of useless notes when I left them. I found a bank tucked away in a corner of an old street in Briançon, and there I changed my Italian lire for

French francs at a loss of 50 per cent. But at other notes, some new and shiny and others old and dirty, the cashier turned up his nose. Only Paris and London would touch such things, he said with obvious disgust. I tried to keep a tally of what was spent each day, but I wondered what the Paymaster would say to my accounts.

As we drove northwards along the old French front I found the same grumbling over the delays in rebuilding. The workers were ready to work, but the planners were still in hopeless confusion. Advances of money which had been passed by the Senate were not being paid. The wretched owners were asked again and again to sign papers, which they did not understand, but nothing came of them. All through, the patience of the French people seemed to be infinite.

I now wanted to study the positions of the two great bastions of the Allied line. The British one at Ypres I knew like the back of my hand, having spent long years fighting in it—from October, 1914, to March, 1916, as GSO1 and later GSO2 to the 6th Division, during the time when there was no relief for the troops in the line for a whole year and in some cases more. Then from March, 1916, to January, 1918, as GSO1 to the 4th Canadian Division when we captured the Vimy and Passchendaele Ridges. The French positions at Verdun I had never visited, but I had seen the map of the great salient which the Germans had driven in the line to the south of the old fortress. I wanted to know how they had come to make this salient. How had they held it for years, and why had they not made use of it? Why had the French allowed them to stay there so long without pinching it out? I had arranged for the curator of the Verdun battle-area to take us over the terrain. So many people used to ask me about this salient at St Mihiel that I was not going to remain ignorant about it any more.

The curator proved to be a retired Major of Artillery. He was in charge of all the cleaning up of the area, a terrific job with the removal of thousands of tons of barbed wire and the making safe of as many unexploded shells. He had a thousand men working under him. In addition to this he was a Member of the Board charged with the erection of numerous chapels and monuments, dedicated to those Frenchmen who had given their lives in the area.

He took us straight up into the ruined fort of Les Paroches, from whence we could look down into the valley of the Meuse upon the little village of St Mihiel. It was here where the Germans had crossed the river on a front of three miles and to a depth of two miles, thus forming the point of the Salient or *hernie* of St Mihiel as the French called it. For ten minutes he pointed out the various places on the ground before we adjourned for a quick lunch.

After lunch the Major explained to us on the map how the disused fortifications of Verdun, Nancy, Douaumont, Vaux and a host of other small forgotten strong points had been the means of breaking up the original German advance on this part of the French front. The German columns had passed them by on either side, hoping to isolate them until they could be dealt with at leisure. This they failed to do, with the result that the line had to stop in order to deal with the French salients still holding out. Away to the west the old fortress of Paris had the same effect. Behind the fortified area of the capital the French were able to bring up Manouty's Army to win the Battle of the Marne, and greatest of all to frighten von Kluck into giving up his task of outflanking the left of the French line, as Schlieffen had planned, and to turn in to the east.

As a desperate effort to counter the Allied victory on the Marne the German High Command managed to collect a force of three Corps, with siege equipment from Metz, and launch it from the Woevre against the Heights of the Meuse to the south-east of Verdun. They encountered little to oppose them but French reserve divisions, for the regulars had all been withdrawn to take part in the fighting on the Marne. Though they were eventually stopped, within two days they had succeeded in driving in their wedge to St Mihiel and then some two miles further across the Meuse.

We walked down into St Mihiel and then up towards the French line until we stood in the line the Germans had held so long. It was truly an impossible place from which to start a fresh attack, to enlarge the salient or to isolate Verdun. Then why did the Germans hold it at such a great expense? The only reason that I could see was that to keep it meant keeping the French guessing, so that they were compelled at all times to keep a large force ready in the area. As regards to the German losses I think that they must have been very heavy, despite the system of deep dugouts which they had built both on the Bislée spur and the spur south of the village of Chauvoncourt. We could not enter any of these dugouts as they were labelled '*infectés*'. The curator told us that the trouble had come from coal gas. The authorities were still considering how to deal with the situation.

From a strategical point of view the salient was of little use to the Germans as a starting point for the capture of Verdun. Nor was it of much use to the French. The mere wiping out of the *hernie*, which looked so menacing to Verdun on the map, would have been a very expensive operation in casualties and could not have led to any strategic advantage.

After taking leave of the curator we moved on to Longuyon, where we spent a good night in the comfortable inn. The second car was now going so badly that I decided to let it go straight to Calais, while I went on to have a look at the British bastion at Ypres.

14 May, the date upon which I paid my visit to the field of Passchendaele, was one of the most interesting I have ever spent. Like so many other British officers, I had spent long periods in the Ypres salient, holding first one then another of the sectors of defence. The period I was now going to try to reconstruct was the final attack of the 4th Canadian Division, which at last took the village which had defied so many attacks. During the long-drawn-out assaults of 1917, divisions had been thrown in to capture the high ground overlooking Ypres. Some had gone forward a few hundred yards and others had been stopped short at their jumping-off positions without gaining a yard.

I recall that my appointment as GSO1 to the 4th Canadian Division came as a very nasty shock, as I had hoped to be made GSO1 of the old 6th Division. The chief part I did not like about it was that I had to go home and prepare the Division for war. I did not want to do six months or so at home as one got so very quickly out of the picket if one had a long time away from fighting, and I felt that I might just as well have been posted to the War Office. I knew how good the Canadians were, but I did not want to break my life with the 6th Division.

However, it was once more a case of fate being kind to me and had I thought for a minute I would have realized that it was almost a miraculous chance to get on in the Army. The making of the Division would be mainly in my hands and I should most certainly be in the limelight. The General who was to command it was an old volunteer soldier and an important man in peacetime, being the proprietor of a Montreal newspaper, but he knew little of war and I was told that I should have to lead him. I thought of how these Canadians might look on me and I felt it depended largely on how I began. Turning it over in my mind I was confident that I would make a good impression on them; after all, I was a fighting soldier with some shrewd idea of war and I had worked in rough countries. As it proved, they received me with open arms and 'Dave' Watson, the General, treated me very well indeed and I could not have had a more happy and successful two years than I had with the Canadians.

I had an amusing time finding where the 4th Canadian Division was training. No one at the War Office knew where the Divisional Commander was. He had not yet come back from France, where he was serving as a Brigadier in the 1st Division, and the Canadian Government officials told me that they thought the man for me to report to was Major-General John Wallace Carson who had a suite and an office in the Savoy Hotel. To him I presented myself, escorted into his magnificent first-floor office by a very smartly dressed subaltern in the Canadian Grenadier Guards, who was very anxious to show me in to his boss. As I went in I encountered an enormous desk in the corner of the room at which, facing me was sitting an oldish man, wearing pince-nez, dressed in khaki, and looking more like a professor than a major-general.

He got up to shake me warmly by the hand and by the way he kept on welcoming me to the Canadian Army one might have thought that the 4th Canadian Division was lying gasping for breath just waiting for my arrival. While I was talking to the General my eye became fixed on a large notice which read as follows:

'Get to the point, but don't camp on it.'

He wanted me to stay in London until the Divisional General arrived, but I was keen to get down to Bramshott camp and make a start. Then I was told that I ought to go and see Sir Max Aitken, who was a liaison officer with the British Government, and Sir George Perley, who was the High Commissioner; so I paid my respects to each of them and found them very helpful and kind.

I arrived at Bramshott camp on 3 March, 1916, full of hopes, but I found the situation far from happy from our point of view. It looked as if politics were going to ruin our chances of getting the 4th Canadian Division into the field. There was the 10th Brigade of Infantry, ready for war but without a brigadier, and then some twenty battalions of different kinds which had been enlisted and brought to England under the man who had enlisted them with a promise that they should not be broken up when they reached England. Nine battalions would have almost constituted a division if we had the power to break up one of these odd battalions, but each colonel wired straight to the Canadian Parliament refusing to allow them to break up his regiment. Their training was being neglected and none of them had any war experience. I went to Max Aitken and told him how serious things were. He understood in a minute and went off to confer with the War Minister of Canada, Sam Hughes, who had just come over to Britain. Within forty-eight hours they had seen all the twenty colonels in question, and by talk and political promises they had some sort of a toss-up as to which battalions should remain as part of the 4th Canadian Division and which should be broken up.

I found Dave Watson easy to compete with. He was as anxious as I was to get out to France with his new division and I was able to make a programme that forced us to work at high pressure. I warned him that unless we got to France soon, the other three divisions might stop us from going by demanding our men as reinforcements. He knew nothing about training, but was able to understand what I was trying to do and could give a good deal out as if it came from him. This I urged upon him more and more as he gained confidence in himself, although he could not understand at first why I didn't mind his 'cribbing', as he called it, my work. I told him that was what I had been sent to do, that I was a trained officer and could make plans of a simple nature, which were easy to learn. And so he and I got on very well. I never had a row with him and would never have had one. All the advice

5 The Turkish Palace at Ismid where General Ironside set up his Headquarters.

6 The Town Guard at Shilé, on the Black Sea.

7   The British Residency at Baghdad.

8   General Haldane and General Ironside in a launch on the
Tigris at Baghdad.

I gave him he could take or leave just as he wished. I was not jealous, but was there to advise him and he had the responsibility of making the final decision.

I never had any anxiety as to whether we should turn out a good division or not and we had far more of the Canadian-born lads than the other three divisions and fewer of the old British soldiers. Each month we increased our training programme until we could go no faster.

When we came out to France the Canadian Corps was just moving up north out of the Somme to the Ypres Salient. We were ordered to go in and receive our baptism of fire under Gen Sir Ivor Maxse, a Guardsman, and General Jacob, afterwards the Field-Marshal. Both were excessively kind to us and we did two successful attacks just at the end of the Battle of the Somme. We did a month in the line before coming out and were then told to march up slowly to the north to join the Canadian Corps which had been located at Vimy Ridge. This was held with two divisions and two in reserve until the great battle was fought.

The story of how we tackled Vimy is an interesting one. When we took over from the French we found ourselves holding the very edge of the Ridge with a deep hollow behind and none of the view that the enemy had. They were looking over us and threatened to have us off the Ridge at any moment. They had beaten the French on the Ridge by mining under them, blasting them continually and driving them steadily off. The Canadians had very good and numerous Engineer Companies, almost treble the size of those in a British Division. They also had a battalion of miners, which was the saving of the position and the beginning of our famous victory. The Colonel of this mining battalion planned to tunnel well back and get under the German workings so as to blow them up. We all hoped that the mining would succeed and it did beyond all hope. Within a month we were blowing up the German miners and eventually drove them out of their positions until they ceased work altogether. The whole Canadian Corps were on top of the world and made the Germans very jumpy and never gave them a moment's rest. We found that about a fortnight in front of us was enough for most German divisions, but we still did not overlook them and they overlooked

F

us everywhere. With a valley on our side we had to have the guns much further back from our lines in order to be able to hit the German front line, which was some 200 yards from ours at most points. Great use was made of mortars and even at this game we got the better of the Germans. We had command of the air and from the air photographs we discovered the new positions on the German side as soon as they had been occupied. Our mortars were right down in the valley and the Germans could never get at them properly.

The great battle was to extend away to the south and the 4th Division held the left hand of the Canadian Corps and of the whole attack. We were ordered against all our protests to maintain a brigade in reserve and not to attack the German extreme right, which was situated at the end of the Ridge with the valley on its right. We thus had two brigades in action, and as they went forward their left flank would be exposed to fire from the circular hill, nicknamed the 'Pimple'. I argued against this for many days, but was overruled. I was told that the Germans on the circular hill would be kept quiet by a terrific bombardment and amongst other things a great deal of smoke, and that we should have no trouble. I didn't like it at all as the artillery had to cover our left flank against an actual infantry attack, but it will be remembered that the great attack was a complete success all along the line. Our reserve brigade was never used and we had to tackle the circular hill three days later. It was done on a narrow front of two battalions with two in reserve, and when I saw the number of guns which were going to take part on the front of 400 yards I could hardly believe my eyes. All was fixed for dawn, and on the afternoon before it began to blow a hurricane of snow straight from us into the faces of the Germans. I knew the attack had to be made and Corps HQ was informed of the weather. We had to go on with it and then at about 5 pm my chief clerk reported to me a telephone call made by the Divisional Commander to the Brigadier in charge of the attack on the circular hill 'not to attack if the weather kept so bad.' I tried to get the Divisional Commander to verify if he had given such an order, but he was reported to have gone to Corps HQ some miles behind us. I was in a quandary. I told the G2 what had happened and to report to the GOC that the attack must go on. It would take hours to get in touch with all the artillery which was widely distributed and I did not know what had happened at the Brigade HQ as the line was now down. I had to go and see the Brigadier so that he could inform the other two brigades in cipher that the attack was on and it took me and my orderly two hours to walk to the Brigade HQ, tumbling and fumbling in the snow. When I got there I found the Brigade Major in a state of collapse. The Brigadier had gone off to enjoy a little rum and taken too much and was now lying unconscious on his bed. The two battalions were still preparing to attack, but had reported the weather was damnable. I told them all was well and the attack must go on. The wind was behind us at gale strength and it would help us and impede the enemy. I asked both Colonels if I should come up and see them and they both reported they were ready. I did not tell them what had happened to the Brigadier. Never have I had such an anxious time and I sent a runner back to Divisional HQ to report that the attack was on (it took him three hours to get there) and we then got our watches out and waited. Zero hour came and the most awful noise imaginable. Our men ran straight through the Germans and could see nothing but dim figures in front of them. Our casualties amounted to a dozen and no more, and I think we must have taken prisoner any Germans who escaped the bombardment. With all the Ridge now taken we set off for home and by this time the weather had abated, but we still had the wind against us.* After Vimy we had many visitors to see the field of battle and one was the CIGS Wully Robertson. I met him at his car on the road behind the Ridge and he got quickly out, shaking me by the hand in a friendly way, with the remark, 'I see you ain't got no smaller'.

My old bulldog Gibby stood beside me at these visits and many the photographs there were of him; one led to a column in a newspaper. His Mons ribbon on his collar was noticed and it was reported that he had been slightly gassed at Vlamertinghe and

---

* I found the General and reported our success. I never told him that I knew he had telephoned the Brigadier about the attack and what had happened to him, and I never did say anything to the Corps Commander or to the Brigadier. The incident remained unreported.

had been taken to the top floor of the château and given a breath of clean air. This report appeared in the Canadian and American papers and I was called a Canadian Officer. In due time a letter arrived at 10 Downing Street from America enclosing a cheque for $1. A little girl, through her guardian, had sent it so that Gibby could be supplied with a proper gas mask. The cheque had been made out to Lloyd George and had his endorsement. After this publicity old Gibby became a hero and people always asked to see him if they visited the 4th Canadian Division. No one ever opposed his right to be at the front and I don't suppose I could have been told to get rid of him, but there was ever the chance that some busybody might interfere.

We remained on to hold the new Vimy Ridge and the plain below. We had earned our field of view and we enjoyed it for some months. It was a happy relief from being overlooked by the Germans. When mobile warfare was altering into trench warfare the Germans were more wide awake than we were and they fought stubbornly to seize the heights before they built their permanent trench lines.

My last great fight was at Passchendaele and I suppose it was the greatest the Canadian Corps ever finished so brilliantly. There has been much talk about whether Haig was right in pursuing the struggle against the Passchendaele Ridge or not. There can be no doubt that all that autumn and late summer the British were bearing most of the weight of the German Army and the French were at a very low ebb indeed. But as we know, it now seems very wrong to have put in the magnificent Corps of four Canadian Divisions when there was brewing the Cambrai Tank attack at the same time, and I think it must be acknowledged that neither Haig nor Byng, the Army Commander concerned, had much belief in what the tanks could do. On the other hand Hugh Elles and Boney Fuller, who were respectively the Commander and the Chief of Staff of the Tanks, believed that on this occasion, the first time when tanks would be employed properly, they would do well. In fact the Field Ambulances of the Canadian Corps were ordered behind the Cambrai Front to conceal the fact that we were going to be thrown in on the Passchendaele front. It can be imagined what the Canadian Corps might have done, backed up by the cavalry and other divisions on the Cambrai front.

A thing which has always puzzled me was this. Had we, the Canadian Corps, broken the front, and at Cambrai, was there a general or the troops to meet a mobile attack by the Germans? Had we been trained to mobile warfare we must have succeeded in making a break, but the cavalry were not so trained and could not have opened a gap in the enemy line and maintained it. We certainly did not have an army ready to fight a mobile war and we would never have got any French troops to fight in the open. I remember every incident of our final attack in November, when the cold and the mud were at their worst. My story may add a little to the problem as to whether Haig was right or wrong. The whole Canadian Corps had been out of the line for well on a fortnight after heavy trench fighting further south. Never had I seen our men so fit or more determined to win any battle into which they were sent, in all the two years I had served with them.

The 3rd and 4th Divisions were ordered to take over the line, and I as GSO1 of the 4th Division was ordered to reconnoitre the position on the right. I motored up to the western edge of Ypres and then walked forward to the Menin Gate. There in the ramparts I found General Monash, commanding the 5th Australian Division which we were going to relieve. The German heavy shells were still crashing down over the whole of the rear of the Salient, but towards the front both sides had abated their artillery fire as if they were verifying the position of their respective lines after the recent fighting. The General told me the story of their last attack, in which they had made an advance of about two hundred yards. They had hoped for more, and he attributed this partial failure to the fact that their men had arrived at their jumping-off line worn out after a long night advance. The Division before him had failed in the same way, coming up so late that they were an hour behind their barrage.

When we had finished our discussion on the map, the Australian G1 and I started off with our orderlies for the front line. When we emerged from the Menin Gate it was as if we had come into another world. Mud reigned supreme. The whole area from the ramparts to the Roulers Ridge was pitted with shell-holes filled with mud and water, and so close together that their outer rims

met. For the first two miles up to the gun line a beaten track had
been maintained, more or less along what had been the old *pavé*
road. Along this we joined an endless stream of artillery horses,
each laden with four rounds of field artillery ammunition and led
in pairs by an artillery driver. Day and night this stream never
stopped, so that the means to keep up our terrific barrages might
be maintained. This track was kept open by large working
parties, filling up ever-renewed shell-holes and throwing up the
débris on either side. In the months of this long battle this track
had become a sunken lane, with banks composed of broken carts,
dead horses and equipment of every kind. The stench of death
was almost overpowering. Before us in the distance stood the
menacing Ridge, from which the enemy could look right into
the very innards of our back area. It seemed incredible that men
and horses could escape complete destruction. And yet the stream
never ceased.

Just short of the gun line we came to an old enemy pill-box, in
which the Australian Brigadier had established his headquarters. It
was crammed to overflowing with staff, orderlies, clerks and
telephonists. Linesmen and runners lay around the pill-box in any
hole they could find, ready to go off to mend telephone wires or
carry messages. At the side of the pill-box were seated two
Australians crouching over a little fire. Both were dead, though
they looked so peaceful that one had to go near to them to see if
they lived or not. One still had his pannikin of tea in his right
hand. An orderly told me that they had been killed only a few
minutes before by fragments from a shell. The enemy never
ceased to spray the whole place with field-gun fire. The Brigadier
explained that the front lay some two miles further up the slope,
and that there was at the moment a temporary lull in the front
line. He had not yet been able to get all his wounded down, but
he hoped to get them away that night.

From the pill-box forward there were now no tracks of any
sort. We had to follow the edge of the shell-holes, zig-zagging
round one until one met the next, which caused us to be looking
continually up in order to keep our general direction. Unloaded
as we were it was a physical effort of no mean kind to get forward.
It was no wonder that the fighting soldiers had become exhausted

by a night advance over such terrain. Each mud-crater was a trap from which no man could have escaped unaided, and we encountered bodies around these craters which had been lying there for days. I made up my mind then and there that we could not risk a night advance. The men would have to be filtered up in daylight, and some place would have to be found close to the top of the ridge, where they could spend their time unseen until zero hour. They would then be in good heart for the daylight attack the next morning.

At last we arrived at the edge of the final plateau, on which the village of Passchendaele lay, to find the Lt-Colonel in charge of the line in another pill-box, the last remnant of the permanent German fortifications in front of the Roulers Ridge. From here we could get a clear view of the country over which we had to go. It was completely free of any strong defences. The enemy and ourselves were lying in two opposing lines of fox-holes, somewhere about 200 yards apart. To the crest from our front line was about 600 yards. This was our task, to cover that distance and drive the enemy over the hill, so that he would lose his observation into the Salient.

There was an uncanny silence on the plateau. Shells from both sides were passing over and bursting far beyond where the front lines lay. We could see men on either side doubling from fox-hole to fox-hole, throwing out ammunition, food and water-bottles for the men in them. Neither side was making any attempt to stop this. I heard neither rifle nor machine-gun fire going on anywhere on the plateau. It was fascinating looking at the wide stretch of apparently unoccupied ground. It looked a simple enough thing to put down a heavy barrage or smoke-screen at some unusual hour, and then to race the men across the space they had to cover, instead of always attacking at dawn and sending the men across at a steady walk. One ought to be able to catch the enemy unprepared at, say, 5 pm of an evening. It would have been easy and quick if the men had done no night advance. I would put the suggestion up when I got back to headquarters.

I and my orderly then began our search for a lay-by for the troops who were to carry out the assault. A possible one appeared at once just behind the edge of the plateau. In the end we found a stretch of 1,000 yards long and 150 yards in depth. The ground was strewn with hundreds of rifles with their bayonets fixed, ready to be used as markers. It took us just over two hours to drive these rifles in to make a pen for the men who were to wait there during daylight. We were both pretty tired when the task was done. Time was getting on and we had to go over the shell-hole area in daylight.

I set off in the lead with my orderly some ten yards behind me. I halted every (what I took to be) five minutes and all went well. Then, when we had gone half-way to the Brigadier's pill-box, I heard a cry behind me. Looking back I saw my orderly right in the middle of a big hole, already engulfed up to his armpits in the mud. He was struggling hard and it was only his kilt which had spread out round him which kept him from sinking beyond help. I turned back, shouting to him to be still. I had a muffler and a belt, and these I tied together, and I began casting as if for a fish, with the buckle-end of the belt at the forward end. The lad was shouting at me not to come too close and so fall in with him, but I got him to be quiet. Three, four casts and then he caught the fifth. Very slowly I towed him in and up the bank. When it was over I could hardly stop laughing at him. The mud on his kilt weighed him down so that he could barely stand. I got the kilt off him and with an old piece of a rifle I scraped most of the mud off, while he stood shivering by me. He was pretty near done by the time I managed to get him down the next mile as far as the ammunition track. From there he had a ride on a horse. It was pitch dark by the time we reached the Menin Gate and so into the Australian headquarters. Hot Australian tea well laced with rum for both of us, and a pair of khaki trousers and a coat for him made us ready to stand the car journey homewards. It was midnight before we reached our billets.

Four days later our assault on Passchendaele was a complete success. Our men were brought to the front in twos and threes and, with a very strong body of Sappers, we were able to lay down a couple of lines of duck-boards over the shell-holes.

We were now approaching the field of Passchendaele from the enemy side. I wondered whether I should recognize any of the ground after two and a half years. We had a short meal in a café at Roulers and then drove up to the Ridge and left the car there at a police post.

Taking Kostia with me to carry my binoculars and various maps and papers, we crossed the ridge and on for twenty yards or so till we had a clear view. The view which the Germans had always had of our operations against them. My first impression was one of surprise that the whole panorama in front of us looked so uniformly flat. The slope up to us from the Menin Gate now looked a very paltry affair to what it had seemed to me when I tackled it on our reconnaissance two and a half years ago. Then it came upon me that all slopes must seem steeper in war to those who had to face armed men at the top of it. When I had first seen it it was all uniformly brown, but now it looked like a lush green field of grass. Looking closer I saw that the shell-holes were still there, but now there were large tufts of reeds and bulrushes growing in them up to a height of three feet. The ruins of Ypres looked bare and open with all the roads leading up to the town very clearly marked. Nothing much had yet been done to clear away the *débris*. The sunken road from the Menin Gate to the gun line was still there, and there were still muzzles of guns sticking up from the mud amidst what appeared to be a mass of broken wheels. The objects which now struck one most were little white tents, hundreds of them dotted about here and there about the land as far as we could see, each surrounded by a series of tin shanties, with here and there a red or a blue flag fluttering at the top of a long pole.

Ypres is to us the best known of the Flanders battlefields and, as GSO2 of the 6th Division which was holding most of the Ypres Salient under Sir Walter Congreve, VC, it was my responsibility to escort VIPs around the town. One of these was Lord Curzon, who had been asked by the King of the Belgians to inspect the conditions of the ruins, and I had been detailed to conduct him and his party of senior Belgian officers.

I met the party at Vlamertinghe and guided them and their cars into the outskirts of Ypres. The party got out and their cars were sent off to shelter a little further back. We had halted for a minute and I was just explaining what I proposed for his tour when he asked if he could step to one side to 'micturate' as he called it. He moved over to the buildings I pointed out to him and was commencing operations when the great 16-in howitzer in Houthulst wood suddenly let off a shell. It fell 100 yards beyond where Curzon was standing and he turned to me with the words, 'And what is that?' I told him that it was the big 'how' to the north which usually fired some eight rounds each time it opened fire. He made no answer, but at the second shell I said to him that I should have to take him under cover until the 'hate' finished. He looked at me somewhat superciliously and said, 'I am not afraid'. I replied, 'Well, Sir, neither am I, but I am in charge of your person and I must take you under cover for a short time'. I then led him off to the side and to one of our big hot baths we had rigged up in the cellars of the prison. Inside we saw the process gone through. Each man stripped naked and jumped into the steaming water. There they bathed and played like children until a whistle called the batch out. They filed out to a dressing room, where they were completely refitted with washed and disinfected clothing. When they had come in they were smothered in mud from head to foot and looked like monsters come from some deep sea. They looked so healthy and pink in the water and so smart in their clean kit that one could hardly believe that there had been such a transformation before our eyes. I found it very difficult to engage his Lordship in conversation and I pointed out to him that our young soldiers looked so happy and healthy, with their clear skins when once they had been given a bath. To this he did not reply for some time, but then he said, rather pompously, 'Yes, once before I have seen the lower classes in their baths. I used to think they had dark skins all covered with hair, but I see they have not'.

Two or three people must have heard this choice remark, but no one even smiled. We then came out when the hate was over and walked round with the Belgian officers. As we passed an angle of the Cloth Hall one of them picked up the head of a small figure exquisitely carved and offered it to Curzon as a memento and I have never seen a man's face so filled with disgust. That he, the noble Curzon, should be offered a souvenir was too terrible. I dare say if it had been taken home for him and put up in his garden he would have accepted it with alacrity.

While I was sitting there up strolled a Belgian Corporal of Police. He had evidently seen our car at the post and identified it as British, and now wished to pay us a friendly visit. He addressed Kostia, who was standing behind me, asking him if there was anything he could do for us. I turned to him and explained that I was a British General, who had fought long in the Ypres Salient, and now wished to see the battlefield from the German point of view. I had addressed him in Flemish, as I knew from the few words of French he had used to Kostia that he was a Fleming. This confused him for a moment, but he was soon explaining to us what the white tents were and what the flags meant. It appeared that the position of each farm-house of every holding had been marked on the ground from a general survey. Each farmer was allowed to start work from that point outwards, until they met the confines of their old farms which were soon to be marked on the ground. It all seemed very business-like and quick. Infinitely better that the steps the French were taking to re-establish their farmers.

The Corporal then walked down with us to introduce us to some of the farmers. It was a homely sight to see the old father or mother taking a short rest in a camp chair, the old woman knitting and the old man still shouting directions to his various children. The cook-house was in a shanty next to the tent, and I saw a heap of *débris* ready for firing, though the cooking was all done on an oil stove. An orchard had already been planted, and I even saw some espalier pears already planted to climb up the south walls of the house when it was built. The flags all had a reason. A red flag meant that they had several shells ready to be defused by the Government experts. They told me that these unexploded shells were for ever appearing like a growing bush. They seemed to turn their noses up and force themselves above the surface. Before they used a plough upon a new piece of ground they had to inspect it well, by prodding every inch of it with a supple stick, which bent if it struck any metal. This work was very dangerous, but everyone shrugged their shoulders with a smiling, 'Ça va bien. Nous gagnons!' A blue flag was to denote the fact that a heap of barbed wire was ready for pressing. The owners had all been supplied with gloves to prevent cuts and infection when the wire was being dragged towards the entrance to the farm. Soon a man would arrive with a lorry and a machine for baling the wire and crushing it into a small space. It was then taken away to be dumped in the great craters which had been blown along the front. Everybody was happy and I heard no complaints about the Government. Apparently their currency was rising in value. I had my health drunk in many a glass of *péquet*.

One of the most difficult things to put right was the land drainage. The years of heavy shelling had completely obliterated every outward vestige of the ditches and streams. Even this knotty business was being tackled energetically and courageously. Already the main directions of the lines of drainage had been marked with plans. Human remains were being dealt with great reverence, and identity discs found on bodies were very carefully kept till the visiting inspectors charged with their collection arrived on given days.

I was so interested with what was going on that it was too dark to get to the coast in daylight, so I decided to put up at the inn at Roulers and make an early start the next morning. That night there was quite an assembly in my honour, and I had to make several speeches describing the various parts I had taken in the Salient. And when that had been done, I had to tell them stories about Archangel and the fighting there.

On my arrival in London I duly reported myself at the Foreign Office, but my mission had long ago been forgotten. I sent in my card to Lord Curzon and after waiting an hour I received a polite message that the Secretary of State had no time to see me. As his underling explained—and I shall never forget the wording—'His Lordship did not wish to be confused by reports coming in from various parts of Europe, as he wished to be able to have an unprejudiced view of the general situation'. I wondered how he made a picture without seeing reports.

II

COMMAND OF THE ISMID FORCE

18 July to 18 August,
1920

Ismid lies at the end of a long narrow gulf on the coast of Turkey by the eastern shore of the sea of Marmora. It was little known but was situated at a strategic point in terms of road communications. Ismid lends its name to the Gulf, the peninusla and to the force which had been established there to deal with Mustapha Kemal's guerrillas. The Ismid Command was part of the Army of the Black Sea, whose job it was to restore order in the region and to enforce the Treaty of Sèvres; in other words to sort out the new Greek and Turkish boundaries.

CHAPTER I

Journey to Constantinople

In England the weather in May and June of 1920 was fine and sunny. I found it pleasant enough in our little Mill House in High Wycombe, for I had saved up enough money on my Budapest trip to buy a small and very old car. In it we were able to go round and visit the many friends my wife had made in my three months absence abroad. One who lived just above us at Daw's Hill was Lord Lincolnshire, and many was the night we went up to dine with him or to spend the afternoon in the grounds of his beautiful house. I well remember the day upon which we were introduced to General Sir George Higginson, a Crimean veteran who lived to well past a hundred years before he died. Lord Lincolnshire had been his fag at Eton and insisted on having his photograph taken between the oldest and the youngest Generals in the Army. Sir George had been the Adjutant of a battalion of Coldstream Guards in the Crimea and described to us some of the mismanagement which had taken place out there. He spoke so vividly that it was hard to believe that the events he was describing had been enacted seventy years before.

But with all the little amusements which came my way I found it difficult to settle down to anything serious. How could it be otherwise with a half-pay General? I was still the junior Major-General on the list and was no nearer a permanent job than I had been the year before. My relations and friends were trying hard to persuade me that I should take up something in civil life. They argued that wars were now over for a long time to come, and that there would be nothing but stagnation in the Army just as it had been after the war in the Peninsula. They told me that I ought to make a change while I was still young enough to learn a new trade. But from what I had seen in Eastern Europe I thought that the world was very far from being peaceful. Some of the offers of employment were tempting enough, but I always came back to the thought that I must be true to my salt. I loved the Army and had been very happy during my service in it. And how could I tell whether I should be happy in civilian life? I simply could not contemplate leaving the Army for good.

The first inkling that there might be something brewing for me came on 1 July, when my wife and I were invited to Aldershot to spend a week-end with Lord Rawlinson who was the Commander-in-Chief there. As a fellow guest I found Mr Winston Churchill, then the Secretary of State for War. My relations with him dated back to the South African War, where we had been subalterns together. Even in those young days I had realized that he was a person of importance. And he had already served in two campaigns. The first in Cuba against the United States, and the second in the Sudan at the battle of Omdurman. We had always got on very well together. After dinner on the Saturday night the question of the stagnation in the Generals' list came up for discussion. An Army List was sent for and Mr Churchill went through the list from top to bottom, considering each name in succession for several minutes. It was surprising how many of the Generals he knew personally, and when he did not know any particular General he listened most carefully to what Lord Rawlinson said about him. It was often embarrassing to hear their opinion of my seniors expressed so vividly. When my name came up at the very end of the list, Mr Churchill stopped and asked me what I was doing. To this I replied, 'Just waiting with all the patience I can muster.' At this he replied with a smile, 'Never mind. You may find the list a good deal shorter before long.'

Within a month I was summoned to the War Office for an interview. There I saw my old friend Tim Harington, who was DCIGS to Sir Henry Wilson. He informed me that the War Office had received a wire from Sir George Milne, the Commander-in-Chief of the Army of the Black Sea, in which he asked for the services of 'a young fighting Major-General' who could speak French. The General Staff thought that I would fill the bill. Was I prepared to go out to Constantinople at once? I accepted on the spot. He told me that my name would be telegraphed out to Sir George, and that if he accepted my nomination I should probably be interviewed by the Prime Minister before I left the country. Meanwhile I was to go to the Intelligence Branch of the War Office in order to make myself aware of what was going on in the Middle East.

I was given no hint as to what my job was going to be. As they required 'a young fighting Major-General' it looked as if I were to be given a command. What the French was needed for I could not conceive, as there were now no French troops working with us in the Middle East. It was all very mysterious. I had never served under Sir George Milne, and to tell the truth I had never even seen him. I knew him well by reputation as a hard-fighting General, and as a brother Scot from Aberdeenshire and a Gunner I was proud of his distinguished career. With many other officers in the regiment I thought that he had been shabbily treated in not having been raised to the peerage as all the other Army Commanders had been at the end of the Great War. I felt glad to have the chance of fighting under him, and was in high spirits at the thought of more active service.

I spent a good many hours in the Intelligence Branch. The political situation in the Middle East seemed to be growing more and more complicated. With the greatest difficulty the Allied Council had succeeded in drafting a treaty for the reconstruction of the broken Turkish Empire—the Treaty of Sèvres. The details of this treaty had not been disclosed to the Turkish Government till 24 April 1920, and by 9 July it had still not been signed. From what I could hear it seemed to be dying for want of the power to enforce it.

I had lately seen how the treaties with Austria and Hungary had been implemented. No Allied troops had been used to enforce the clauses of these treaties, and the Council had grasped eagerly at the military aid offered by the so-called successor states, with the result that they had been forced to acquiesce in a much more drastic partition of the Old Empire than had been originally intended. It was only natural that the new states should

G

grab as much as they could of the booty available, and the Council had no means of keeping order in the demarcation of the new frontiers.

In dealing with the affairs of the Turkish Empire, the Allied Council found itself faced with still more difficult problems. Time had been going on and all the Allies had grown tired of war. The Turks had been given time to draw breath and consider the terms of the treaty. They had probably passed over the loss of the Arabian possessions, but now they saw that Anatolia, their homeland, was to be cut up and distributed in pieces at the will of their conquerors.

Long before the defeat of the Turkish Army in the field had been achieved there had ensued an ugly rush on paper to seize the spoils which might be expected on the break-up of the Turkish Empire. Russia had been promised the guardianship of the Dardanelles. Italy had been allotted the Dodecanese Islands and a large slice of the Smyrna vilayet as a reward for joining in the war on the side of the Allies. A new state of Armenia was to be set up on the Caucasian border, largely at the behest of President Wilson. France was to be given a mandate on a strip of territory extending from the Mediterranean to this Amercan sponsored state. From this picture it will be seen that there was to be little left for the Turks of their ancestral territory. Unfortunately for these grandiose plans a gigantic rot had set in amongst the Allies. President Wilson's project for an Armenian State was rudely rejected by the US Congress, and no one else could be found to take up the mandate. Britain was already assuming the mandates of Iraq and Jordan, besides that of the new state of Israel, and she could not spare any more troops. France and Italy had come to the conclusion that they could not find any troops who were ready to continue fighting for the new mandates which they had demanded. The Allied Council had fallen into a predicament from which they could see no escape other than a complete abandonment of the Treaty.

To the British statesmen it seemed unthinkable that after all they had done to defeat the Turkish Army in the field, unaided by any of their Allies who were now demanding so much of the spoil, everything should be thrown away. One plan only seemed to offer an alternative to total abandonment of the treaty. Ready at hand stood M. Venizelos, the Greek leader, willing to employ the whole of his forces against the Turks. Before his eyes he had conjured up the picture of a greater Greece, and he was ready to stake his all in remaking the old Greek Empire. He believed that his troops were superior to anything the Turks could now produce, and there were moreover a million and a half of Greeks in Anatolia who could be relied upon to fight for their liberty. So persuasive had M. Venizelos become that Mr Lloyd George and his colleagues on the Allied Council were almost mesmerised by his arguments.

His offers of help were accepted, and in May a force of 20,000 Greeks was landed in the Smyrna area to help in the enforcement of the Treaty of Sèvres. As a reward, the Greeks were to be allowed to mark out a Greek State in the vilayet of Smyrna, where the majority of the Greeks in Anatolia might be assembled. This was to replace the land which had been originally allotted to the Italians. It does not appear that any exact directions were issued by the Council as to the actual size of this new state.

There were two dangers attached to any employment of a large Greek Army in Anatolia. Both were very real. First, nothing was more likely to revive the latent spirit of the Turks than the sight of their despised Greek subjects calmly pegging out a new state in the middle of their homeland. Secondly, both France and Italy were violently opposed to the setting up of a third Power in the Mediterranean. Though they themselves were unable to take part in the future partition of Anatolia, their jealousy might drive them to almost any lengths in order to prevent the founding of a new Greek Empire.

It seemed quite evident to me that the Allied Council had made up its mind to destroy the Turks as a nation, just as they had done with the Magyars. It did not seem to me that they had yet grasped the desperate danger which came with the declaration of power by the Bolsheviks in Russia.

Sir George Milne having signified that he was prepared to accept my nomination, I made ready to be interviewed by Mr Lloyd George who was over in Spa, busy with the affairs of the Allied Council. I had never spoken to him before, and had only seen him once when he came to inspect the 4th Canadian Division in which I was serving as GSO1, just before they went over to France. Late one evening I was ushered into his sanctum by Sir Henry Wilson. It was in Spa. I can well remember him looking at me over his old-fashioned pince-nez, which were askew across his nose, rather as if he were examining a new sort of moth which had been lately captured. He treated me to a long discourse upon the iniquities of the Turks. He told me that he knew there were many British officers who regarded them as good old country-gentlemen, whereas they were in fact the greatest scoundrels unhung. As he developed his theme he took off his pince-nez and beat time with them on a book which was lying on his table. He then switched on to the excellencies of M. Venizelos, telling me that he had regenerated his people. Greek troops, he said, were now amongst the best in Europe. I listened to him in silence, for I knew nothing about M. Venizelos or the troops which he now had. Suddenly the Prime Minister stopped, and looking at me with some suspicion he barked out, 'You're not pro-Turk are you?', with repeated beats on his book. To this, I replied that I was not. There was a short pause and then he asked me, 'Are you pro-Greek then?' To this I replied again that I was not. This seemed to puzzle him, for he plied me with a third question, 'Then what are you?' Somewhat nonplussed by the catechism through which I was being put, I replied. 'I am a British soldier and I am pro-British.' Sir Henry Wilson with his ready wit jumped in with, 'You see, Sir, he is completely mercenary and goes wherever he is told.' At that we all burst out laughing. I was asked a few more trivial questions and then dismissed. I came away still without the least idea of what I was going to be asked to do. It was all damned mysterious.

My orders were to catch the Orient Express in Paris on 14 July. I was to provide myself with an ADC and was given permission to take my servant with me. My spirits went up as I saw the order for an ADC. Surely that must mean that I was to be given a command? Finding one was not so easy, for all the British regiments were being filled up to go abroad, and no colonels were ready to part with good subalterns. I received two flat refusals, but in the end found a Gunner called Brownhill, who had been in Russia with me. My servant Kostia had served in Russia with the Royal Scots and having been made a British subject he elected to enlist in a Highland Regiment. I sent him up to Perth, where he was duly enlisted in the Black Watch and fitted out with a full kit. The whole of our household had great fun with him when he returned in his kilt with a red hackle in his bonnet.

Our journey started badly with Brownhill being directed to cross the Channel to Calais instead of Boulogne, with the result that he missed the express in Paris by a few minutes. It took him a week to catch us up again. I found that the War Office had not been able to book our tickets any further than the Italo-Serbian border, as there was no certainty that the train would get as far as Constantinople. When we did reach this frontier at Logatec the train stopped so that some telegraphing could be done. I got out to learn how things were going, and seeing some tattered-looking soldiers on the opposite platform I crossed over to talk to them. Who should they turn out to be but men of the Czech Legion who were due to come to us at Archangel, when the army of Kolchak crossed the Siberian frontier into Russia in 1919. They had just landed in Trieste from Vladivostok. Some of their officers came out to see who I was, and laughed heartily when I told them about Archangel, telling me that the last thing they wanted was to come there. By that time they had had enough of all Russians, Red or White. They brought out a bottle of plum brandy in order to drink my health in memory of our meeting. They had had a nice long war, but were now going home at last.

We pulled into Belgrade about midnight. There were no lights in the station and there appeared to be nobody in charge. Two porters were busy demanding that all our luggage should be taken out of our carriages, as the train was not going on. I took my torch and walked along to the ticket office to see if I could find any further news, and there I found a very old and fat woman reading a paper by the light of a hurricane lamp. From her I gleaned that she was the wife of the station-master, who had gone into the city to get orders about the train. She had no idea when he would come back. A young man was hanging about the office with a disconsolate look on his face. He turned out to be an attaché in the French Embassy at Athens, and he had been trying to buy a ticket to that place. He had evidently not been travelling much in post-war Europe with so many depreciated currencies, and had been insulted by the old woman offering him dinars for his louis d'or, the only money he had with him, on an equal footing. With the depreciated dinar she ought to have been giving him thousands for a gold piece. I tried to cheer him up by telling him that I had not a ticket either, but I proposed to pay when I reached my destination.

Finally at about 5 am the station-master returned very drunk indeed. He must have been indulging freely in plum brandy, but after much prodding I learnt that the train was to go on at 9 am.

At Nish, where the Athens portion of the train was to be cut off, we found ourselves surrounded by hundreds of Serbian ex-prisoners of war lodged in a camp close to the station. They had been working on the land in North Germany and were now being returned to their homes. They were all shouting for cigarettes or tobacco at the windows of the restaurant-car, where one misguided waiter had thrown out some cigarettes. We were only saved from a combined raid when the train moved on.

It was late when we reached Sofia, but here the station was ablaze with light. Demobilized soldiers thronged the platforms waiting the carriages which were to take them home. Seeing in the Paris *Daily Mail* that I was on the Orient Express, the Military Attaché in Sofia had come down to see me. He was full of interest as to what I was going to do in the Middle East, for the chief topic being discussed in Bulgaria was the employment of the Greeks in Anatolia. He wanted to know whether British troops were going to be employed with them, and if I was going to command. No one would believe that the Greeks could fight Turks all on their own. The down-trodden Greek subjects of the Turks could never be turned into good soldiers. As regards Bulgaria, he told me that all was quiet, though there had been some trouble over the demobilization of the many young Bulgarian officers who were now redundant. They had all refused to be sent back to the land as labourers.

We moved on again at about 4 am, and I had hardly got to sleep when I was wakened by a furious hammering on the door of my bunk. I then heard Kostia's voice in Russian shouting to someone to stand still, and I opened the door of my compartment thinking that we were in for a rough-house of sorts. There I found an elderly American shivering while he faced Kostia and his revolver. He stuttered out that he was a man who made travelogues, which he used for lecturing in the USA. After he and his photographer had boarded the train at Sofia he had suddenly realized that his passports were not in order. Losing his head and with the idea of getting help from me, he had hammered on my door in his fright. I gave him a good cursing at his folly in making a scene for nothing and sent Kostia off to his bed again.

When we reached the Turkish frontier I was awake, but got up when I realized that the train was not stopping. As we moved along at a snail's pace I saw that the two sides of the permanent way were crowded with Greek soldiers. A large siding was packed with trucks loaded with more Greeks. In about half an hour we stopped at a point where a trench ran away into the distance on either side. It was occupied by Greeks who were busily clearing the field of fire with scythes. Field guns had been brought close up to the recently built trench and were being dug in by their gunners. A Greek NCO entered our carriage and ordered us in French not to get out. After half an hour, in which I tried to think what was going on, the train moved off slowly once more. The Greeks had evidently crossed the Turkish frontier and were preparing to advance against Adrianople. The Greeks must have started earlier than had been expected. Had I missed the bus? There was no one whom I could ask. Even if I had been able to speak Greek no one would have dared to answer me. They must have known that I was in the train and in uniform, and yet no one was sent in to make contact with me. Just before we were due in Adrianople we crossed a similar trench, this time occupied by Turkish soldiers, and we drew up and halted in the main station a few minutes later. The station was obviously the headquarters of the force opposing the Greeks, for I saw a field office established on a platform. Though I got out and stood by my carriage to watch the scene, no one came to ask me what I was doing. Orderlies were coming in with messages and staff officers were using telephones. They were all very busy, but there were no planes moving about and I could hear neither artillery nor machine-gun fire. Evidently the fight had not begun yet.

As I stood there wondering how all this was going to affect me, I became aware of a civilian in a light cotton suiting who was addressing me in French. When I had pulled myself together I realized that his business with me was a very prosaic one. Had I got a ticket? he asked me. I told him that I had been unable to get a ticket in Paris, and I intended to pay what was needed from the Italian frontier to Constantinople. Quite politely he explained that the Turkish railways in Europe had been taken over by a company registered in Paris, and he was responsible that everyone travelling on the line had a ticket. I had so many things being turned over in my mind that I told him to go away and bother me no more. At this rebuff he began to be more offensive, roaring at me, 'Why will you not be sensible? Even Franchet d'Esperey buys a ticket.' As the great French General had left the Middle East a long time ago, I told the little Frenchman to go away, adding in the calmest way I could, 'And who is this man Franchet d'Esperey of whom you prate?' That finished him up and he went sadly away. Poor devil, probably the only pay he got was from odd people with no tickets.

It was not till we were close into Constantinople, at a point where the railway ran along the shores of the Sea of Marmora, that I got my first sight of a British soldier. The train pulled up at a tiny station with the waters of the sea lapping right up to the low platform. A large tented camp lay literally on the shore of the sea, and on a great expanse of beach were thousands of British Tommies, disporting themselves in the water or playing ball-games on the beach. As soon as they saw the express drawing up, hundreds of them ran back from the beach to see it arrive. With a minimum of clothing, they were still wearing their topees. I think they were just as surprised as I was when I stepped on to the platform and they saw a British General in khaki looking straight at them. Much abashed, some saluted and others took off their topees and stood to attention. Then out came the traveloguer with his photographer, shouting to the men and, I suppose, to me also, 'Hold that! Hold that!' I am afraid I growled at him in my rage.

I was taken in to see Sir George Milne on the morning of 17

July. He greeted me kindly, saying that he was always glad to have another Gunner in his command. He looked a strong, sturdy man in his early fifties, with just that Scottish accent which marked him as a man from the north-east. He had a reputation for being gruff with any visitors who came to see him, but I certainly saw nothing of that. He told me that he wished me to take over the command of the Ismid force at once. It was about a division in strength, consisting of both British and Indian troops from the two divisions under his Corps Commander, Sir Henry Wilson. The Indian troops were steadily being sent home as ships became available to take them. My immediate job was to clean up the Ismid Peninsula, into which Mustapha Kemal had introduced some considerable number of guerrillas in order to harry us. Some of these gentry had even penetrated as far as the Bosphorus, where they had sniped the Flagship of the Mediterranean Fleet, the *Iron Duke*, as she lay at anchor at Baikos. There had been no casualties, but Sir John de Robeck, who was also the British High Commissioner, had been very angry at the insult to his Flag. Two colonels for my staff had been found, both of whom had served with me before. Sir George specially asked me to deal with his Corps Commander as much as I could, but as he had no administrative staff I would have to deal in all administrative matters direct with the Army. As he dismissed me, Sir George's last words were that he thought I should find that the Ismid force required a good shake-up.

Not one word was said about my going to have Greeks with me, nor of the curious position which I had encountered near Adrianople. I did once allude to the fact that I had seen some Greek troops, but from Sir George's face I saw at once that this was obviously taboo. As I learnt later, it was not till 22 August that the Greeks advanced against Adrianople. Their success was so quick and so complete that the whole of European Turkey was cleared of all regular Turkish troops.

I spent the afternoon paying three visits. The first was to the Corps Commander. He had not yet received any orders about my taking over the Ismid force, though it was at the time commanded by one of his infantry brigadiers. As the two divisions each had a major-general in command of it, the reason for my having been brought out to command some of their troops appeared more mysterious than ever. I told him that I had received verbal orders from the Army Commander to clear up the Ismid Peninsula. I had nothing in writing. Sir Henry was most polite and told me to come and see him as often as I wished. As a matter of fact I never did receive any orders, either verbal or written, from him or his staff. None of them came out to see me. He made no allusions to any manoeuvres being carried out by the Greeks, and he had no idea what the Greek force at Smyrna was doing. I then went on to see the chief of the Army administration, General Welch. He was also reticent upon the question of any Greek operations. He made it quite clear to me, however, that there was no chance of any British forces being engaged in large operations either on their own or with the Greeks. All the second-line transport had been sold to the Greeks, and he advised me to see that I retained all the first-line transport handed in by Indian units going home. While I was with him I asked if he would ask the CGS to come in and take part in our talks. He was away and I never set eyes on him then or later. My third visit was paid to the head of the Intelligence Branch, Major Donald Cameron. He and I had been at the same preparatory school at St Andrews in Fife, and we knew each other very well indeed. He had a distinguished career in the Army, having come into the service a little late after three years at a University. How he came to be in charge of the Intelligence in the Middle East it is difficult to understand. He could speak neither Greek not Turkish, and he had to depend completely upon the good faith of his agents. He had it firmly fixed in his brain that the Allied Council, through the British Commander in Constantinople, had such control over the Sultan and his Ministers in the Turkish capital that no important leader could arise in Anatolia. He knew of Mustapha Kemal and of his fine career as a soldier, but he assured me that he was in such a bad state of health that he could not cause much harm to the Allied cause. He shied off giving me any information of what Greek troops were doing in European Turkey. My interview was the last I had with him. He never came out to see me at Ismid and I was not on the list of commanders who received the weekly Intelligence report.

It was therefore in great confusion of mind that I spent my last night before I went out to take over the Ismid force. The situation as regards the Greeks must have changed very drastically since my interview with the Prime Minister.

CHAPTER II

Ismid

Early on the morning of 21 July I crossed over to Haidar Pasha, the terminus of the Baghdad Bahn, on my way to take over command. The great array of platforms, hundreds of yards long, stood desolate and empty before us. Away at the end of one of them stood the trolley which was to take us out. The three of us, Brownhill and I followed by Kostia and a hand-truck pushed by two seedy-looking old Turks, presented an unimpressive party as we made our way down to the two figures near the trolley. The first was the chief stationmaster, an enormous Turk in khaki wearing a long string of medals, who saluted me as he flung out something in Turkish. Seeing that I did not understand, he repeated that all was ready in German. As I looked at him I wondered whether one of his medals was the one the Kaiser had given when he declared the Bahn open so many years ago.

We climbed in and were soon chugging down the line, which had been laid closely along the southern shore of the peninsula, following every twist and turn of the coast over numberless little bridges. Only a slight breeze from the south was blowing, but so close were we to the water that the spray from the waves blew right into the trolley. It was a bright and sunny day, the mountains on the other side of the Gulf showing up very green as they rose straight from the water's edge. Behind that screen lay the Greek main forces. I wondered where they were and what they were doing. Our little operations would be completely cut off from them, but it seemed very stupid to keep me in ignorance of what they were doing. Were they having a stiff time settling themselves into the Smyrna area? How close were they working up towards the Gulf of Ismid? It took us exactly three hours to reach the little town, nestling under the hills at the extreme end of the Gulf. A British battleship lay anchored off the town. The Brigadier was at the station to meet me, bringing my two future staff officers, Colonel Barne of the Royal Artillery, who had been a cadet at the 'shop' with me, and Colonel Lavie who had commanded a battalion so well in Archangel. Later was to come a Captain Pirie of the Gordons. It was good to have under me men whom I knew so well.

After lunch we rode up to see the positions we were holding above the town. I found a curious state of affairs. The force of some 8,000 men lay on the top of the ridge 1,500 feet above the town, holding a line of trenches bristling with guns and machine-guns, a distance of three miles with the flanks thrown back to the sea. The whole line was protected by a most formidable wire entanglement, in which I could see no entrances leading to the front. The terrain in front of the ridge rose slowly to the north as far as the eye could reach, affording a field of view for several miles. In the centre there was a small height about 800 yards in front of the line. I was told that this had been held for some time as a totally enclosed detached post, but that after severe night-sniping the decision had been taken to evacuate it. The with-drawal was very inadvisedly arranged to take place during the hours of darkness instead of under an artillery barrage. The result was that two companies of an Indian battalion had lost their way, drifting down into a valley where they lost twenty men in an ambush. From that moment the troops along the front had been closely confined to their defences. We had in fact reverted to rigid trench-warfare tactics. The only thing which was wanting was an enemy. No sign of a Kemalist had been seen for a fortnight and all sniping had ceased.

So close behind the barbed-wire had the men been kept that all day reconnaissances had ceased. Even night-patrolling in front of the line had been stopped. A cavalry regiment, the 20th Hussars, was with the force, but this was kept in idleness behind the line. It was a most unsatisfactory position in which to keep British troops of the regular army, however young and inexperienced they might be. And they were doing no good, holding this half-circle-shaped line at the end of the Gulf. In the forty-mile space between the line and the Black Sea there was ample room for any number of guerrillas to slip in to the Bosphorus unobserved.

Though it was true that the officers in the Ismid force all had experience of war, yet the younger ones had no conception of what was wanted for mobile warfare. Also I had some trouble with three of the CO's of the British regiments. They had been captured early in 1914 and had remained prisoners of war till the Armistice of 1918. They had now been sent back to their battalions in order to let them qualify for the full retired pay of their rank. Poor fellows, it would have been better to keep them in England for preliminary training. I felt that I had to go easy with them, so that they could pick up their lost experience, but it was not fair to the men to send them out fighting under untrained leaders.

By holding Ismid with a system of fortified points I was able to do away with a mass of the clogging barbed-wire, and yet provide a force with which I could organize the training of at least the British troops. I found that the young soldiers had been well disciplined and that they took eagerly to mobile work. A squadron of the 20th Hussars was turned out every morning to spend the hours of daylight reconnoitring the rough ground to our front as far as the field guns could reach, while all the battalions in the line had to organize night patrolling on a large scale. For the first ten days I rode with the squadron each morning, accompanied by the Captain of the battleship, who was a keen horseman. With the help of an interpreter I was able to interrogate the peasants on a wide and increasing area. Many of the men had been old soldiers who had fought in Palestine and Mesopotamia and were quite willing to talk. The country was dotted all over with Roman remains, including several fine bridges with tiled roadways leading up to them. The water supply for Ismid was brought into the town from a dam in the hills by means of stone pipes. In one corner, all covered with thick undergrowth, we discovered a monument to two officers and nine ratings of the Navy who had been killed in the bursting

of a 32-pounder gun in the year 1878. A party from the battleship soon set this in order again.

Then on the 23rd there came a welcome surprise. Without
previous warning, a Greek regiment of light infantry was
signalled as going to land at the little port of Derinje, which lay
just behind our lines. It was to come under my command for the
clearing of the Ismid Peninsula. I found that the regiment came
from Crete and was commanded by a young colonel who spoke
very good French. As they came off the boat the men impressed
me as being just the sort of light infantry we needed for the job
in hand. Judged by our standards, their khaki drill clothing was
lamentable, being of all shades and fitting nowhere. Some had
leather leggings and some puttees, but most of them wore their
slacks without finishings. One thing they all had, and that was a
pair of serviceable, well-nailed boots. They drilled almost
entirely to whistle, and there was neither shouting nor loud

words of command. No fussing by excited NCO's trying to show their authority. All their transport was pack, and I was delighted to see how fit their mules were, apparently all bought from the British Army. Their packs were not loaded till the last minute, and when they were loaded they balanced well. I had brought an Hussar orderly with me, so that he could guide the regiment to the camp which had been chosen for them, but the Colonel asked if one of his orderlies might be shown the camp first, and then he could run back and guide the regiment in according to custom. Both the young Hussar and his horse were considerably surprised when the enormous kilted Cretan, in all his flowing draperies, stepped up and seized the trooper's left stirrup-iron. I think that we all thought he was about to jump up behind the saddle. The trooper certainly did. It was then explained that all the Cretan wanted to do was to run alongside the horse. They trotted off amidst the jokes and laughter of the Greeks.

In camp they might well have been men of the Light Brigade under Crauford in the Peninsula. They formed line to one blast of the whistle, and to another they piled arms and lay down. To a third they broke off. The weather being fine they made no attempt to set up their little tents. All cooking was done in squads on the French system, and they had a hot meal going in a matter of minutes. I also noted with great interest that the Colonel at once sent off two officers to reconnoitre the position behind which they were going to camp. It was refreshing to see how well trained they were to field work. I wondered how long it would take me to get my men as well trained.

I had a long talk with the Colonel as to how his regiment could best be employed. My idea was that his first drive should come as a surprise—straight across the Peninsula to Shilé on the Black Sea, where I could revictual him by sea. In order that he might move on a broader front I offered him a squadron of the 20th Hussars, and this he accepted with enthusiasm. For a second drive against the north-west corner of the peninsula I proposed that he should be based on the road which ran from Shilé to Scutari on the Bosphorus. I could then supply him at either end.

When we had finished our arrangements for the coming

drives in the Ismid Peninsula I drew the young commander out to talk of the task which lay before the main Greek Army in Anatolia. He was immensely proud of this crusade, as he called it, which had been entrusted to the Greek people. He told us how limitless, in his eyes at least, were these plans for Anatolia. There was now no question of the setting up of a small Greek State in the Smyrna vilayet, where the majority of the million or so of Greeks who had been subjects of the old Ottoman Empire could be congregated. Now it was a question of setting up a second Greek Empire. He did not even hesitate at the prospect of having their old task-masters, men who had never been subjected to the rule of any foreigner, as a strong minority in their new empire. I had not the heart to tell him of my fears as to their plans being brought to a successful conclusion. I began to wonder whether the British Government had already made up its mind to have nothing to do with the Greek campaign and to leave them to their own empire building.

The Commander-in-Chief had kindly lent me his yacht to help me in my operations in the peninsula. It was manned by naval ratings and flew the flag with a crown and crossed swords when a general was aboard. The Bosphorus was a great sight of activity as we steamed our way to Shilé in the Black Sea. A host of warships of various nations were anchored in the stream, even a flotilla belonging to General Wrangel's army in the Crimea was there, flying the old imperial flag of Russia. On the Asiatic side we saw the sandy coves occupied by British bathing parties with women and children in them, guarded by launches mounting a machine-gun on their decks. Everything seemed most unwarlike. We were kept busy saluting other ships who had saluted our flag, and it was amusing to see at close range the signal officers searching in their books to find out who was on board our ship.

On arrival at Shilé there was no sign yet of our Greek column, but I decided to go on shore to view the little town. I was met by a Greek guard of twenty men armed with rifles, and was informed that the Greeks had now taken over control in all the towns and villages as far east as Trebizond, fresh evidence of how the Greek advance had been extended over the Turkish homeland. These Shilé-men were a nondescript lot of people, varying

H

from old men with grey beards to boys of fifteen and they seemed to wear an apologetic air for being under arms. They told us through our interpreter that the Turks had offered no resistance when they took over authority in the town, but they had not carried out any search for weapons in the Turkish houses.

It was common knowledge in the town that the Greek column would be coming in towards evening, and it was rumoured that there had been a brush between them and some Kemalists in which the Greeks had killed some Turks and taken ten prisoners. We wandered round the little streets with their overhanging upper storeys, until we met a Turkish deputation under a venerable old Turk who informed me through my interpreter that he wished to show me the pile of weapons which had been collected from the Turkish community in Shilé. A motley collection of old and rusty rifles and brass-handled swords, presented so shamelessly, did not impress me much.

The column arrived in fine fettle exactly at 6 pm. They had killed ten Kemalists and taken six prisoners. Two of their men had been wounded and a sergeant of the 20th Hussars had been slightly wounded in the arm. I received a most excellent report about our Hussars and arranged to leave them with the Greeks for another drive, when I would send another squadron to take their place.

That evening after dinner Brownhill and I were sitting out on deck, talking lightly of what we thought was going to happen in the Middle East, when there arose the most dreadful shouting and screaming in the town. It didn't take long to get into our little boat and row ashore with two ratings to see what was happening, and there we found that the venerable old ex-headman was in trouble. He was being held by two Greek soldiers ready for twenty-five strokes of the bastinado on his feet. As soon as he saw me approaching he redoubled his screams and appeals to me to save him. The Greek Colonel explained that his house had been searched, with the result that two heavy machine-guns and two dozen modern rifles had been found hidden away in the rafters. I had to explain that I could not allow such summary punishment in my command, and I ordered it to be changed to a fine of 2,000 piastres.

After making all arrangements for the second drive, I picked up the wounded sergeant and deposited him in hospital at Scutari on my way back to Ismid.

Life at Ismid was pleasant enough. Bathing from the yacht was delightful. Brownhill had developed a wonderful technique for catching red mullet by bombing. This kept the mess well supplied. Mobile training was going well, and I had got to the stage when a column consisting of a battalion, a battery and a squadron went out two days and three nights on small schemes. The whole force was becoming alive again. I hoped that stronger columns would soon be working out as far as the Black Sea. I had a flight of planes attached to me. The departure of the Indian battalions was diminishing my force considerably, but I was glad to see them go, for their discipline had deteriorated badly for lack of senior officers to keep them straight. I was left severely alone. No one came to see me. I received no news telegrams. My staff officers could glean no news, though I gathered from a newspaper man who reached Ismid by devious ways that the Greeks had turned all the Turkish troops out of European Turkey with very little loss. A Naval Intelligence officer turned up one afternoon to see the Captain of the battleship and kindly came on to see me before he went back to the flagship. From him I learnt that Mustapha Kemal, the man I had heard so much about, was the real leader of the Turks in Anatolia. He had been sent there by the Sultan towards the end of May for the special purpose of ensuring that all orders were obeyed. After a very short time it was discovered that he had become the leading spirit in an effort to raise the spirits of the beaten Turks, and to prevent their complete destruction by the Allied Council. The Navy reported that he was a man who had fits of dissipation, in which he lay useless for days at a time, but he always recovered with renewed energy to continue his fight.

Two incidents also took place which showed the disunion which had set in between the Allied Powers. I discovered the first purely by chance while talking to one of the CO's of a departing Indian unit. He told me casually that he had spent some amusing evenings talking to an Allied officer who was making liaison with the British forces. I put Brownhill on to ferret him out, since I had never heard of him before. When found he came most unwillingly. A cheery, amusing individual who spoke very good English and told a very good story when he tried to. He had no papers of any kind and would not disclose from whence he hailed. For many years I had studied the various shibboleths of different peoples and I soon discovered that he was a Frenchman and had come up from Syria. When searched we discovered a very clear report of the arrival of our Greek regiment at Derinje, and the dates of departure of our Indian battalions. I sent him in to the Intelligence Branch. The other incident was more serious. An Allied plane, with French markings, made a forced landing to the east of Ismid. The two occupants were badly concussed. Luckily the crash was seen by a patrol of the 20th Hussars under an NCO. The men were brought in, and the sergeant had the sense to take all the papers he could find on the men or in the plane and put them in a sack, before he set fire to the wreckage which lay beyond our lines. A search revealed some very useful papers showing that one of our Allies was in direct communication with some of the Turks in Anatolia. The two men were sent in to the Intelligence Branch.

On 8 August I was ordered by telephone to go over to Broussa on the southern side of the Gulf, and to make liaison with a Greek Commander who had suddenly appeared there. I was given no instructions as to what to find out or to say to him. I knew that we had a British General and several other officers working as liaison officers with the Greek main force, so that I suppose there was little for me to find out. A British destroyer, *Shark*, under Commander Simpson, a brother Scot, was sent to take me over and back. The Greek General was a young active-looking man, very smartly dressed in khaki overalls and patent-leather Wellingtons. I was given an excellent lunch in the shade of a mulberry orchard, while we talked of various generalities. No maps were produced and neither of us could get any satisfactory answers out of the other, though we both fished hard for information. As I said good-bye the General expressed the hope that our two forces would soon be co-operating, when he reached the end of the Gulf of Ismid. I bowed and smiled and left it at that. There were certainly no British troops fit to go fighting

Turks, and even if I had possessed good troops I had no transport to go with them.

I returned to Ismid full of doubts. What had I been sent to see this man for? It was clear to me that the Greeks were steadily pushing on into Asia Minor without any fixed objective. I wondered if they had enough resources in men and material to conquer the whole country. By this time they must have realized that the Turkish resistance was growing fiercer every day, and that if they were to take over the country, they must defeat the Turks in battle at the end of long and difficult communications. Every mile they went forward without bringing off this victory must make things more difficult for them. I was now sure that the British Government had no intention of seconding them in their seeking of a new Empire. I was not so sure that the Greeks had been told this in definite terms.

On 10 August I was summoned to Constantinople. All my doubts were quickly resolved. I was informed by the CGS that the Ismid force was to be dissolved as soon as I had handed over the defence of Ismid to a Greek Commander, who might be expected to arrive in a few days. I was given no explanation of what had happened. It made me smile to think that only two days before I had been making liaison with a Greek General, who did not know whether I should be fighting alongside him or not. I was told to wait, as the Commander-in-Chief wished to see me before I went back to Ismid. After a meal at a hotel I was ushered in to see Sir George. He expressed his sorrow at losing my services and thanked me for what I had done. He made no allusion to what had happened. Then quite casually he told me that he had been told by the War Office that Sir Aylmer Haldane in Mesopotamia had been wiring for some time for my services. They now wished to say that I was at liberty to accept what General Haldane had to offer me, but would like an early acceptance if I wished to go there.

All this came to me as such a surprise that I was left speechless. I had known that my job at Ismid was probably coming to an end, but I felt that I was being handed on to another in a most extraordinary way. I asked for twenty-four hours to consider my position. I took a room at an hotel, and there at dinner I con-

sidered what I should do. I went to bed early and went on thinking till I had made up my mind. Then I fell asleep. The War
Office was evidently trying to be helpful. They were not ready
to offer me a permanent job. If I went home I should at once be
placed on half-pay once more. I knew General Haldane well and
had always been happy soldiering under him. I therefore decided
to accept his offer of employment. After all, there was a rebellion
going on in Mespot and there might be something important to
do.

At 11 am the next day I saw Sir George for a few minutes,
telling him that I had decided to go to Mesopotamia. He shook
hands with me and that was the end of the command from which
I had hoped for so much.

I went back to my hotel to pick up my kit and tell Kostia that
I was going back to Ismid for a few days before we went further
east. He saluted me smartly while handing me a copy of the
Paris *Daily Mail*. There in large headlines stood the paragraph,

> 'What is General Ironside doing on the shores of the Gulf of
> Ismid?'

That was a question that I could not answer. I though of Mr
Lloyd George as he beat on his book with his pince-nez. I had
been a mere pawn in the game of politics.

My fears of Bolshevik aggression in Europe and elsewhere were
being further aroused by the news coming in from Poland. With
all their internal difficulties the Bolsheviks had been able to
launch an offensive on a gigantic scale against this, the strongest of
the newly formed states in Eastern Europe. On 13 August they
were approaching the Vistula on a wide front, and the fate of
Warsaw already seemed sealed. When he started his invasion the
Russian Commander-in-Chief, Tuchachevsky, had issued the
following arrogant Order of the Day:

> 'In the West the future of the Universal Revolution is being
> fought out. The course of World Conflagration is passing over
> the dead body of Poland.'

Daily I ready the melancholy news from London and Paris.
Allied statesmen and ambassadors with their accompanying

posses of military advisers were crowding the hotels of Warsaw. They could offer no other advice to the 'dead body' than to make what terms it could with the victorious Bolsheviks. They brought no military help with them. And even as they gave their cowardly advice they were arranging their special trains to enable them to get away before the débâcle took place. It was not a pretty picture of Allied might. I was relieved on the 18th and 19th, before I left Constantinople, to hear the news of the miracle of the Vistula, as great a miracle as that of the Marne in 1914. Marshal Pilsudski, in disgust at the defeatism in Warsaw, had slipped quietly away by himself with two of his staff, to launch the counter attack against the widely dispersed columns of Tuchachevsky's army. Just as Samsonoff's army was destroyed at Tannenberg, so was Tuchachevsky's destroyed on almost the self-same spot.

On 17 August I handed over to my Greek successor. The Union Jack was lowered while we both saluted it. The Greek flag was hoisted while we saluted again. We shook hands and saluted each other. I turned away and walked down to the little railway station, followed by Kostia, who had rolled up the Union Jack and brought it away under his arm. It still hangs in my room at home.

Sir George was kind in offering me hospitality until the time came for me to embark for Port Said on 22 August. My heavy kit had been sent off in a slow cargo-boat from England, and was not due to reach Constantinople until long after I had left. I wondered where or when I should see it again. I never tried to get the Commander-in-Chief to disclose to me what had happened over our backing the Greeks in their adventures in Anatolia. I felt that he had too many worries of his own to have mine added to them.

I spent my days of liberty in seeing the sights—the Navy playing polo; the disembarkation of the Russian imperial stud of stallions, which had been rescued from the Crimea by Wrangel; and the Sultan's Palace; followed by some wanderings in the old town.

The Palace was in charge of an old Pasha of over eighty years of age, but he detailed a young captain to take me round the rambling old building. It had been empty since the departure of Abdul Hamid. It was a place of tiny rooms and long dark passages to which the light of day never reached. Each new sultan was wont to leave the apartments of the last sultan to his dependants, and to arrange a new set of rooms for himself and his household. One might easily have lost oneself in the labyrinth of passages. The Palace was quite uncared for despite the large number of caretakers who emerged from every hole and corner to pray for *bakshish*. The young Captain jumped up on a chair, in order to show me a spy-hole through which one could see unobserved into a private room. He was wearing tight overalls with patent-leather bespurred Jemima boots, and as he made a bad jump to get down he ripped off the covering of priceless red silk.

The finest room was that in which foreign visitors were assembled, offering a lovely view of the Golden Horn below. In a small alcove of this room we were served with China tea in a service of Sèvres, which had been presented to the reigning sultan of the day by the Emperor Napoleon III.

The Library contained the oldest book in the world, the writing being painted in Persian characters upon some leathery substance, each page being done in different colour. There was no protection for this priceless volume, and it disgusted me to see the captain's none too clean hands turning over the pages for me.

The last thing I was shown was the great collection of Chinese porcelain, received by each reigning sultan from time immemorial from each new Chinese dynasty. The collection was housed in good glass cases, the only things which were well cared for in all the Palace.

I spent a morning wandering about the Turkish quarter, where I saw the young bloods coming into their favourite café to have a cup of black coffee and to have their fezzes cleaned and ironed. Round the shop stood on shelves many brass head-shapes which were kept warm by means of small charcoal fires. As the young man came in he bowed his head, while the attendant lifted the fez reverently from his head and placed on its appropriate shape. There it was groomed and ironed. The process took about twenty minutes in all. When the young man rose to go, the cleaner ran forward to place the fez on his head once more, at the proper angle, and to receive the expected *bakshish*. It was much the same spectacle as one might have seen in Victorian days in Jermyn Street when a young man came in wearing a topper.

I was asked to visit the Island of Prinkipo, of ill-fame, where all the dogs of Constantinople were taken and left to die of hunger. I could not bring myself to face it.

III

COMMAND OF THE NORTH PERSIAN FORCE

4 October 1920, to 17 February, 1921

In 1971 Persia celebrated 2,500 years of monarchy, but the rise of the present Pahlevi dynasty dates from the *coup d'état* of 1921. The Kajar dynasty finally ended on 31 October, 1925, after 130 years of rule, and the Sardar Sepah, Reza Khan Pahlevi, was temporarily nominated Shah by the Mejliss. He was formally elected on 13 December, and the Crown of Persia was made hereditary in his family when he was enthroned on 16 December, with succession limited to sons born of a Persian mother.

The situation in 1920 was near to anarchy, and the British force stationed at Kazvin was there primarily to prevent Bolshevik agression, which through Imperial British eyes was seen more as a menace to the Indian Empire than as a threat to the infant British oil concessions. The British Resident at Bushire still held the main sway in the Persian Gulf region and was responsible to the Government of India.

British policy in Persia had been fathered by Lord Curzon: 'For something like 30 years I have been connected with the politics of Persia and if at any time I have been inspired by any lack of regard for the independence or integrity of that country, I hardly think I should have been honoured as I have been during the whole of that period with the confidence of successive Persian ministers and statesmen. On the contrary, I believe—and I say it in no love of vanity—that they regard me as a true and consistent friend of their country.' Curzon wanted to feel that he still had prestige in that country, even though his Persian policy was being torn to shreds and his Anglo-Persian Agreement of 1919 remained an object of contempt while still unratified by the Mejliss. Owing to the new fear of Bolshevik aggression the Persians were gambling on the fact that the British would be obliged to continue giving them support in any case. The only native forces in the country were the Persian Cossacks commanded by a White Russian called Starosselsky who derived his position from the old Russian sphere of influence in Persia and the Czarist agreement with the Shah to officer the force with White Russians.

Curzon's Persian policy was pursued without regard to expense at a time of increasing economy at home and it gave rise to much bitter controversy. In the House of Lords he was forced to defend himself in detail. Clearly his plan was to replace the old Russian sphere of influence and assume Protectorship over the whole of Persia, but the military situation did not allow this. Whilst the Foreign Office jogged along, they were being overtaken by events. The ousting of Starosselsky, the Commander of the Persian Cossacks, was achieved painlessly as a result of swift action by those on the spot and Curzon reluctantly supported it. He said, in the House of Lords, 'It was impossible to regard the combined presence of this officer and his Russian colleagues, representing, as your Lordships know, the old régime as anything but a menace to both Persia and ourselves in that part of the country (Kazvin). It was these considerations that only a few weeks ago decided the Shah to dispense with services of so dangerous an ally. This decision on the part of His Majesty was strongly supported by General Ironside who has only recently gone to Persia with a great reputation for clear-headedness and capacity. He was, at the time, in command of British Forces at Kazvin, and he earnestly recommended that the opportunity should be taken to get rid of these incompetent and treacherous men and of reorganizing the Cossack Division.' But by his deportment in Teheran he implied his displeasure at not being consulted: 'General Ironside and Mr Norman have incurred a grave responsibility which can only be justified by success.'

In command of the North Persian Force, 'NORPERFORCE' as it was called, my father had been given a fairly free hand by General Haldane to act as he thought fit. It was a semi-independent command and those who served in it were later awarded a 'North Persia' bar to the General Service Medal. This appointment was exactly suited to my father's temperament and capability.

After rebuilding the morale of his own force and stabilizing the situation at Kazvin he was able to turn his mind to the reorganization of the Persian Cossacks. The story of his choosing Reza Khan to command them is known to many and although he could not know at the time that this man would one day become Shah of Persia, he clearly paved the way for him.

Before my father actually left Persia, Reza Khan carried out a *coup d'état* in Teheran, but true to his promise he declared his loyalty to the reigning Shah. In his diary he says, 'I fancy that everybody thinks that I engineered the *coup d'état*. I suppose I did strictly speaking.' The promise

made by Reza Khan was faithfully kept until, as a point of honour, he sought release from it in 1925 through his personal envoy who presented himself at the Staff College, Camberley.

In reviewing his time in Persia later, he said, 'Luckily my opportunity for carrying out my two main objects arrived quickly. The Persian Cossacks collapsed in front of the Bolsheviks and I was able to dispose of the Russian officers *en bloc*. We certainly had luck, but the opportunity was only a fleeting one. I was then able to undertake a small operation against the Bolsheviks with practically every unit of my force and to carry it out with complete success. I thus rehabilitated the force completely and showed them what a contemptible opponent the Bolshevik was, and I made any future scandalous withdrawal an impossibility.'

CHAPTER I

Journey to Baghdad

I left Constantinople on 22 August in a small BI ship bound for Port Said. From there I was to make my way as fast as I could to Baghdad to report to General Haldane, the Commander-in-Chief in Mesopotamia. But beyond that I had no idea of what lay in store for me. General Haldane had been my chief in the VIth Corps in France and I had always soldiered very happily with him. It was flattering to know that he had been making so many efforts to get hold of me once more. I still had Brownhill and my servant Kostia with me, but I had only the meagre kit I had been allowed to take with me on the Orient Express. My heavy kit had only left England a few days before, and it was too late for me to prevent it from being sent to Constantinople. It might be months before I saw it again. However, my spirits were rising quickly at the thought of getting something to do and I had almost forgotten my disappointment at losing the command of the Ismid force.

As we steamed southwards I had a marvellous view of the Dardanelles which I had always wished to see, but though I had tried hard to buy or borrow a book on the campaign I had failed to find one. In fact I never saw a decent bookshop in Constantinople. Thus, as so often happened to me in my travels, I had no background upon which to base my observations. There was no one on board who had served in the campaign. Even the skipper was unable to point out to me the important places. Luckily I had an excellent map and did some good work with that, but could only imagine the plan which had been so brilliant in conception and yet so badly executed by incompetent

subordinate leaders. The failure was a most dreadful catastrophe
for the Allies. As things turned out I could not have taken much
of my opportunity to read, for as we drew out to sea the weather
became abominable. I was laid up with sea-sickness in my
dingy little cabin in the afterpart of the ship, subsisting upon
toast and weak tea till we reached Port Said on the 26th. There I
was told that I had no chance of getting a direct passage to
Basra, and that even getting one for Bombay I should have to
wait for at least a week. I was advised to go up to Cairo and there
wait in comfort till something could be done for me. It was a
most annoying delay. My old brother cadet at the 'shop',
Geoffrey Salmond, was AOC in the Middle East, and to him I
confidently appealed for a passage by air to Baghdad. But he
would have none of it. The rebellion in Mesopotamia was in full
swing and he was allowing no planes to cross the desert, least of
all those containing odd generals as passengers. Nothing would
move him. I thus lost the chance of getting to my new job in
seventeen hours flying instead of what would be at least a month
by sea.

I settled down at Shepheard's to see as much of the country as
I could. It was getting uncomfortably hot and I had no khaki
drill, but with luck I found an Indian tailor who ran me up some
jackets and Jodhpore breeches in a matter of hours. They weren't
very regimental but they were good enough for campaigning in
Mespot. Prices were everywhere running high, but I secured an
advance on my detention allowance which covered the bill for
myself and Kostia at the hotel. Cairo was full of high-powered
American cars and money was being spent like water, the result
of the high price of cotton and the high wages paid in the war.
The excitement over the new Constitution was at its height, and
the little tables in restaurants and cafés were occupied by Gyppies
in tarbooshes, eagerly discussing the situation over endless cups
of coffee and cigarettes. The Staff in Cairo told me that the
centre of interest was already quickly shifting to the question of
the Sudan. The local papers were demanding that the dual
administration there should be brought to an end. Democracy
had sprung up in the night and gone mad. How could these
café-effendis ever rule such a country as the Sudan? They had

tried to do so once before with disastrous results. It did not seem possible that we could abandon Africans to an alien Oriental rule in Cairo.

To my great pleasure I was able to spend a full day with the Horse Gunners at Abbassia. I had not been in a Gunner mess since 1914 and I received somewhat of a shock. My own contemporaries in the regiment were still majors, some a considerable distance from the top of the list. I had completely failed to realise how far I had outstripped my fellows. The two majors of the horse batteries had both been senior to me on the Gunner list, but they were very kind in putting me at my ease. I remembered how happy I had been as a subaltern in 'I' Troop in India, and I felt a considerable nostalgia in the realization that I should never again enjoy the pleasure of a regimental mess. At dinner that night I met Sir George Gorringe who was commanding the troops in Egypt. The last time I had met him was when he was a Column Commander in South Africa and I a Gunner subaltern. He told me that he had served for over twelve years as a Major-General and was now being passed over for promotion to Lieut-General. He pointed out to me that the promotion on the list of regimental officers could never be accelerated until the retiring age for Generals was reduced. At the moment a Major-General retire at sixty-two, a Lieut-General at sixty-five and a General at sixty-seven.

Sir Walter Congreve, the Commander-in-Chief in Egypt, was away when I arrived, but I spent two nights with him when he came back. I had been his G2 in the 6th Division in France and had the greatest of admiration for him. He was a Rifleman with all that which is meant by the name. Though not of strong physique, his spirit was simply terrific. I can remember once remonstrating with him one morning in the Ypres Salient when he turned up with his three sons to accompany him on his daily visit round the trenches. Billy, a Rifleman like his father, who had also been awarded a VC, Geoffrey a Lieutenant in the Navy and Christie a Boy Scout in all his finery. I told him that he ought to divide the party up and allow one of the boys to go with me. He just smiled and started off without a word. When we came to the Wieltje Salient, where there was a dried human hand sticking out

I

of the parapet, even Christie followed the universal custom of all ranks by shaking hands with this grim relic. The next time I saw Christie was a year later—in an Eton jacket at his prep school.

I found the General as cheery as ever, though he had just suffered a nasty accident while out riding. During the latter part of the war in France he had been hit by an enemy whizz-bang while returning one evening from the trenches. This had removed his left hand and forearm, and he now wore a hook when on a horse. While out on an exercise he was standing listening to a conference, with his reins held in the hook. His horse took fright and he was dragged for some 200 yards before the straps of the hook broke and released him. His staff told me that he at once remounted and rode home, though suffering great pain.

Sir Walter told me that Egypt had become the clearing-house for all traffic going east or west. It was a veritable sink of the war in the Middle East. There were huge camps of troops and refugees dotted all over the area, waiting for shipping which never seemed to come. Some of the refugees were Russians who refused to clean either themselves or their camps. They were always demanding more pay, though they were getting the same amount as British soldiers—and for doing nothing. He was having endless correspondence with officials of the War Office, Colonial Office, India Office and Foreign Office, not to speak of the Indian, Australian, New Zealand and Egyptian Governments. All were demanding the impossible for their own particular people. He had a stream of men coming from the Army of the Black Sea, all long overdue for discharge. These men could not understand why they were not being sent back to India, when as they sat on the banks of the Suez Canal they saw ship after ship going east to Australia and New Zealand. The discipline of these Indian soldiers had sadly deteriorated during their long waiting, and there were few British officers left in the units in which they were serving who could speak to them in their own tongue.

At last on 1 September I was ordered to embark in the P & O ship *Delta*. I had been in a great hurry to reach Basra, but I felt that the few days I had spent in Egypt had not been wasted. For there remained indelibly printed on my mind the fact that the Suez Canal was the real centre of the British Empire's communications. No roads across the desert from Haifa to Baghdad and thence to Basra and the Persian Gulf could ever replace this canal. It was true that we had stated over and over again that we intended to terminate our occupation of Egypt, but after what I had seen there I could not conceive that we could consider handing over the defence of the canal to any weak state. The United States had been careful to ensure the neutrality of the Panama Canal before they had built it. With the memory of the Great War in our minds, had not the time come to settle the security of the Suez Canal in the same manner?

I found Sir Percy Cox a passenger in the *Delta*. He was going out to take over the High Commissionership in Mesopotamia. He had been the Chief Political Officer with the Indian Expeditionary Force in the latter half of the campaign against the Turks and knew the country well. He had spent most of his career in the Persian Gulf, where he was familiarly known as 'Cokkus'. I had never met him before but had heard a good deal of his prestige amongst the Arabs, but I found him curiously reticent with strangers. Indeed he hardly spoke to anyone on board. He did ask me when I first met him, whether I was going out to succeed General Haldane. When I told him that I was going out to take over a subordinate command under the General, but did not know what it was going to be, he looked at me very suspiciously. From that moment he never addressed another word to me. I think he thought that I was being sent out by Mr Churchill to report upon his affairs. I could only think that a lifetime spent in the Persian Gulf had made him adopt the suspicions of the Arab.

At Bombay there was a wire for me from Lord Rawlinson, inviting me to come up to see him in Simla. But there was another from General Haldane, telling me to hurry my journey up as I was needed to take over the command in North Persia. It was a relief to know what my future was going to be after such a long delay, and I was delighted to know that I was to have a semi-independent command. As my departure for Basra had been fixed for the 17th I had most reluctantly to refuse the invitation to go up to Simla to see my old chief. However, before I embarked I was able to spend some hours with Colonel Muspratt of the General Staff, who had come down from Simla to explain to me the views of the Indian Government as regards their troops in Mesopotamia. It was the old story of watertight compartments. Just as the Indian Government had told the War Office little of what they intended to do in the early days of the Mesopotamian campaign, so the War Office and Colonial Office told the Indian Government little of what they were doing now.

Half the regiments of the Indian Army were still serving abroad after a period of over six years of war, and it was only a matter of time before recruits would no longer present themselves under such conditions. The Indian Government was fully aware of the acute shortage of shipping, but it had lately come to their ears that Turkish prisoners of war were being repatriated from Basra by way of the Suez Canal. Why had not the men of the Indian Army been given preference over these Turks? No one in India had forgotten how both British and Indian troops had been made to march the long way from Kut to the Bosphorus. Surely the Turks could be called upon to make this march now.

There appeared to be a general rumour running round that I had been sent out to supersede General Haldane. I assured Muspratt that I was going to command in North Persia, and had that day bought a copy of Sykes's *History of Persia* at Thackers in Bombay.

On the 17th I embarked in the *Cocanada* which was taking two British battalions to Mesopotamia—the East Yorks and the Duke of Cornwall's Light Infantry. They were typical of the newly re-formed units of the British Army. Very young and very keen. Not a medal-ribbon to be seen on the jackets of the men and very few on those of the NCO's. They were all beautifully turned out in their laundered khaki drill, as all units are in India and the East. On arrival in India they had been split up in company stations and neither battalion had been able to carry out any regimental training. Both were under 600 strong, having been compelled to leave all their details behind; those details which are always exacted from British units, to make up the signallers, orderlies and clerks which are needed for the staffs of the larger formations such as divisions. They had been ordered to embark in a hurry, while their married families were up in the hills, and these were to stay in India until they could be shipped home in the cold weather.

I did not fall in love with the Persian Gulf. Everything was hot and clammy. We stopped only once, at Bushire, where we put the mails ashore. From the ship it looked a dreary sandy hole. On the 23rd we ran up the river and anchored off the port of Basra. The heat had risen to 120° and it felt clammier than ever. The glare was intense. All the European troops seemed to be wearing dark glasses. After several minutes I saw a launch making towards us from the quay. Who should emerge from it but my old friend of the Rifle Brigade, Alan Paley. He had been in command of one of the battalions of his regiment for two years and was now waiting to go home with it. He had been offered the command of a brigade several times, but had always refused. He looked upon the country as the nearest thing to hell as any could be. His ambition was to get a Terrier Brigade at home, where he could hunt a pack of hounds till he could ride no more. His report on the country was not a happy one and I began to thank my stars that I was going to Persia.

My orders were to go up to Kut with the river steamers taking the two battalions up country, and then on to Baghdad by the railway. I tackled the Inspector of Communications with a view to getting a launch or a plane to get up to Baghdad more quickly, but neither was forthcoming owing to the economies which were being made. The steamers were to start at about midnight, which gave me a few hours in which to look at Basra, but I saw little but miles and miles of abandoned camps which had served the Expeditionary Force. Now they were all rotting in the sun. The little traffic there was between the town and the port was carried out by boats plying in the backwaters of the river. All work ceased between 10 am and 4 pm to avoid the great heat of the day. I saw only two small freighters alongside the quays.

It was only on the morning after we had started that I realized what curious affairs our steamers were. There were two of these, each with a long flat lashed to each of its sides. In the flats the men lay packed like sardines under a very thin canvas shelter stretched over their heads. To add to the dullness of the voyage, we were so low in the water that nothing could be seen from the decks of the steamers or flats. On the steamers one had to go up on the bridge to see anything of the surrounding country. These bridges were heavily lined with iron plates, to protect the officers against sniping. The steamers had come from the Irrawaddy and with their heavy 600 hp engines they could make ten knots against the three-knot current. We proceeded like crabs zig-zagging across from bank to bank, the flats hitting hard and then slithering off on a fresh tack to the other side. The old skipper was an Australian who had been at the game since the beginning of the war. On the first evening of the trip he called me up on the bridge to see one of the sights of the country. We were passing the reputed tomb of the Prophet Ezra. As the sun went down in a great ball of fire behind the little white shrine, which was surrounded by a row of date-palms, it showed up clearly against the desolate landscape behind it. For a few moments we were treated to a marvellous spectacle, and then as the sun passed below the horizon the picture suddenly faded. Behind me stood a Colonel of the Indian Army who had probably seen this sight many times before during the long campaign. I turned and asked him what he thought of the shrine. He waited till the sun had gone and then said to me in a gruff voice, 'Well, I think that old Ezra must have been very glad to get into his tomb.'

On the second night, an hour before sunset, we tied up while all the men turned out for half an hour's exercise. They went tumbling ashore like schoolboys let out of school, and within a minute dozens of footballs were being kicked about. Then the siren went after twenty minutes of hard kicking, and they all trooped on board again much refreshed. British troops are unlike all others. A football revives their spirits at once, whatever the weather may be and however dull and tired they may be. I have never known them to suffer from that fabulous disease the 'cafard', which so often attacks the soldiers of the Latin races. On the flats once more they recommenced their beloved game of 'Housey', as if they had never left it.

Navigation at night was difficult despite the great searchlights with which the steamers were equipped. We could see the lights of other steamers on a wide arc in front of us, marking how sharp were the windings of the river. As the lights swung round on the banks there showed up the weird shadows of men and beasts in the beams. Both were drinking their evening handful or mouthful of river water. The whole country was alive with jackals, their eyes shining like pin-points as the beams swung round, and their howls rose at times to the highest pitch and then died away to complete silence.

The next afternoon I had my first experience of the daily Mespot dust-storm. They were far worse than the storms I had seen in India and Africa. The air at first became still and all animal noises ceased. Then a slight breeze sprang up, with the temperature rising as if someone had opened the door of a furnace. The sky became as black as ink. Within a matter of minutes we were tied up to the land to posts driven in by the crew, and everything was battened down. Then came a hurricane of thick biting dust, accompanied by the stench of musty putrefaction. The drinking water was at all times well sealed up in steel tanks, but the dust penetrated into every nook and corner of the steamers and their flats, making all uncovered food quite uneatable. These storms lasted usually less than half an hour, and when they had gone the air seemed to have grown fresher and lighter.

The Arabs all drink the water of the muddy river and I saw many of them coming down to slake their thirst after sunset. They all went through the same process. They washed their hands and faces and then rinsed out their mouths. A hand was brushed across the surface of the water, as if to sweep away any filth which was floating there. Finally water was poured into their mouths from a cupped hand. I never saw a man put his head down to suck the water up.

We were into Kut, the scene of Townshend's disaster, early on the morning of the 28th, to be told that a suspected case of cholera had been discovered in the crew of the *Coconada*. We were to anchor in mid-stream until further orders. No doctor came to see us until about 7 am, when one appeared in company with a worried staff officer. Orders had come for me to be sent up on the early train, but by this time it had gone without me. The doctor now refused to let me go up country until I had been inoculated with the remainder of the troops, so down I went to the disembarking sheds to receive the first shot of vaccine, before they began with some 1,500 men. It was quite the most damnable shot I have ever received, running straight through me in less than an hour. The three of us then left for Baghdad on a light engine, feeling like nothing on earth but desperately hungry.

The General greeted me most warmly and of course wanted to know why I had been so late in coming. He had thought when he first wired for me that I was still on half-pay in England, and no one told him that I was mixed up with affairs in Turkey. Apparently Sir George Milne had not passed on to me the first telegram he had received from the War Office, because at the time he had not finished with me. Neither he nor the War Office informed Haldane that I was not yet available. It had taken me thirty-eight days to get from Constantinople to Baghdad, and he had already been wiring for me a fortnight before I started. His original intention had been to put me in charge of the operations at Samawah, but he had been forced to appoint someone else. Operations were still going on there, but he hoped that they would be over by 10 October, the date upon which the new High Commissioner was taking over. Now he wanted me to go up to North Persia at once.

He then told me the story of what had been happening there. A curious sequence of mishaps and mismanagement. His position had been a difficult one. As C-in-C in Mesopotamia his military policy had been laid down by the Colonial Office and the War Office, and he had been fully occupied with the quelling of the rebellion in the Euphrates area. Though the North Persian force was under his command, the military policy there was directed by the Foreign Office and the War Office, through the British Minister in Teheran. He had pressed the War Office hard to get a policy from the Foreign Office, but with no success. Affairs in Persia had appeared to be so peaceful and secure that military life had been allowed to drift very much on to a peace footing. The Commander of the North Persian force was a Brigadier in the Indian Army who had little experience of war and none of an independent command. He had been allowed by the Indian

Government to have his wife and family of two children and an European nurse up with him in Kazvin. The Indian troops had a good deal of their heavy kit with them, including band instruments. Many officers had their full-dress uniform with them. All seemed to be a happy party. But at the little Port of Enzeli on the southern shore of the Caspian Sea, there lay interned what had been the White Russian Fleet. It had sought refuge there after the defeat of the White Russians in the Caucasus, and had been legally interned by the Persian Government. There was a small detachment of fifty British soldiers, which was virtually in charge of the fleet, stationed in Enzeli. The guns of the fleet had been made useless by the taking away of their breech-blocks. No one in authority seemed to have realized what a prize the fleet would be for the Bolsheviks, could they but lay their hands on it. Information as to what the Red Russians were doing in the Caucasus was meagre both in Persia and at Baghdad. That they might make a raid against Enzeli does not appear to have been considered. No instructions had been issued to the C-in-C in Mesopotamia, the Commander of the North Persian force, or the British Minister in Teheran as to what action should be taken against any Russian force which made an attack on Persian territory. Resht was occupied by a British force of two battalions, but there were no Persian forces in the Resht area, the nearest being in the Persian capital.

Early one morning in these peaceful conditions the news was brought into Enzeli by some Persian fisherman that Bolshevik ships were lying off the port concealed by the mists of the Caspian. Nothing could be seen from the land. A few hours later there arrived a summons to the Persian Government, demanding the handing-over of the interned fleet. This demand was handed to the British officer in command at Enzeli. There were no Persian officials there. No one knew what to do. It happened that the Commander of the North Persian force was at Enzeli with his family on a week's leave. He immediately motored back to Resht, where he telephoned his news to the British Minister at Teheran, then Sir Percy Cox, and to the C-in-C in Baghdad. He asked both for instructions. Both these messages reached their destinations, but he received nothing from Baghdad owing to the communications breaking down. Sir Percy Cox had no authority to issue any orders to the Brigadier in command of the North Persian force, but he did advise him to oppose any landing which the Bolsheviks might make.

As can be imagined, with so many high authorities concerned, the Brigadier received no orders. He had been placed in a very difficult position and had not the military experience to act on his own. His next news from Enzeli was that the Russians had landed and seized the ships without opposition. The British detachment was withdrawing on Resht without having been engaged. Further reports stated that the Russian force which had landed was 'large', and that a Persian force under a rebel named Kutchik Khan was being hastily raised under Russian officers. It had been named 'The Persian Army of Liberty'.

Without any orders from his superior, he made up his mind to withdraw his troops from the Resht area. Undoubtedly the responsibility for allowing hostilities to commence between the Russian and British forces was a great one, and the making of a decision weighed heavily on his mind. Probably his decision was a right one, not that all hope of saving the fleet had gone. But the operations by which he extricated himself from the low country round Resht were badly executed. He made no attempt to reconnoitre the enemy positions and ascertain their numbers or indeed whether they had brought the means with them for penetrating further inland. It must have been very doubtful whether they had any transport with them. His withdrawal could have been executed in his own time and without loss, had he not been in such a hurry to break off all contact with the Russians. Large quantities of stores were left behind, including clothing and blankets, ammunition and food, besides the most important thing of all—hundreds of thousands of gallons of petrol, which the British had brought away with them when they evacuated Baku. No one seemed to know who was responsible for leaving this petrol in Resht instead of bringing it up in safety to Kazvin, where it was urgently needed.

British prestige suffered a heavy blow. The Persian Government very naturally asked us why we had not opposed the Russians in their landing. They pointed out that they had delib-

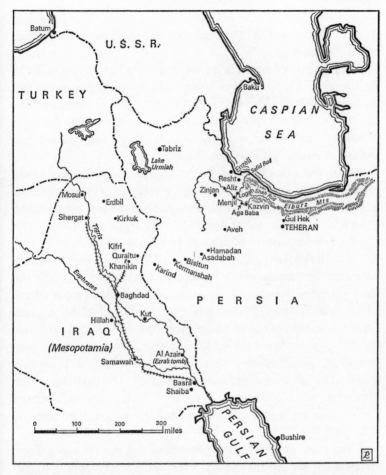

erately refrained from sending any troops to Enzeli because we were already there.

The C-in-C warned me that I should find things in Persia in some disorder. He still could not give me a military policy because he had not been given one from London. I was to get into touch with Mr Norman, the British Minister in Teheran, and to keep myself informed of any instructions which came to him from the Foreign Office. I was not to undertake any operations in the Resht area without further orders from him, and must confine myself to preventing the Bolsheviks from reaching the Persian plateau. I received no orders as to what I was to do should the Persian rebel, Kutchik Khan, attack me. I did not press the matter as I did not think that he could attack me without strong Russian help.

On 1 October I set off in a troop-train for the Persian railhead at Quraitu. The train was being sent up to bring down the married families which had been summering in the Persian hills. It thus came about that I was once more going to face the Bolsheviks on the second anniversary of the day upon which I had landed at Archangel in North Russia.

It was 397 miles by road from Quraitu to Kazvin, the headquarters of the North Persian force, a piece of fine engineering, crossing as it did three considerable passes, the most northerly of which lay at an altitude of 7,000 feet. As I drove up the long road I gained no impression of urgency in Persian affairs. I hardly saw an army lorry throughout its length. We were, however, much impeded by strings of pack-camels and donkeys carrying up civil stores to Teheran. They used the road whenever it suited them, but in the hilly sections they struck off along ancient tracks to avoid the curves in the motor-road. The road was well graded and banked throughout its length and its surface was excellent. Small military posts had been established along the road, all linked by telephone to one another. The maintenance of this road must have been very expensive, even with cheap Persian labour, and I saw no toll being exacted from Persian transport.

I had been given a touring Vauxhall for myself and a Ford box-car for my servant and kit. Two lorries were standing by for my heavy kit, and everyone was much relieved when they heard that I didn't possess any. They told me that the British Minister had required ten lorries to take him to Teheran. Off at 7 am we did the 117 miles to Kermanshah by 6 pm, including a long halt in the married families camp at Karind. After the heat and clamminess of Baghdad, the fresh air of the Persian hills was a great relief, though by evening we needed our coats. The tribesmen were all coming down to winter in the plains. Every animal—camels, ponies, donkeys and even sheep—were carrying their share of the family's worldly goods. One could often see the head of a baby sticking up from amongst the shapeless bundles and old kerosine tins which were dangling from the pack-saddles.

Kermanshah was the headquarters of the Persian communications, and here I found Colonel Lakin of the Indian Army in charge. He was installed in a comfortable Persian house with his wife and daughter, preparing for his second year on the road. He greeted me with the news that he was expecting an addition to his family, and for this he intended to keep his wife with him throughout the winter. From his description it was clear that the road would be closed by snow from the middle of December to the end of March. He had thousands of Persian coolies ready to shovel snow, but the terrific winds on the Asadabad and Aveh Passes closed the drifts again as soon as they were shovelled clear. He warned me that the state of the mechanical transport on the Persian road was bad, and he was trying to economize in its use in every way he could, so as to be ready for hard work in the spring when we would probably be evacuating the country.

I wondered whether the Persian force was getting all it wanted for the winter under such conditions of economy.

I was to have left early on the 3rd but the wretched Vauxhall needed repairs, so I had to use the Ford for the 140 miles to Hamadan. After a series of punctures we did not get in till midnight. It was an eerie drive in the dark with the perpetual howling of the jackals. And just before dark we came upon two great shaggy wolves standing in the middle of the road. They stayed watching us until we were nearly on them and then lumbered away into the bush. The manager of the Imperial Bank was waiting up for me, a most interesting man who remembered the country when it was divided up into British and Russian spheres of interest. He impressed upon me most forcibly that the natural economic entrance to North Persia was through Russia and not through the Persian Gulf. Russian communications were now closed, but even with a railway to Teheran from the Persian Gulf, we should never be able to compete with them when they were reopened. By road, rail and river it was 1,000 miles from Basra to Teheran, and the road was only open for six months in the year. On the other hand the road from Teheran to the Caspian, a distance of 200 miles, was open all the year round and after that there was only the short sea-voyage to Baku before the main Russian rail-system was reached. He thought that the British Government had forgotten this elementary fact.

On the 4th I completed the 140 miles to Kazvin with the Ford running well. The road over the Aveh Pass was as good as any Alpine road in Europe. I lunched on the summit and stayed looking for some time at the desolate country all round us. Everything was uniformly brown except in the bottoms of the valleys where the villages were. The view to the north was magnificent, row after row of hills rising gradually towards the Caucasus. It was already getting very cold as I started down on the last stretch of road to Kazvin, and I was glad to stop at the RAF landing-ground for a cup of steaming tea. I then drove on and took over command.

CHAPTER II

Kazvin in October

I did not meet the Brigadier whom I was relieving. He was going down to Baghdad for passage to Britain, but for the moment he was in Teheran paying his respects to the British Minister on handing over the command. The two Staff officers of the force, Major McCleverty of the 2nd Gurkhas and Major Macintyre of the 15th Hussars, however, were able to give me a clear picture of the situation. The North Persian force (36th Indian Brigade) was made up as follows:

'A' Battery Royal Horse Artillery (the Chestnut Troop).
The Guides Cavalry.
Two Batteries of Indian Mountain Artillery.
Armoured Car Company (16 cars).
2nd Bn York and Lancs Regiment.
1st Bn Royal Berkshire Regiment.
2nd Gurkha Rifles.
122nd Rajput Regiment.
42nd Deoli Regiment.
Flight of RAF.

It consisted of some 6,000 of all ranks, and was composed of some of the most distinguished units of the British and Indian Armies. It was a compact little force, well suited to the country in which it was operating. It was composed of well-trained and experienced soldiers, able to compete with any Russian force brought against it. It was well equipped and very mobile.

After our hurried withdrawal from the Caspian the Persian Government had sent their only formed body of troops—the

Persian Cossack Brigade—down to Resht with orders to deal with Kutchik Khan and to drive the Bolsheviks out of Persia. This Cossack Brigade was a relic of the old Imperial Russian sphere of influence, consisting of 3,000 men enlisted upon a volunteer basis. They were officered as far as the higher ranks were concerned by Russians, backed by a smaller body of Russian NCO's. All these Russians had come from the old Czarist Army, and though some of the original men had fallen out they had managed to maintain themselves through every crisis, even through the 1917 Revolution and the withdrawal of Baratoff's army from Persia. As White refugees they were not looked upon with disfavour by the Persian Government, because they were unlikely to take sides with either the British or Soviet Governments in any future struggle for power in Persia. The Shah had come to regard the Cossacks very much as his own bodyguard, a protection against his own Government as much as against foreign pressure from abroad. The Commander of the Cossack Brigade was a man called Starosselsky, ranking as a Colonel and reputed to be high in the Shah's favour.

Owing to the ill-feeling which had been caused by our withdrawal from Resht it had not been found possible to leave liaison officers behind with Starosselsky. Consequently we knew little or nothing of what the Cossacks were doing. They were thought to be still holding the town of Resht and to be still in action with the Bolsheviks who had landed at Enzeli. In the three months they had been in the low country on the shores of the Caspian they had carried out some spasmodic fighting, but were reported to be suffering much from malaria.

The main portion of our force was holding a strong position at the head of the Menjil Pass, down which ran the old Russian road to the Caspian. On its left was a detached battalion of Indian troops at Zinjan, which lay a hundred miles away on the main Kazvin to Tabriz road, The remainder of our troops were in Kazvin or stationed in posts along the Kazvin–Menjil road. All was reported to be quiet.

Two matters struck me at once as being unsatisfactory. Throughout the force the incidence of malaria was very heavy, there being more than 200 cases in the main hospital in Kazvin. Then I

9   Kazvin aerodrome.

10   Aerial photograph of Kazvin.

11 Northern Persia; a forty-foot snowdrift about to close up.

12 A very deep snowdrift at the summit of the Asadabad Pass.

found that no preparations for winter hutting were contemplated, and I was told Baghdad did not favour any hutting, apparently on account of the expense.

Communications were good and I was able to talk to Major van Straubenzee, the Major of the Chestnuts, who was in command of the Menjil Pass. He verified that he had no touch with the Cossacks, but was quite satisfied that he would get ample warning of any collapse on their part, and of a consequent Bolshevik advance from Resht. He was holding a very strong position with good observations right down the Pass. I told him that I was going to Teheran to see the British Minister, but that I would be back to see him as soon as I possibly could. I instructed him not to leave his present position without a personal order from me. He could call upon Kazvin for any support he needed. I also ordered him to send down a reliable officer to act as liaison officer with Starosselsky. He was to inform Starosselsky that I had taken over command in North Persia.

We had a curious unit of specialists under a lieutenant in the Gunners, which had been sent out to intercept messages on the enemy wireless. To make quite certain of getting information about what the Cossacks were doing, I ordered this unit to tap all the wires between Teheran and Resht at a special office in Kazvin. After dictating orders about hutting I started off in the Ford for Teheran.

The hundred miles to the capital took me about three hours and a half. The surface of the road was good, though running as it did along the base of the Elburz mountains, it was intersected every few miles by Irish bridges which slowed us up considerably. These bridges were paved surfaces, often as much as twenty yards broad, designed to allow the various mountain streams to cross the road without causing any damage.

Mr Norman was still out at his summer residence at Gul Hek some miles north of Teheran, a charming place tucked away in a hollow of the foothills and surrounded by the Persian garden of one's dreams. I found him finishing his breakfast at a little table placed close to a lily pond. The scene looked all too peaceful to be real, when one thought of the dreary waste outside the garden wall. There were little trout in the pond, which came up to take a

K

fly on its surface and then raced off with a whisk of their tails to the weeds below. Little streams of water ran tinkling down from rosebed to rosebed, guided in turn by numerous Persian gardeners. I thought how all Orientals love to play with water, a precious thing at all times. I was soon sitting with the Minister drinking some of his French coffee and sampling some of his fruit.

The Minister told me that he had arrived after the withdrawal of our troops from Enzeli, and that he was a newcomer to the East. He had failed utterly to secure a ratification of Sir Percy Cox's Treaty with the Shah. All the money advanced as a proof of goodwill when it was first drawn up had already been dissipated without result. He thought that a great deal of it had gone into the pockets of the Shah and the Commander of the Persian Cossacks. Nothing had been done to start the formation of a national army as had been agreed, and of the large mission of British officers which had come out to train the army, only a few remained. The others had drifted home to England in disgust. The Imperial Treasury was empty. The Government seemed to exist from the sale of Governorships. The Governors were always in great haste to recoup themselves for the money they had expended in buying their offices. The taxes extorted from the wretched peasants never reached the capital. The gendarmerie under their Swedish officers had ceased to exist. Footpads roamed the roads not controlled by the British. 'How can one deal with such a country?' he pathetically asked me.

The withdrawal from Resht had been a disastrous mistake. He still had no instructions on the subject of a military policy from the Foreign Office. He knew that the War Office was pressing hard for the evacuation of all British and Indian forces from North Persia, a policy which was being strongly opposed by Lord Curzon. It seemed certain that the North Persian force would now remain for the winter. I explained to him the orders I had received from General Haldane, and assured him that no Russian force which could be brought against us could force the Menjil Pass. I proposed to go straight back to inspect the positions there and would report to him again.

On my return to Kazvin I started investigating our administrative position. The main hospital was situated in a disgraceful temporary building. The huts in which the patients were lying were exposed to every wind that blew. No attempt had been made to screen them with matting. The Chief Medical Officer was worn out with service in Mesopotamia and badly needed a rest. He was in fact long overdue for retiring on his pension. Blankets and warm clothes, stores and hot water-bottles, even the stores necessary for competing with such an outbreak of malaria as had overtaken us, were sadly wanting. Every day I had to send off new demands to Baghdad. Persian towns and villages offered no buildings suitable for billeting troops, and I was sure that hutting for the winter was indispensable. Though I knew that the temperatures would never sink so low as they had in North Russia, I was pretty certain that the winds in North Persia would make conditions very severe. I wired my opinion to Baghdad, asking for specific permission to commence hutting for the men. I added that I had already given the order to reconstruct the hospital.

It was not till the 10th that I got clear of my various problems and could pay a visit to Straubenzee at Menjil. On the way I inspected the posts occupied by the British battalion along the main road. They were serving no useful purpose there, since no enemy could come in behind us or through the mountains on either side of us. Their summits were already deep in snow. What was being done by 500 men could be better done by a section of Armoured Cars. I found the troops in a pitiable condition. They had been dumped down at any point where an old shed or a derelict caravanserai offered itself, often in malarious hollows. The men were still in their summer kit, for the most part ragged shorts and torn shirts. Many had no coats of any sort, though the nights were already growing cold. Quite a number were suffering from malaria and the general state of the sanitation of the posts was lamentable. No attempt had been made to deal with mosquito breeding-places by means of sanitary squads. I ordered the whole battalion back to Kazvin to be reclothed. When I looked at them I thought they were like a batch of newly-released prisoners of war from a German camp. I had to send home the CO, as soon as I saw him on my return to Kazvin, as being quite useless for further military service.

Straubenzee's men were in much better fettle, though most of the units were short of necessary warm clothes. The Chestnuts, the Guides Cavalry and the 2nd Gurkhas were in excellent order. The Chestnuts had even got hold of some skis and were eagerly awaiting the arrival of the first snow.

The position Straubenzee was holding at the head of the pass was impregnable to anything but an attack carried out by a large force well trained to mountain warfare. His observation posts looked right down into the deep gorge in front, and his guns could cover every yard of the curves in the road as it wound its way up from plains below. He was holding the position with a small portion of his force, with the remainder in reserve. I checked all his posts on the ground and then decided to go forward as far as I could to inspect the gorge. With an armoured car I ran down the first half of the pass—twenty-five miles to the Menjil bridge over the Safid Rud. The bridge had been destroyed by blowing up the centre span during the panic retreat from Resht, and was now being repaired by our RE. We crossed the temporary bridge and ran on for another twenty-five miles until the gorge began to open up on to the low-lying flats of the Resht area. We had not met a soul on the road, not a cart nor a man on horseback or on foot. There were no signs of the Cossacks and we could hear no sounds of firing.

I made up my mind that we must hold the Iron Bridge at the bottom of the first half of the gorge. Even this would be impregnable to the attacks of such an enemy as we were facing. On my passing through Straubenzee's headquarters I gave him orders to start on the Iron Bridge position, which was to contain a battalion and a section of mountain guns.

My wire-tapping at Kazvin had produced good results. The Cossack Brigade were reporting that they had made no impression upon the Bolsheviks, who had prepared a strong position at Enzeli, covered by the fire of their guns in the fleet. Operations against them had now come to an end. Colonel Starosselsky was asking for permission to withdraw from the Resht area for refitting. The Shah was wiring to him that he should withdraw to Teheran for a month at least. He was evidently missing his bodyguard badly. Both Starosselsky and the Russian officer he had left in Teheran, Colonel Philipoff, were loud in their abuse of the British and everything to do with them. Both of them were urging the Shah to get rid of us as soon as he could. I gathered the impression that it would not be long before they would be forced to withdraw. Half their men were down with malaria and their morale had sunk very low.

I had to make up my mind what action I should take if the Cossacks should come tumbling back in disorder through our lines. They had done little enough towards turning the Bolsheviks out of Persian territory, but so long as they were in the Resht area they formed a buffer for us against them. If they came away they might be followed up by the Bolsheviks, or what was more likely by Kutchik Khan's nondescript forces. I had no wish to come into contact with either of them, even at the top of the Menjil Pass. It was better to let them stay and stew in the malaria of the low country. The important question was what to do with the Cossacks. Was I to hold them at Menjil or Kazvin or was I to allow them to pass through to the Persian capital? I felt that this could only be decided by the British Minister. I felt that once they got through to Teheran, nothing on earth would drag them out again. Their presence there might have a most injurious effect upon British policy in Persia, about which I knew nothing. I felt that I must go back and consult with the Minister as soon as I could.

I had much on my hands and little time in which to do it. I was considerably concerned at the continued reluctance of GHQ to agree to my programme of hutting. I felt that living as they did at sea-level in a warm climate, they did not realize what a winter in the mountains at an altitude of 5,000 feet meant to us. If they went on havering much longer I should have to go down by air, to put my case personally to the General. Luckily I knew him well enough to be able to do this. I had to gamble upon how long the Cossacks would stay in the Resht area, but I felt that with my wire-tapping I could keep my hand upon the pulse of affairs.

On the 12th, therefore, I set off for Teheran armed with all my inside information. I found the Minister much worried. He had seen the Shah twice, pointing out to him that if the Cossacks were withdrawn they would be abandoning the defence of Persia. The British troops would not be sent to Resht to replace them, though they would continue to hold the Menjil Pass. He told the Shah that the Cossacks could be much more easily refitted in Kazvin than in Teheran, and when they were refitted they would not have so far to go to reach the Resht area. He also told him the presence of White Russian officers in a Persian unit was a disturbing factor, and the Soviet Government had complained that it obviously meant that a plot against Soviet Russia was being hatched in Persia, under the auspices of the British Minister. After a long discussion it had been decided to refit the Cossacks at Kazvin under my supervision, if they found it necessary to withdraw from Resht.

Feeling that I was bound to communicate to the C-in-C in Baghdad the trouble we had been having in the Resht area, and not wishing to commit the story to a cipher telegram, I wired for permission to fly to Baghdad. Weather reports being good and the news from Resht unchanged, I started off on 16 October.

It was my first trip in a DH.9A and I did not find it a comfortable machine for a man of my size. Only with the greatest difficulty could I force myself into the back seat with all my flying clothes on. The observer's machine-gun ring fitted tightly round my waist and I could not strap myself in. The morning at Kazvin broke fine and bright and I had good observation all the way. For most of the journey we followed the course of the main road, and I employed myself in picking up the various points I had noted on my way up by car. We crossed the Aveh Pass at 12,000 feet, but for most of the time we were flying at 3,000 feet, which gave me a good view of the country. When passing the Bisitun Rock my pilot, Flt-Lieut Robinson, came down until we were on a level with the great carvings. We seemed to be only a few feet away from them as we swept by, raising a cloud of dust as if we were giving them a spring clean. The gardens and orchards of Hamadan and Kermanshah were the only spots of green to be seen. South of Kermanshah we could see the scars of the Turkish and Russian trenches standing out plainly on the hill, marking the limit to which Baratoff had advanced in his attempt to join up with us in Mesopotamia.

After Karind we left the road, striking off across line after line of knife-edged ridges on the shortest route to Baghdad. Just over five hours flight.

All operations in Mespot had ended with the relief of Samawah and I found the C-in-C in high spirits. My business with him went well. He saw at once that our men could not be condemned to live in tents with snow and slush alternating round them. I think that the administrative staff thought that I was making too much of my experience in North Russia, and the General had been inclined to listen to them. After consultation with the medical staff it was decided to keep all the malaria cases in Persia, for they would do better at Kazvin than at Baghdad if we could be sure of keeping them warm.

There was a heavy thunder-storm on the night of the 17th, but by dawn on the 18th the landing-ground had dried enough for me to start for Kazvin. With a following wind we were back in three hours and twenty minutes. I remember that I took back with me a copy of John Buchan's *Mr Standfast* and read it throughout the trip. The position at Resht had not altered materially. Starosselsky was still trying to engineer his return to Teheran, while sending in favourable reports about his operations against the Bolsheviks. Our liaison officers reported that all fighting had ceased long ago.

On the 20th I drove the 120 miles to Zinjan in the RAF tender, the most reliable motor vehicle we had in the force. The valley up which we drove was the most prosperous I had seen in Persia, and I would have dearly loved to go to Tabriz, but 330 miles there and back was out of the question with only one motor. The British Legation had a capable political officer there, to whom I spoke on the telephone. All was quiet with him. After consultation with the Commander at Zinjan I ordered him to reconnoitre the road from there to the Iron Bridge at Menjil through Aliz, as soon as the squadron of Guides Cavalry arrived, which would be in two days time. He was told to hold himself to reinforce the Commander at the Iron Bridge, on receiving orders from me.

As I had expected, the collapse of the Cossacks was not far off. After a despairing wire to Teheran on the 21st, Starosselsky began to withdraw from Resht in the early hours of the 22nd. He made no effort to inform the Menjil command of his intention to do so, and he took no steps to control the traffic southwards through the long fifty-mile gorge. Manoeuvring down in the Resht area must have become a hideous nightmare, for the continuous rain had turned the fields on either side of the main road into quagmires. His men were full of fever, and I was certain that they would put up little fight if they were followed up by anything like a formed enemy.

Colonel Francis of the Berks had now taken over the command in the Menjil Pass. He had held a brigade in France and was a first-class soldier. We discussed the situation fully, coming to the conclusion that Starosselsky would require most help at the Iron Bridge, where a traffic jam was almost inevitable. We had to be ready with a force below the bridge, so that the mass of the traffic could be passed across it in peaceful conditions. Under the commander at the bridge two senior officers were appointed, the first with troops on the line Aguzban—Logah, well up the hills on either side of the road so as to cover with their fire the long straight stretch as far as Naglobar. They were to be ready to put in a counter-attack from the hills on the road, if the enemy came on hard. The other was to be in charge of a posse of police to direct the traffic.

Though impeded by the vehicles, both military and civilian, trying to escape to the south, the Cossacks extricated themselves successfully from the town of Resht. By midday on the 22nd they were holding the mouth of the first defile at Sarawan, at which time the traffic block was being felt at the Iron Bridge. The police at the bridge worked magnificently, pushing the vehicles over it to the flat ground at the foot of the second defile. There another batch of police reorganized it for the second long climb to the top of the pass. It was late on the afternoon of the 24th before the first of the Cossacks began to cross the bridge and by three hours after midnight they were all over. Luckily the Russian officers obeyed all the orders given by the British commander at the bridge. They too were ordered to stop on the level ground until they received definite orders to tackle the final defile. Again the Russian officers obeyed their orders.

Only a small body of Kutchik Khan's men, supported by a few Russians, followed up the retreat of the Cossacks. Our concealed infantry did not use rifle fire, but killed some thirty of them with their bayonets, including eight Russians.

The operation had so far been executed most successfully, but there remained the tricky business of shepherding the Cossacks into a camp at Aga Baba some miles from Kazvin. I had made my plans for carrying this out, but at the last minute I was informed that the task of separating the Russian officers from their men would be left to me. Luckily for me Starosselsky played into our hands. As soon as he saw his men into the second defile he set off in his car to Kazvin and Teheran. He stopped at the post office in Kazvin long enough to wire to the Shah that he was motoring there at once, and a long wire to his Brigade to camp to the north of Kazvin. Our wire-tappers suppressed his wire to the Shah and altered the order for camping to Aga Baba.

From the top of the Menjil Pass the Cossacks were closely followed by the 2nd Gurkas in lorries, and they were met at the entrance to Aga Baba camp by a British detachment. They entered the camp peaceably enough, though the major in charge complained of being shadowed into the camp by so many British and Indian troops. The camp was well picketed all night, the Guides Cavalry standing by to stop any move in the night.

In the meanwhile Starosselsky had reached Teheran and been granted an audience by the Shah. He was told that he had been dismissed from his post, that all Russian officers and men were to be moved from the Cossack Division and sent to Baghdad as soon as they could be shifted there. His dismissal must have been a sore shock for him, but he did not give up hope. Driving to the nearest telegraph station outside Teheran he telegraphed to the Brigade to concentrate at Anjala, a village half-way to Teheran from Kazvin and just north of the main road. There he would meet the Brigade and issue further orders to them. This telegram was altered in the usual way by the wire-tappers. The Cossacks were told to remain in the Aga Baba camp, while all the Russian officers and NCO's were to meet Starosselsky in the government building in Kazvin. When Starosselsky turned up at

Anjala he was picked up by an armoured car and brought to Kazvin to join his officers, who were now in custody.

We were lucky that the trick we played on the Russians succeeded without a hitch. It might have led to a nasty scene with some shooting, but they were so sure of their position that they never dreamt of falling into such a trap. They had been embezzling British money for years and at the same time openly boasting of their hatred for us. They were the centre of all intrigue in Teheran, and it was certain that our affairs in Persia would go far more smoothly after their departure, whatever the policy of the British Government might be.

CHAPTER III

November/December

The departure of the White Russian officers from Teheran relieved the political situation considerably. Commanding as they did the only formed body of Persian troops in the country they had exercised great power, becoming during the last two years of their reign in Persia the centre of various intrigues. Starosselsky and his predecessors had been astute enough to keep on the right side of the Shah, who was always in open disagreement with his Mejliss. The Mejliss suffered their power in the capital, because they thought that whatever they did they would not join with either the British or the Red Russians in any future division of power in Persia. They left the country quietly and without raising any trouble. They were allowed a few days in Teheran in batches of twenty to arrange their affairs, and as these batches returned to Kazvin they were sent off to Baghdad under military escort. They were given passages to any country which was prepared to take them, but some 80 per cent of them went to Vladivostok.

The affairs of the Cossack Brigade had been handed over to Colonel Smythe, one of the senior officers who had been sent out to raise the new Persian Army under Sir Percy Cox's Treaty. He soon discovered how greatly the Russians were implicated in the wholesale robbery of government money which had been going on. The regimental books were found to be in hopeless confusion. They had been kept by the Russian Adjutant of the Brigade. There were now about 3,000 men in camp, while 500 more could be accounted for in various ways. Some were in hospital in Teheran and others had cleared off to their homes to convalesce from various ailments. From the pay and ration books it soon became clear that the late Commander had been maintaining at least 1,000 'blank files' for a period of years. How the money thus embezzled had been shared amongst the various authorities connected with the Cossacks it was impossible to say. The strength of the Brigade was fixed at 3,500 for the future and there were to be no additions. A general medical inspection of all ranks was being made, and all unfits and old men drafted out at once.

The Persian Mejliss lost no time in appointing a new Commander to the Brigade. I was still struggling with the despatch of the White Russians to Baghdad when he came to call on me. He was the Sirdar Hamayun, a member of one of the junior branches of the imperial family who had been serving as a diplomat in Europe. Like so many Persians he was so polite that he took a long time in coming to the point, talking away aimlessly and smoking innumerable cigarettes before he told me what he wanted. It was for me to introduce him to the Brigade personally. He was quite frank in acknowledging that he was not a soldier, and that he had been appointed to ensure the fidelity of the Brigade to the Shah. He was sure that I knew that the man who commanded the Cossacks was in virtual control of the capital. I promised that I would introduce him to Colonel Smythe, the British officer now in control of the administration of the brigade during the process of reorganization.

When I walked round the Brigade with the Sirdar and Colonel Smythe I found everything in a pitiable condition. Neither officers nor men had any winter clothing, and they were all literally shivering with cold and fever. Many of the men had no boots and appeared in front of us with their feet wrapped in sacking. Smythe explained that within a week all would be clothed in a good Persian coat and breeches made of wool. He was concentrating for the next month on good feeding and simple physical exercises. After that he would know where he was. The little Sirdar was hopelessly at sea. He did not shake hands with any of the Persian officers and he hardly said a word to them. They all bowed obsequiously to him but he had no cheery word for them. He did not thank them for what they had done down at Resht, nor did he tell them that a better future awaited them, now that they would be completely under their own officers. He had no intention of living in the camp or even near them, and it was obvious that he could neither command them nor administer them. Colonel Smythe and I decided that we must find a deputy at once.

It was interesting watching the Persian officers and men at their work, and I paid several visits to their camp. They were all volunteers and as their general health improved they made a better impression upon me, now that they were free of their old masters. The weak point lay, of course, in the senior ranks, who had never been allowed to have an opinion of their own or to take any responsibility on their shoulders. For a long time they all behaved like lost sheep. I was told that the most welcome change to them in the new régime was that they received the pay due to them without any reductions. Gradually both Colonel Smythe and I found our attention was being drawn to the work of the Tabriz *otryad* or troop. There the simple training was always the most advanced. The men were cheery and contented, taking a great interest in the small schemes they were set to do, an interest which was mostly absent in the other troops. Their Captain was a man of well over six feet in height with broad shoulders and a most distinguished-looking face. His hooked nose and sparkling eyes gave him a look of animation which was unexpected. He reminded me much of the Mahomedan Rajput gentlemen I had met in Central India. His name was Reza Khan. Thus gradually came to notice the man who was to affect the fate of his country so greatly. I remember that the first time I saw him he was shivering from a severe bout of malaria. I marked that he never went sick. We decided to make him Commander of the Cossack Brigade at least temporarily, and at once.

As far as I was concerned, one of the most important matters which affected the Cossack Brigade was the date upon which we should loosen our control of them. It seemed almost certain that the North Persian force would be withdrawn in the spring of 1921, and I favoured the loosening process being operated some months before we actually went, and not at the actual moment of our departure. I referred the question to the British Minister for his decision.

I had many administrative affairs on my hands. I thought that I had had sufficient financial trouble to last me a lifetime up in Archangel, but now I found a young financier who had discovered a quick way to make a fortune on the side. When I was inspecting the wires which had been sent off from Kazvin, I realized that someone was running a financial ramp every day between Bombay and London. The same sender was operating a simple code which looked very suspicious to me. I sent for him and asked him what he was doing. He was quite frank and told me immediately. Nearly everyone in Persia was on the Indian establishment, and so drew their pay in rupees in India. As the war had been going on for a long time, many officers had sent their wives away from India, where living was comparatively dear, and sent them to the United Kingdom or to some country in the Commonwealth like Australia or New Zealand, or perhaps even Canada. And to help these officers they were given a preferential exchange with the pound sterling. Also to help the officer serving in Persia he was given the same preferential exchange between the rupee and the Persian toman. All he had to do was to buy tomans and pounds at the preferential rate with rupees from Bombay, and then to sell them back to Bombay at the normal rate. I told him to stop his game at once and I should say nothing more about it. After a certain amount of thought I then limited all officers to one transaction a month and the total sum of rupees sold should never be more that the monthly pay of the buyer.

Nearly all officers did a little trading in Persian carpets and rugs, but that was perfectly legitimate. Many succeeded in bringing home some very good specimens.

I mentioned before that a Listening Station had come out to Persia under a young Gunner subaltern called Muntz. He and his men had helped us to tap the wires when we were dealing with Starosselsky and his men. The reason for this section coming to Persia was this. After the Revolution in 1917 in Russia all the telegraph lines in the country were destroyed, and the Bolsheviks made very free use of the wireless stations they had captured. Owing to lack of clerks they were unable to use a cipher, so they disclosed all their plans to listeners all over the world. One of the most favourably situated places for listening was on the Persian plateau. Muntz proved himself a wonderful success. Unlike other experts, Muntz took a positive delight in discovering that the Bolsheviks had changed their cipher, instead of cursing at the extra work thrown upon him. He specialized in Russian ciphers and, of course spoke the language fluently. I had many a good laugh at the rows that went on between the generals and the men put on to watch them. All Muntz's work was secret and he had the added work of sending off the results that he had obtained in a British cipher. We only heard some of the amusing snippets which did not affect the main situation, or something which directly affected us in Persia.

So good were his interceptions that we were told of an attack which was being prepared against us, to test our defences at the Iron Bridge over the Siah Rud. We had nearly a week's notice of what was going to happen, so that I was able to send the Deoli Regiment down from Zinjan along the road they had reconnoitred to join in the fray. The attack failed immediately under our heavy fire, and the Deolis were able to put in a counter-attack with the bayonet. The enemy lost fifty-two killed and wounded, while our casualties amounted to two killed and seven wounded. It was a successful action well commanded and carried out. On the next morning we discovered that the enemy had withdrawn to Resht.

The Minister passed on the news of our little fight to the Shah, and His Majesty expressed a desire to see me if I was able to come over to Teheran. The result was a formal invitation for me to present myself as soon as I could. I was ushered into what I took to be his private office, a simple room with walls hung with Persian carpets and one large table in the middle of the room all covered with papers. When I was introduced by the Court Chamberlain the Shah was busy signing papers with some minor official. He motioned me to a chair on the opposite side of the table. He at once offered me his warmest thanks for having defeated the Russians in such a signal way. He then told me how great his sorrow had been at parting with his Russian officers. They had served him well for many years. He hoped that they were being treated kindly as they so well deserved. I was able to assure him that they were being given a passage to Vladivostok at the expense of the British Government. Now that they had gone he wished for an assurance that the British would not put British officers in the Cossacks in their stead. That would ruin all chance of Sir Percy Cox's Treaty being ratified. The Mejliss would never agree to such a thing. I told him that the Cossacks would in future have only Persian officers and that we were busy going through all available officers for the various posts which existed. His Majesty must understand that we could never again allow such flagrant embezzlement to take place as had existed under the Russian officers. As I saw the fat young man in a grey frock-coat wriggling with nervous jerks at my words I thought that it was painful to see such a wretched specimen of a man in so great a position.

Rather abruptly the Shah then changed the subject. He told me that the lack of gendarmerie in the country had brought affairs to an almost desperate state. The only roads which were safe for travellers were those under the British authorities. This had placed him in a difficult position. He hoped that I would do my best to help him in his trouble. He found himself compelled to transfer a sum of money to his bank in Bombay, and the only safe way of doing so was to consign it by way of our convoys to Baghdad. At first I hardly understood what he required me to do, but gradually I elicited the fact that he had some Persian tomans, large silver coins about the size of French five-franc pieces. The value of this enormous weight of silver amounted to about half a million sterling. I was taken aback because I had no idea what the actual weight of the consignment was. I knew it must be a number of lorries and a number of men as guard to take such a valuable load down to Baghdad. And then the enormity of the crime he was proposing to commit suddenly dawned upon me. We had been advertising all over the East for Persian coinage with which to pay our men, and doubtless our demands had reached India. The Shah was exporting currency to a place where he knew he could get a good price, instead of selling to us and the Imperial Bank of Persia. I asked him why he could not pay what he had into the Imperial Bank in Teheran, but he brushed that question aside as if it did not need answering. I then

13 The Cairo Conference, March 1921. *Seated, left to right*: Sir Malcolm Stevenson, General Sir Walter Congreve, Sir Herbert Samuel, Mr Winston Churchill, Sir Percy Cox, General Sir Aylmer Haldane, General Sir Edmund Ironside, General Sir Percy Radcliffe. *First row, left to right*: Sir Geoffrey Archer, Miss Gertrude Bell, Sassoon Effendi, General Sir Edward Atkinson, Jafar Pasha, Colonel Lawrence, Air Vice-Marshal Sir Geoffrey Salmond, Colonel Trevor, Mr Young.

14   Boarding the aeroplane at Shaiba.

15   The final state of the aeroplane.

said that I thought he would be doing something very wrong to export what we were forced to import at great expense. He looked at me with a wry smile while he said, 'Peut-être que oui, mon général, mais n'oubliez pas qu'au fond tout le monde est égoïste!'

What could Persia do with such a ruler? Was it a wonder that she had sunk so low? She needed a strong man to bring her through, and she certainly had not got that. It had been a continual mystery to me how she had been able to preserve her independence. At one time it did look as if she had lost it, when her territory was divided between Britain and Czarist Russia. Would the same struggle begin once more with Soviet Russia? To a Western eye the country looked ripe for Communism. She had a thoroughly effete and rotten upper class, and the lower classes were bitterly poor. The mass of the population knew nothing of either Democracy or Communism. Kutchik Khan had not made any visible progress with his revolution. Everybody I met asked me what I thought would happen when the North Persian force evacuated Persia? I wondered whether the Mohammedan faith of the Persians would act as armour against Russian Communism. At the moment I noted in my diary that the people of Persia seemed quite apathetic as to what happened to them. There were no military forces capable of withstanding even a weak assault on their freedom. But I also noted that the Russians had much too much to do at home to think of starting a foreign campaign.

By the end of November we were in the full grip of winter and through traffic to Baghdad was interrupted in several places. The men of the Chestnut Troop were enjoying their ski-ing and I hoped that we should not be bothered much from outside. The Persians had begun their long hibernation. Then on the last day of the first week in December in came a long cipher wire from Baghdad. An order for the North Persian force to be withdrawn as early as possible in the spring had been received from the War Office. I was summoned to Baghdad for consultation. My peace had been disturbed. I had not made a flight in snow conditions since I left Archangel, and I was most annoyed. We could not use skis, as we had done in Russia, for we had to

L

land on an aerodrome which never had any snow on it. With Robinson I made a careful reconnaissance of our landing ground. It was covered to a depth of two or three feet of soft snow. We decided that we could get off if we could produce horses and camels to the number of at least 500 to beat down a run-way This was carried out in two days.

On 11 December we made our first attempt. The weather was passably good with us, though less favourable at Kermanshah where it was reported to be snowing. I decided to have a try at it. We got off easily enough, but failed to see the Verey light recalling us on a very bad report from Hamadan. We soon got through the thin layer of the lower clouds into clearer air, and turned to face the Aveh Pass. Twice we rose to sufficient height to cross it, and twice the upper layer of clouds seemed to be closing down on us. We could see the pass well with its two little peaks standing up on either side of the road, but the gap between the two layers looked perilously small. At last Robinson signalled defeat and turned to land again at Kazvin. I was never more thankful in my life. When I got back and read the report from Hamadan I was even more thankful.

On the 12th there was more heavy snow, which necessitated more work by the horses and camels. Then on the 13th in beautiful weather we got away. I had lunch on sausage-rolls with hot coffee in a thermos as we passed over Kermanshah. All the way from the Aveh Pass we saw strong bodies of coolies working on the roads. The journey took us exactly five hours.

At Baghdad there was lots to be done. We were to clear out of Persia lock, stock and barrel. What we could not take away with us was to be sold by auction in the country. Petrol, oil, unfit vehicles, tyres, clothing and stores. The date of our departure depended upon the weather. As the melting snow would cause many washaways, the date might even be as late as April. The withdrawal was to be carried out as a military operation, all useless mouths being sent down before the fighting force came away. The line of communications was to be rolled up as we came away. I was to discuss the evacuation of civilians with the British Minister. This item carried me back to the days in Archangel, and I layed a small bet with myself that the people would

be equally loth to register for a passage. I found the staff at
Baghdad very helpful and there were no arguments of any kind.
I was treated very much as an expert in risky withdrawals. Of my
own future when we reached Baghdad after the withdrawal, of
course I could learn nothing. I could see little chance of work in
Mesopotamia, for I knew nothing about the country and I
could see that the force there was being reduced at great speed,
all depending upon the shipping available.

During the three days I was working in Baghdad it had never
ceased to rain, making the aerodrome an impossible quagmire.
As more was predicted, and that meant more snow in the hills, I
decided to go back by road. It would give me a good idea of
what conditions would be like when we came down in spring
After much telephoning I got through to the Sapper officer at
the Aveh Pass. I could ride over the summit by a track which
would be kept open for me. A pony would be ready and a car
would come up on the northern side from Kazvin.

It was a long and troublesome journey I made, but it was well
worth it if only for the experience. I saw what we might have to
face in the way of washaways between Baghdad and Quraitu and
I did not reach Kermanshah till the evening of the 19th. On the
20th I pushed through the 180 miles to the southern slopes of the
Aveh, which I did not reach till dark. The road was reported to
be open but very difficult, and with the bad lights of the Ford
cars I decided that I would not attempt such a night drive. It was
lucky I did not try, for a regular hurricane blew up about 11 pm.
We should certainly have been caught on the northern slopes,
which were exposed to the full force of the wind. I started the
next morning on the pony, which was a good one, and the
saddle big enough for me. A Persian guide went with me on foot,
and the hour was some time before dawn. It was bitterly cold
and the wind drove into my very bones after the warm heat of
Baghdad. The guide took me well away from the main road,
zig-zagging up what appeared to me to be a quite indistinguish-
able track after the night's storm, wallowing on for three hours
until we reached the summit of the ridge. Here we found a hut
buried in the snow, crammed with coolies sheltering from the
wind. After an hour's rest and several cups of scalding tea we

set off again along the nine miles of track leading to the main road. We were exposed to the full force of the wind, battling against it for four hours. For myself I saw nothing in the drifting snow, with my feet freezing with the cold coming from contact with the stirrup-irons. I was heartily glad when we stumbled on my own Vauxhall with my servant Kostia waiting anxiously for us to appear. 'Ochen kholodno' was all he said as he packed me into the front seat. He had brought two coats and a thermos with hot coffee with a double ration of rum. I stumbled into bed at Kazvin and slept for twelve hours.

I and my staff then settled down to all we had to do before we left Persia some four months later. The sales we proposed to hold at once caused trouble. The Persian Customs were run by Belgian officials, and I received an early visit from their chief. He announced that everything we sold in Persia would be subject to duty, and that we should be responsible that the tax was paid by all buyers. I had to be stiff with the poor devil, telling him that neither he nor anybody else in Persia had the right to dictate to us, after what we had done to help the country. Even the British Minister could not order me to pay anything. I soon found that the wretched Belgian officials had not been paid for many months and that they were all depending upon the nest-egg they would get from us to pay their salaries. In the end the duty to be charged on our discarded motor vehicles was solved in a curious way. As soon as the news of these sales reached Mesopotamia, the head agent for Ford cars wired me that he was coming up at once to see me. He did not disclose how he proposed to reach me. Somehow or other he came up with two Ford cars from Bushire. What he came to say was that he proposed to buy every car which was offered for sale, whatever price it went for. He had no intention of allowing a glut of old cars to spoil his sale of new ones, as his depots down country were all crammed with those waiting to go up country. As soon as the sales were finished, the first thing he did was to apply for the help of the troops to break up and burn what he had just bought.

On Christmas Day we had a Church Parade and the usual festivities for the troops. I thought they had very good dinners, helped by any number of partridges and haunches of venison. I also issued a double tot of rum, not omitting the 2nd Gurkhas who are very partial to such an issue. I thought back to my service of twenty-one years, my coming of age so to speak. When I counted up I found that I had spent only four Christmases in England.

On the 30th there arrived a cipher telegram from the War Office. I was asked what the chances were of my being able to evacuate all my troops from Persia at once. The Government wished to economize all it could, and wished the operation to be completed before 1 April—that famous end to the financial year for all Service Departments. I wish I could remember how often that date has managed to obtrude itself into my service life. I could only reply that no such withdrawal should be contemplated except in a military crisis, and that did not appear to exist at the moment. I then telegraphed a short account of my last journey up by road from Baghdad. I heard no more of the project.

On 31 December I went over to Teheran to spend the night with McMurray, the head of the Imperial Bank of Persia, and so see in the New Year. After dinner we went to the club to meet the rest of the European community. They had all been offered transportation to Baghdad when the British troops left in the spring, and all said that they had refused. They ridiculed the idea of a Bolshevik invasion of Persia, despite the obvious inability of Persia to protect herself. Some asked me what I thought. I replied that I didn't believe that the Bolsheviks were capable of carrying out a serious invasion. They had far too much to do in their own country. I told them of our evacuation of Archangel and of how everyone had refused a passage. Then at the end they had all come clamouring for passages when there were no more ships available. Most of the European officials in the service of the Persian Government had been through a number of crises already, and in most cases these people had nowhere to go if they left the Persian service. They had lost touch with their own countries, and they all said that they would be left stranded in Baghdad, with no money to pay for a passage anywhere and no Government to do it for them.

CHAPTER IV

Last days in Persia

I spent New Year's Day wandering about Teheran. Few people were about and the city gave me the general impression of being down and out. There were no troops to be seen even in the main square, and I saw only one tired-looking policeman patrolling the main bazaar. When I thought of the bazaars of Peshawar and Lahore and other places in India, with their merry uproar rising from their tightly packed crowds, I almost got a shock to see the Teheran bazaar. All the townspeople looked sad and lugubrious. There was no badinage between the passers-by and the shopkeepers, and there were no picturesque hillmen carrying a rose behind their ears or in their mouths. No swaggering Pathan out for an escapade of any kind. I had expected to see some of the men from the Elburz mountains in sheepskin jackets. Not a single individual looked sturdy or proud to be a native of the Persian Empire. I soon got sick of watching such dejected-looking beings and turned into one or two of the second-hand shops, which were mostly in the hands of Armenians .They were all eager to learn what the English intended to do. Did I think that the Bolsheviks would invade Persia? They were quite open in saying that if the Bolsheviks did come they would not stay. They intended to make their escape to the east through Baluchistan. All the goods of these men were cheap trash made in Europe, gaudily painted chairs and sofas, gramophones and musical boxes made in Birmingham. For these they were asking prices that must have been ten times that originally paid. I had thought that I might find some remnants left behind by Russian refugees— old imperial china, samovars and ikons—but saw not a vestige of anything interesting. Persian lambskins, obviously dyed and badly cured, were being offered at thirty shillings apiece. Every shopkeeper demanded British or Indian currency, and I was never given a quotation in either krans or tomans. The meat shops were filled with partridges at three shillings a brace, and outside were festooned with haunches of venison at a few pence per pound. There was not a single car in the streets, not surprising perhaps with petrol at £1 a gallon. I saw five new Overland cars in a garage, which the proprietor told me he hoped to sell when the panic came with a Bolshevik invasion. I wondered how much he would charge to fill the tanks of these cars, and how far down the road would a full tank take them. Still I didn't believe in any coming invasion. Hordes of beggars stood in the streets begging for alms, and amongst them many blind men, led by a boy. It was all a horrible picture of acute despondency. When would the strong man come to rule Persia? Surely she was doomed unless a leader was spat up from somewhere. I spent an hour in a carpet-dealer's, which offered me a happy relief. I was shown some beautiful rugs but the prices asked were beyond anything I could possibly pay. The dealers did not seem very eager to get one to buy, and I decided to wait till it was nearer the date for our departure.

I found the Minister in despair over the thought of a winter withdrawal, but I quieted him by telling him that I had said that it shouldn't be attempted except in a crisis. He was taking his responsibilities towards the other European communities very seriously. He had sent to all of them the British offer of transport to Baghdad, but had received not a single application in return. The situation had become very like that which had presented itself at Archangel in the last days of 1919. Very few people believed that we were going to withdraw, and all had decided to wait and see what others did. The numbers involved in Persia were very small, probably well under two hundred in all. Perhaps half of these belonged to the Legation staffs, who had their own transport and would merely require petrol for the road. The people to be pitied were the few Europeans in the service of the Persian Government. They had long been separated from their European homes, and even if they reached Baghdad they would have nowhere to go. They would have to wait in desert camps for ships that never seemed to arrive, and eventually might have reached their homelands in a state of despair. Their Persian pay was always months, if not years, in arrears and they would soon be without resources of any kind. Many of them were quite insignificant people, who would certainly elect to remain in Persia whatever happened.

My own opinions about an immediate invasion after we left were quite clear. The Bosheviks had just suffered a heavy disaster before Warsaw, and they were engaged with difficult operations in the Caucasus against the Turks. I did not think that they would engage in operations in Persia, which might at least be lengthy and expensive. If we left the Persian Cossacks in sufficiently good shape to deal with the disintegrating forces of Kutchik Khan, there would be little danger to the Persian State for a long time to come.

During the month of January travelling became more and more difficult. Frost by night and thaw by day rendered the roads unsafe for anything but the slowest driving. Our accident returns rose steeply, especially upon the hill sections of the Baghdad road. Our vehicles were deteriorating fast, and I was hard put to it to accumulate a reserve for the final withdrawal. Though Persian labour on the road south was still plentiful, the work of clearing sections to allow the convoys of 'useless mouths' to get through was very heavy indeed. I dared not crowd the road too much and yet I had to reduce the force to a fighting minimum by the beginning of April at the latest. I did not expect that I should have to make a fighting withdrawal, and I fully intended to give Kutchik Khan a good healthy knock before I turned my face southwards. If the worst came to the worst, I could easily make the fifty miles of the defile from Naglobar to the top of the Menjil Pass impassable for many months to come.

I made regular visits to the Cossack Brigade at Aga Baba. Reza Khan had now become a Lt-Colonel and the Brigade was making rapid steps towards efficiency. I had been given the responsibility for fixing the date upon which we should release them from our control, and had it in my mind that it should be done about a month before we started on our march to Baghdad. I therefore put two matters to Reza Khan. I told him when I proposed to release him, and asked him to promise me not to take any offensive action against me during our withdrawal. I warned him that if he did so, I should have no compunction in halting and turning upon him. His country would then be in a more precarious position than ever. I did not want to do this, and asked him to remember that we had not resuscitated the Cossack Brigade in order to destroy it as we went away. I also asked him not to take or allow to be taken any violent measures to depose the Shah. To both these requests he gave me his most solemn promise that he would do as I wished. He talked very openly to me, expressing his dislike of the politicians who controlled the Mejliss for their own benefit. He was a soldier and came of a family of soldiers, and hated their interminable talk without ever making a decision. He seemed to me a strong and fearless man who had his country's good at heart. Persia badly needed a leader in the difficult times ahead, and here was undoubtedly a man of outstanding value.

My plans for withdrawal were suddenly complicated by hundreds of Assyrians from Lake Urmiah, men women and children with all their worldly goods. They had been despatched to us by an American Mission, in order to save them from Turkish violence, and they came without warning and mostly without money. They arrived by way of the Tabriz main road in horsed transport, mostly in very bad condition. Most of these people had been over to America, but had returned to their own country when it had been announced in the USA that a Christian Armenian State was to be set up under American protection. When I interrogated them they seemed to be more terrified of the Kurds than of the Turks. It was a miracle that these sturdy hill-men had maintained their position so long in the midst of their Muslim neighbours without losing their identity or their fervent belief in the Christian religion. I sent them all off to take their chance on the road to Baghdad.

I had always kept up a close correspondence with Lord Rawlinson, ever since he had come out to Archangel in 1919 to superintend the evacuation of North Russia. I now received a letter from him, offering me the command of a District in India. He had heard from General Haldane that my command in North Persia was coming to an end, and wished to have me under his command once more. It was a kindly thought, but for me it meant another jump still further to the East and I wanted time to think things over. With all I had on my hands I could not tie myself with a new job.

On 30 January we carried out a very successful action at Menjil. News of our coming departure had of course leaked out, and the Bolsheviks had been very talkative on the wireless. With the help of Muntz's radio section we were able to listen to the whole plot, just as if we were sitting at table with the plotters. First came a political message from Moscow to the commander at Enzeli, telling him that he must exert himself. There followed wires to Moscow by the commander and the head commissar, explaining their difficulties and making complaints about each other. The next thing was a peremptory order to do something, with a demand for details of the proposed plan to be forwarded at once. On the evening of the 29th our observation posts picked up an enemy body setting up a camp at Naglobar at the entrance to the defile. The commander at Menjil decided to attack them early the next morning before they could get to work. The camp was rushed just before dawn by three platoons of Gurkhas, with a troop of the Guides Cavalry in support. The surprise was complete, the Gurkhas getting to work with their kukris without any opposition. The enemy suffered thirty killed and twenty prisoners, most of whom were wounded. The remainder fled into the fields, pursued by the Guides. We had no casualties. The next morning Gikalo, the commander at Resht, reported that he was having great difficulty in keeping the Persian Army of Liberation in being.

The retention of our little force in North Persia had now become very unpopular in Parliament and in the Press. It was almost like Archangel again. Our affairs were alluded to as the Persian Imbroglio. Lord Curzon had delivered a long speech in the Lords justifying his policy, but this was greeted with many angry replies. One of his critics demanded to know why we did not come home at once. He asked sarcastically, 'What is the good of remaining in Persia till spring? What is General Ironside being asked to do? Is he to strew leaves from a Persian rose-garden in front of the advancing Bolsheviks?' There must have been many men in Parliament who knew what the physical conditions were like in North Persia, but no one stood up to answer these questions. I should have liked some military author-ity to have explained that we had already strewn something more effective than rose-leaves in the path of the enemy. This was the third time since the Armistice in 1918 that I had found myself commanding unpopular military forces in widely separated parts of the world. I was rapidly becoming a bird of ill-omen.

February broke with a howling blizzard, one of the worst I have ever experienced. It lasted all day and most of the succeeding night. Telegraph poles were blown down and roads became impossible. It took us the best part of a week to restore our communications with Baghdad. And it was during this short period that we suffered the very few cases of frostbite which overtook us that winter.

When communications were reopened once more we were subjected to a spate of telegrams from London. Now that definite orders for our withdrawal had been issued, all the various departments concerned began to send us afterthoughts. I was told to organize a network of Intelligence posts throughout the country, without telling me where I was to get the personnel for the posts, or from whence the money for paying them was to come. They seemed to have forgotten that Persia was still an independent state, and that she would most certainly have protested at our behaviour. I was ordered to send down four officers to Baghdad, as they were to sit for the Staff College examination. My solitary General Staff officer was included in the number. He would be a great loss to me in the coming operations, but I could not ruin his career by refusing to let him go. I am glad to say that he arrived in time and duly passed his dreadful ordeal after six years of continuous active service. I had to take my ADC in as helper and did the GS work myself.

They were busy days but I was well up in all the little difficul-ties involved in the evacuation of foreign countries. There were always a certain number of men who had contracted liaisons with women of the country or with refugees. They wanted to get married and bring their wives home with them. There were often children to be considered. Curious people of doubtful character and even more doubtful nationality emerged from the burrows in which they had been living and asked for visas to go all over the world. Stateless people who had no passports and no one to turn to in order to get one. Very few would admit to having any money, and the stories of how they had reached Persia in the first instance were quite incredible. A Turk appeared in a large car and applied to be given free petrol to take him back to Anatolia. He had been in Teheran for a month and wanted to go to Erzerum. He denied being a Kemalist, but when we had himself and his car searched we discovered that he had been interviewing Persians belonging to revolutionary societies. He must have been a very inept spy, for he had a book on him with the names of a hundred Persian rebels in it.

Late on the evening of the 6th, there presented himself a curious little figure in my office. He proved to be Prince Firouz, who had been Persian Foreign Minister at the time of Sir Percy Cox's Treaty. He had just arrived back from Europe, and told me that he had abandoned his cars at the Aveh Pass and taken to a horse in order to reach me. He was wearing a sports coat and very baggy knickerbockers, finished off with gaudily coloured stockings. On his head was a Persian Astrakhan hat. He was in a terrible state about our withdrawal, telling me that there would be a revolution in the country a very few days after our departure. He prayed me to give him a car to take him over to Teheran to see the Shah. The little man's conversation was all in French, and interlarded with expressions of 'vie et mort', 'résistance à outrance', 'attaquer à fond' and the like. I packed him off to see the British Minister, but I had little hope that he would be of any more help than had been the Sirdar Hamayun.

On 14 February, completely unexpectedly, I received a personal and secret letter in cipher from General Haldane. I was to report in Baghdad by the 20th of the month at the latest. I was to be prepared for a short sea journey and was not to bring an ADC with me. When I read the wording of the order it seemed so peculiar that I could not conceive what it was all about. To obey it, the immediate problem was how to get to Baghdad within the specified time. I could not go by road, as the Aveh Pass was snowed up again and the rest of the road to Kermanshah was almost as bad. My only chance was to fly, and to do so was more than hazardous in the weather we were having; regular and heavy snowstorms with frost by night and thaw by day. I had only two moderately sound planes, and my regular pilot had gone off to England. I had therefore to take one of the junior pilots, with whom I had never flown before. The chance of getting through to Baghdad was so slender that I sent off a wire to General Haldane asking if my presence was really essential. To this I received a curt reply that my presence had been specifically ordered from England. I was also told that a Major-General senior to me, Sir George Cory, was being sent up to Persia to take my place there. This left me more confused than ever, for it showed clearly that I was not to see the North Persian force again. The affair must be very secret or I should have received a cipher explanation of what it all meant. I got very little sleep that night turning over what it all meant. Knowing my chief so well, I wondered at first whether he had been angry at the War Office for insisting upon my going down to Baghdad just when he needed me most in Persia. I could make neither head nor tail of it all. The next morning I sent a wire to say that I would make the flight to Baghdad if it were in any way possible.

Before I left Persia I wanted to pay my respects to the Shah and to the British Minister, whom I knew would be considerably disturbed at my sudden departure. Leaving orders for the necessary animals to be collected on the Kazvin runway for the beating down of the snow, and for six-hourly weather reports to be collected from down country, I set off for Teheran just after dawn. I travelled in the RAF tender with a Ford behind us in case of accidents. The road was in a terrible condition, the surface underneath being frozen, with a foot of slush on the top. Every rivulet was pouring down ice and snow across the causeways. Twice the tender turned completely round when the driver checked our speed with the brake, and then within ten miles of the capital it broke down. I finished the journey in the attendant Ford.

I told Mr Norman of my many talks with Reza Khan and arranged with him to settle the actual date when the Persian Cossacks would be released from our custody. I recommended a month before the North Persian force left Kazvin as being the most suitable date. If I saw my successor in Baghdad I would explain matters to him. The Minister had arranged an audience with the Shah and asked me to go with him.

We duly arrived at the great iron gates of the Palace, and leaving our car we slipped unattended into the great courtyard within. I thought of the days when the Minister used to drive up with a carriage and four with two outriders, and escorted by a troop of red-coated Bengal Lancers as escort. We were met in the courtyard by two Eunuchs, dressed in European dress-coats and carrying silver-mounted ebony sticks. Bowing low and walking backwards they led us to a smaller building at the side of the main Palace. This was the *anderun*, or women's quarters, where the Shah had elected to receive us. At the door of this stood a truly gigantic African, who ushered us through a court at the end of which he threw open a door for us to enter the Shah's private room. As we passed I caught a glimpse of a group of women and children, peering at us from a side gallery. They were laughing and giggling at each other, but this was soon stopped by other eunuchs who were with them in the gallery.

The hall which we entered was perhaps a hundred feet long by fifty feet broad. The windows were hung with tawdry curtains which looked as if they had never been cleaned, but the glory of the place was a carpet which covered the whole floor. It depicted the Tree of Knowledge in colours of red, blue, green and yellow, and in the upper branches were perched countless birds in bright plumage. On the way up to the left among the branches stood a very ordinary armchair. In it sat the young shah, wearing a plain black frock-coat with no decorations of any sort. He sat hunched up in the chair with his head sunk deep into his shoulders. Behind him stood a large African, dressed much in the fashion of a mameluke. Two chairs had been placed for the Minister and myself, almost at the foot of the tree's stem, and to these the Shah motioned us when we came in. Small tables were brought in and placed beside each of us, and we were then served with coffee in priceless Sèvres cups. As we sipped our coffee I noticed that the Negro behind the Shah tasted every cup before he handed it to his master. Both he and the Shah were wearing black kid gloves, and I was told later that these were worn to prevent poison beings administered to the Shah through his hands.

The Shah welcomed the Minister and thanked him for coming to see him. We both thanked him for being so gracious as to receive us. The Minister then told the Shah that the British Government was growing tired of the delays in the ratification of the treaty which he had signed. He said plainly that it was impossible for them to go on advancing money unless the treaty was ratified. The Shah was very halting in his replies, not through any lack of facility in French but obviously from sheer agitation. He told us that he found himself in a cleft stick. He would have ratified the treaty long ago had he been an autocrat. He wanted it ratified, knowing that it was the best thing which could be done for his country, but the Mejliss was adamant in its refusal to ratify. He himself had been accused of disloyalty for having agreed to the treaty in the first instance. The Mejliss would never agree to British officers organizing any Persian army, and no argument of his could persuade them to change their minds. He then proceeded to paint for us a lurid picture of what would happen if we withdrew our forces from Persia. His country would at once be overrun by the troops of Soviet Russia. Such an event would bring untold dangers for both Mesopotamia and India. He prayed the Minister not to withdraw the British troops, if not for the sake of Persia then for the sake of the British Empire and India. In a last attempt to escape from the clutches of his cleft stick, he put forward the old plea that officers from some neutral country might be entrusted with the making of the new Persian Army. He was sure that the Mejliss would agree to such a proposition. The Minister had no mercy on him, pointing out how the Persian gendarmerie had behaved under their Swedish officers. He also reminded the Shah how the money advanced on the signing of our treaty had all been dissipated without result. Undoubtedly a large portion of this money had passed into the pockets of the Russian officers in the Persian

Cossacks. How could the British Government be expected to advance money to Persia, so that officers of other countries could embezzle it?

By this time the Shah appeared to be growing exhausted by the efforts he had made to excuse himself, and he had allowed himself to sink lower and lower into his chair. He presented a pathetic picture of defeat. It was obvious that nothing further was to be gained by continuing the conversation. I wondered how our audience would be brought to an end. There was an awkward pause and then he turned to me. He explained that he wished to reward me for what I had done for Persia, and he therefore intended to invest me with the Order of the Lion and Sun. A chamberlain, with a cushion on which lay the Ribbon of the Order and the Star stepped forward and I was duly invested. It was most embarrassing, as I had received no notice of the coming award, and had therefore had no permission to accept it.

More cups of coffee were brought and the audience came to an end. We made our obeisances and then retired. All hope of the ratification of the treaty had disappeared.

I returned to Kazvin on the 16th and inspected the runway that night. It had been well levelled out by the passage over it of 500 camels for some eight hours. All now depended upon whether we got a strong frost and no reports of snow in the south. It did freeze slightly that night, but the morning broke with low clouds and reports of further snow. Reports from Kermanshah were so bad that I put the flight off for twenty-four hours.

CHAPTER V

Flight to Baghdad

No snow fell that night and as I went to bed it began to freeze hard. By 5 am reports from Baghdad and Hamadan were good and I ordered a start to be made at 7 am. My pilot was to be a young Fifer named Kidd, and for half an hour we stood chatting jerkily about St Andrews and how I used to cross by the ferry from Burntisland to Granton, in the days before the Forth Bridge was built. I confess I was a little nervous. At 6.45 am a good report came in from Kermanshah. Kidd had a look at the runway and reported that the flight was feasible, though the cloud ceiling at Kazvin was little over 1,000 feet. Kazvin lay at a height of 4,000 feet, while the summit of the Aveh Pass stood at 7,500 feet, with two peaks rising on either side of it to 11,000 feet. If we could see these two peaks and pass between them all would be well.

The two planes were run out and Kostia and I took our places in the back seats. Both got away to a perfect start on the frozen runway. My plane went first and the other followed at an interval of twenty minutes. Up and up through the snow-clouds we climbed. In the clinging wet the time seemed interminable, and then at 8,000 feet we suddenly emerged into bright sunlight with a thick woolly carpet below us. I heaved a sigh of relief as I saw the two peaks to the south, and then another when the second plane came into the sunlight behind us. It was only a few minutes before we passed between the two peaks and began to drop slowly through the clear air, until we could see the road winding away to the south below us. I settled myself down in my seat prepared for an uneventful flight. As I took out my book which I had

M

brought to read on my way down, I turned to take one more look at the second plane. That was going all right, and I was about to report to the pilot when I saw that he was waving his right arm up and down, and then it stayed steady with the thumb pointing menacingly downwards. Raising myself I leant forward until I could hear what he was saying. Our oil-pipe had frozen up and we had to make a crash landing. It was a horrifying thought. Everywhere beneath us looked white and flat, but my mind told me that there was nothing flat there, and that our only hope lay in striking a deep bed of snow. The ordeal only lasted a couple of minutes in all, but I confess that many things went through my head before we landed. Kidd flew along the road for a bit as if he were going to land on it, but he evidently realized that the road was not broad enough to take the plane, especially with the two banks of shovelled snow rising to several feet on either side. He turned to one side and glided down to a clear space of snow, checked the plane by raising her nose and pancaked into the snow. We submerged with hardly a bump. I remember climbing out of my seat, through the machine-gun ring, and trying to swim upwards through the snow towards the light which was shining above us. Kidd was floundering some-where near me and I heard him shouting. I burst through the frozen crust of the surface and put up my arms to try to hoist myself out of the depths. My weight was too great and down I went into the suffocating snow once more. The road was about some 400 yards from us, but it took an hour to get to it, flopping forward in great jumps like stranded fish. We waited a bit to get our breath and then slithered down exhausted on to the surface of the road. Low over our heads flew the other plane, circling round above us. They must have seen us gain the road, for I saw an arm waving and then the plane turned to the north, evidently gaining height to cross the Aveh on its way back to Kazvin.

We heard later that when Kostia saw us crash he tried to make the pilot come down beside us, but naturally he was having none of that. Much to the consternation of the RAF at Kazvin they appeared back over the aerodrome and signalled that they propo-sed to land. The runway was then unfrozen with a foot deep of slush on the surface. In landing they were both thrown out and a propeller was broken. They had a goose with them, which they were taking to a mess in Baghdad. When it started on its trip it was alive, but was picked up dead after the landing in the slush.

Neither of us had suffered any damage, and as soon as we had got our wind back we walked up to an old Russian toll-post a mile back to the north. It proved to be Ruan, which was occupied by an Indian platoon under a Jemadar. He was just about to set off to see what had happened to the plane he had seen come down. I told him who I was but he was so flustered that all he could do was mutter, 'But why did the General Sahib allow the air-carriage to fall down?' When I asked him why he had not got ready to help the plane quicker, he replied that he had reported to a British officer in the post and had been told to do nothing. I walked into the back room in order to see who this officer was. There I found a young man just sitting down to a late breakfast of bacon and eggs. Even when I told him who I was he did not show much readiness to answer me. I had even to tell him to stand up. He told me that he was a newly-joined officer just going up to the Guides Cavalry, and that he had been given some important papers to deliver to the British Minister in Teheran. He had done nothing about the plane because he did not dare to leave the papers unguarded. I asked him where they were and he called his bearer to bring them in. On interrogating the bearer, I found that the young gentleman had handed over the papers to his bearer, who had had charge of them for nearly ten days. I had not time to deal with the young man, but I left him feeling very sorry for himself. He had avoided his duty to help all other soldiers if he could. He had callously failed to help a crew of a crashed aeroplane. Owing to his delay, by the time that the Indian platoon had reached the plane they found that it had been effectively looted by Persian coolies. Kidd and I had nothing but the clothes in which we stood.

The telephone was working well and I was able to inform both Baghdad and Kazvin that both the pilot and I had escaped injury. I told them that I was pushing on as soon as I could, though there was little chance of my being able to reach Baghdad by the 20th. The Indian officer had pulled himself together by producing some excellent curry and a double tot of rum. The headman of a neighbouring village brought out a light cart with four horses and two grooms, and with these we pushed off at 3 pm. Nothing had yet been heard of our looted kit.

If all went well, I hoped to do the forty miles to Hamadan by dawn on the 19th. At first we got on famously in the springless cart, but owing to an enormous drift across the road for some miles we had to abandon it. Poor Kidd was not a horseman and was soon in an agony from loss of flesh through rubbing, though I had rigged up pads with blankets strapped on the horses' backs. From the point where we abandoned the cart we had to make a five-mile detour high up on the side of the mountain, following a track broken by the Persian pack-transport. It was hard going all the time, especially when we had to cross a stream. At one of these crossings we came upon a dying camel which had foundered in the middle of the stream. None of the horses would face the poor beast, snapping at us viciously in its agony. Neither of us had a revolver with which to put it out of its misery, so we had to go two miles further up the hill to find another crossing which the horses would face. As I looked back I saw a long row of filthy vultures waiting for the end, every now and then one of them hopping down to see how near that end was by attacking the poor brute's eyes. When we eventually got back to the main road we had lost a good three hours of our precious time. I felt fairly tired, but Kidd had to be strapped on to the horse's back. The horses were done too. We struggled on for another two hours to a point where the drivers told us there was a *chai* shop with cover for man and beast. There we found shelter just as it was getting dark. It was bitterly cold and the wind went straight through our heavy flying clothes. Neither of us had any gloves and my hands were so stiff that I could not hold the reins.

The *chai* shop was a long building with two openings, one for humans and the other for animals. It lay buried in the snow and several paces back from the road. We entered the place down a steep slippery slope, which was blanketed off from the main room. Inside, the atmosphere was appalling, from sweating human beings in unwashed clothes mixed with the fumes from a charcoal stove in the middle of the floor. At least it was warm inside and our lungs soon got used to it. I was desperately hungry and enjoyed the small pieces of mutton which were being roasted on short sticks at a brazier. I had to wait a good half hour before Kidd was able to move his jaws, but several steaming glasses of tea, made at a Russian samovar, eventually brought him to. The din of the chattering coolies never ceased all night. They took little interest in us and jabbered away about the pay they were getting and the price of food, just as all coolies in the East are wont to do. In a corner sat an old Hadji intoning verses to himself in an undertone, apparently oblivious to what was going on around him. He spoke good Urdu, having been a wanderer in India for many years. In front of him stood a wooden bowl fairly full of small copper coins. When I had eaten my fill I crossed over to talk to him. He had spent the whole winter in the *chai* shop and proposed to continue his journey to the extreme north-eastern corner of Persia at Meshed as soon as spring permitted. Despite his detached attitude, I was sure that he was a shrewd observer of what went on. If anything important were being discussed, his acute ears would catch it. I asked him how he had fared in the late war. I shall always remember his last words to me as I turned to try to get some sleep.

'You see, General Sahib, Persia is a poor country and no longer rich and strong as it used to be in the days of our greatness. We used to be great fighters but now we are a prey to all other nations. We wished to remain neutral in the last war which broke out in the West, but we were invaded by the Russians and the Turks who fought each other in our country, treating us both like very dogs. Then they disappeared to their own lands. Nothing but ill came to us. The struggle still goes on amidst the Western nations. That is an ill thing for all the world. Each nation gives something to the world in which it lives, and if any one is destroyed that which it gives is destroyed also.'

I asked him what he thought the British gave to the world. His reply came quick and certain,

'General Sahib, you give Justice.'

I dropped a toman in his bowl and received his blessing in return. He told me that I should soon leave the East for a time, and that I should have several years of peace with my family.

I did get some hours of sleep, but being no longer able to keep it up in the foul air of the place I woke up before dawn and went out to ease my lungs. It was still bitterly cold and the wind bit my face like a knife. It took a long fit of coughing to clear my lungs of the air I had been breathing in the night. I was some time waking Kidd and the drivers, but at last I got them all three mounted. We were indeed a miserable party as we rode along at a slow walk over the slippery road, but after two hours of this we came to a bend in the road and there, not three hundred yards off, shone the headlamps of a Ford car which had forced its way out from Hamadan to meet us. The next twelve miles we seemed to cover in a matter of minutes, and we were soon being warmed and fed in the hospitable Bank House. The news was good but there was no time to be lost. The Asadabad Pass was still being held open to a man on horseback, but we must hurry. When once we had crossed the pass we should have ten miles to go before we met the next car, which was being sent out from Kermanshah. From there to the railhead we should have nothing but mud to contend with.

I was determined to reach Baghdad as close to the 20th as I could. We had twenty-two miles to reach the foot of the pass and another six miles to reach the summit. Then there was ten miles descent to the waiting car. A formidable ride of thirty-eight miles. I seriously thought of leaving poor Kidd behind, but he was so insistent that he could now stick out anything, that I finally agreed to take him. Two good riding ponies with European saddles had been found, with a groom who knew the road, and with him we started off very well refreshed at 11 am. Much more work was being done all along the road, with gangs of coolies every five miles or so. There was a high wind blowing and it was very cold even in the sun. Every party we met was ready with glasses of hot tea and I had to limit the time we spent with each to a few minutes. We had no time to gossip. We had four longish detours to make. At one point two Persian carriages were being dug out, and at another I found two Overland cars belonging to the Legation doctor, which had been snowed up for a week. My wretched Gilgit boots were too big to get into the stirrup-irons on my saddle, and the leathers were not long enough to let me use them for support. I found myself getting very stiff, riding without irons, Despite all these troubles and the necessity for me to ride alongside Kidd to hold him in the saddle, we reached the bottom of the pass at 4 pm and the summit two hours later. I must say that Kidd never lost his courage though he was nearly exhausted.

At the summit there was a drift forty feet deep which had been cut through so that a horseman could just get by. We were only just in time, for the wind was increasing every minute as the evening approached. I think I should have wept if I had not got through. Someone took a snapshot of me at the summit, which shows the depth at which the coolies were working [Plate II]. It was quite dark when we commenced wading and slithering down the southern slope of the pass. A stream of icy water was rushing down the road with us, and how the ponies stood up to the atrocious footing and terrific noise was a miracle. Some kind person had supplied us with two good torches which helped us to scramble over two deep washaways. How Kidd remained in his saddle I do not know. I was much too busy picking out the road to look to him. In fact I did not dare to look back to see how he was faring. The Persian groom held the rear torch and shouted to me at intervals to say that all was still well. At last we saw a light twinkling away in the plain beneath us and then we reached the car in about another hour. Hot tea and rum revived us, but Kidd was asleep when we bundled him into the back seat of the Ford. Twice we left the road at a bend and I had to get out and push the car out of the snow wall which had prevented us from going over the *khud* and ending everything.

At 7 am in the morning of the 20th we drove into the court-yard of Lakin's house at Kermanshah. He had gone down country to see if he could pick up Sir George Cory, who was going to succeed me in command of the forces in North Persia. By 9 am we were off again on the last 117 miles to the railhead at Quraitu. The snow had all gone and the road was good. We drove into the station at 3 pm. By some mishap I had missed Cory, but I should have been in no state to tell him much about the conditions in Persia, had I encountered him.

I rang up Baghdad at once, but everyone seemed to be out or taking their siesta. No one took any interest in my arrival. I could not even get in touch with the orderly officer in the General Staff. At last I got on to the General's orderly, who was a Scot. He evidently could not understand that he was talking to me, and thought that he was dealing with an orderly of mine. From him I learnt the first news of what my 'short sea journey' was going to be. Had the Intelligence people heard our conversation, they would have had him under arrest, or perhaps both of us. He began at once:

'Ye neednae fash yersels; the General is awa up country fur twa three days, and the speesial train 'll no go till he's baack. I hope ye'll enjy yersels in Cairo. That's whaur ye're gaan tae. Tell ye're General that his laddie is a'ready. He's got a' hes kit laid out, the lot which is new fra England.'

So the sea voyage was to take us to Cairo. But what for? And why did they need me? A new job? But what and where? I seemed to be tossed about at the will of the authorities, and always under the threat of reverting to half-pay.

In the works section of the railhead I found a trolley car which was reserved for the engineers. After some chat I got it brought out to take the distressed Kidd into hospital and myself to look after him. I did not propose to wait at the dreary railhead station for a couple of days after what we had gone through.

At the door of my room at the General's house stood the faithful Kostia, dressed in his kilt and looking very smart and clean. He saluted punctiliously, saying in Russian, 'Your Excellency, your bath is ready.' I could not help bursting into laughter. There was nothing I wanted more. While I was dressing he told me his story. After their bad landing at Kazvin their plane had been refitted with a propeller, and after waiting a few days for the weather to get better, they started for Baghdad once more. This time they successfully passed the rough country south of Karind, but being delayed by head-winds they ran out of petrol and had to land some forty miles from Baghdad. The pilot was badly concussed and sustained a broken arm. Nothing daunted, Kostia got a pony from a Bedouin camp and rode into the railway line. He managed to telephone into Baghdad to say what had happened. A plane was sent out for the pilot and he was ordered to go in by train.

When I asked him what he thought of his first flight in a plane and whether he had not felt frightened by his experiences, he merely shrugged his shoulders with the expressive Russian word, 'Nichevo', which being interpreted meant, 'Oh, not very much.' He had found my heavy kit and some of his own, which had come out from England a few days before. It was just in time. But now I was off once more to some unknown destination. It was all typical of his attitude to anything which happened to us.

My command in North Persia had not ended quite so abruptly as my command at Ismid had done, since I should have had to hand over in the normal way, when the troops had reached Baghdad in two months time. I had nothing much to complain of, for Fate had so far treated me very well. My service in Persia had not lasted long and I could not lay claim to have gained any deep knowledge of the country. Throughout my time I had been in a perpetual state of wonderment as to how she had managed to keep her independence for so long. Would she be able to keep it after our troops had left? I was sure that I had seen the end of our century-long attempts to maintain our influence in Persia by force, and at first sight it looked as if Soviet Russia would have it all her own way, if she wished to swamp Persia as she had done the Mahomedan States in Central Asia in the days of the Czars. But I did not share the panic feelings of the Persian monarch and of many European officials in Teheran that a Russian invasion would immediately follow our departure. For one thing there was only a diminutive Bolshevik force on Persian territory, and for another Soviet Russia had plenty of trouble on her hands in Europe. The Russians might confine their efforts to peaceful infiltration of their ideas amongst the Persian politicians, combined with wholesale bribery.

What Persia wanted was a leader. The young Shah was lazy and timorous, always frightened for his life. My short dealings with him made me think that he was always on the verge of flight to Europe and an abandonment of his people to their own resources. I had only seen one man in the country who was capable of leading the nation. He was Reza Khan, the man who would be in charge of the only efficient armed force in the country. Would the Shah have the sense to put his trust in this man?

IV

CAIRO CONFERENCE AND DISASTER

11 March, 1921 to 11 April, 1922

Winston Churchill, the Colonial Secretary, had called a conference in Cairo to settle the defence of the mandated territory of Iraq, and, under protest, General Sir Aylmer Haldane released my father to attend, after being peremptorily told that his presence was necessary. The Colonial Secretary had to make out a programme of defence which would come within his budget and it depended upon his using the RAF. Such a scheme was regarded as wildcat by most soldiers and General Haldane had uncompromisingly turned it down. In doing so he recognized that he would very likely be handing his command to my father, but he bore no malice, as can be witnessed in the words he used in the confidential report he later gave.

'Major-General Sir W. E. Ironside served under me as a brigade commander in France in 1918 and is well known to me. He is a very exceptional personality, inspiring confidence in all around him, highly educated and a natural leader of men. His presence with the North Persian force in a very brief time changed the atmosphere of nervousness into one of confidence and contentment. I find it difficult to express my very high opinion of this officer, who is high above the average of his rank.'

The conference was to bring together all those who would in one way or another be concerned with Middle East affairs, and Churchill saw this as being the best way of winning support for his plans and settling the principal points at issue. He knew the capabilities of many of the senior officers in the Army and clearly he had marked down my father for the Iraq command because of his experience in Air Force deployment and his sympathetic views towards the RAF. As he wrote in his diary at the time: 'The Air Force Commanders and Staff have to be trained for future wars and they will never get this without responsibility. As the natural result, probably, of this advocacy I found myself as the Commander designate of the largest Air Force in existence. I had a talk with Winston before I came away and he said he had chosen me because he thought that I would get things moving quicker than anybody else. I dare say even the Air Force recommended me as knowing more about the air than most generals.'

Broadly speaking he had been asked to prepare the levies in Iraq and then take over command from General Haldane in September, 1922, to prepare the ground for an RAF commander to take over later. But before he reached his headquarters disaster overtook him when the DH9 plane in which he was travelling to Baghdad crashed two hours out of Shaiba in a dust storm. This was his second crash within weeks and he suffered only fractured leg bones, which fortunately mended very quickly. But it meant returning to England with the prospect of unemployment and more time on half-pay.

Back at home he waited for a decision about his future whilst battling with the War Office over his pay and allowances. But by July, 1921, these difficulties had dwindled into insignificance, for Churchill had renewed in his mind the plan for employing my father in Iraq and, before this could be put in writing, the CIGS had offered him the post of Commandant of the Staff College which was to fall vacant in April, 1922. My father accepted with alacrity and Churchill, with characteristic magnanimity, did not stand in his way. But there was still a long time to go before moving to Camberley and this had to be filled, still on half-pay. He was much in demand for lectures and shooting weekends. Admiral Sir Charles Madden, C-in-C Home Fleet, invited him on board his Flagship HMS *Queen Elizabeth* for the 1922 spring cruise. This offered a unique chance to study the Navy. The Admiral had said to him in his letter: 'It will greatly benefit the Navy if we can enlist your sympathies and interest in our methods and doings.'

I doubt whether the Navy appealed to my father, but he was able to gain experience of fleet manoeuvres and take account of naval developments, particularly the use of carrier-borne aircraft. The cruise was just what he wanted professionally and at an ideal moment for completing his convalescence. Long afterwards, when I was myself a junior lieutenant RN, a senior admiral said to me, when I was conducting him on a tour of inspection:

'I knew your father, once.'

'Oh, yes Sir?' I said eagerly.

'Yes, he thought all naval officers were bloody fools!'

CHAPTER I

The Cairo Conference

On General Haldane's return from up-country I was given the whole story of the coming 'short sea-voyage'. A conference had been called in Cairo. It had come to him as a complete surprise. Mr Churchill had taken over the Colonial Office, and a new department had been added to it to deal with the affairs of the Middle East as a whole. During the war and after it there had been much confusion and delay in the direction of the affairs in this area, owing to the number of authorities which had to be consulted before even the smallest decision could be taken. During the war the campaign in Mesopotamia had been directed by the Indian Government, until it had grown too big for the resources of India to support. There had then arisen many difficulties between the British and Indian Governments, which had delayed strategic plans. After the war we had had a very good example of difficulties which arose between the War Office and the Foreign Office over the policy to be followed by the troops in North Persia. The administration of our mandated territories was growing ever more expensive, and economies were urgently necessary if we were going to retain these mandates. Governors, High Commissioners and Generals from all our possessions in the Middle East had been summoned to meet Mr Churchill in Cairo to discuss how these economies could be effected.

As regards myself, the General told me that he also had queried the necessity for my presence at the conference, owing to the danger of the journey down from North Persia at this season of the year. The answer he received was that my presence was imperative, but he was given no reason why it was so. He had no idea what was to become of me, but hazarded the opinion that I might be offered something in Mesopotamia. I found that he was more than a little suspicious that I might be going to succeed him in some way, but I assured him that I had had no communication from Mr Churchill. I knew nothing of the country and could not conceive that any such change would be made. The General was certainly much ruffled in his feelings. The War Office had called upon him to send in an estimate of the troops required for a future garrison, giving him very meagre instructions upon which to base his calculations. He had sent in his estimate, but now heard that the Colonial Secretary was contemplating heavy cuts in the numbers for which he had asked. What had troubled him more than this, however, was that news had come to him that the Chief of the Air Staff, Sir Hugh Trenchard, had put in a scheme for the Air Ministry to take over the security of Mesopotamia. He had no exact details of this scheme, but the War Office had now asked him for an estimate of the number of troops required for the 'static' defence of five aerodromes in various parts of the country. As far as he could see the plan envisaged the construction of fortified camps extending to many square miles of country. The construction of these camps would certainly cost a great deal of money, and he was not prepared to recommend the employment of highly-trained mobile regular troops for completely static duties. He disliked what he had heard of the scheme and had said so frankly. Meanwhile the War Office had been asked for further details as to the purpose of the fortified camps.

He showed me the estimate which he had sent in to London and I confess that I was staggered at the size of the garrison he had suggested. It was for thirty-three battalions of infantry and six regiments of cavalry. It seemed to me a vast force for securing peace in such a sparsely populated country as Mesopotamia. I was not surprised that the Colonial Secretary was considering substantial reductions.

My mind went back to the close of the South African War, when the battery in which I was serving found itself at Stellenbosch after peace had been declared. We were waiting to know whether we were going home or not. All depended upon the

size of the garrison which was going to be left behind. We heard
each day rumours of how the original estimate was being steadily
cut down. Many officers who had fought throughout the war
thought that it was being cut down dangerously, and predicted
that we should have the war to fight all over again. But still the
reductions went on. Then when local troops were formed, the
number of British troops required dwindled away to a very small
number. Could not some similar scheme be adopted with
Mesopotamia? We had freed the Arabs from Turkish domination
and the first thing to be done was to raise some local troops.
Our delay in bringing in self-government was one of the main
reasons why a rebellion had broken out. There were now rumours
that we were about to set up an Arab kingdom in Mesopotamia,
and if we did, surely the new king would want to have his own
troops.

It was no moment for the War Office and the Air Ministry to
be haggling over who should have the control of security in
Mesopotamia. The one was saying how insecure things would be
if security were handed over to the Air Ministry, and the other
was saying how cheap things would be if it were. What was
required was a combined scheme, bringing in the two new factors
of military mobility—air forces and motorized infantry. Masses of
infantry were no more required than they had been in the South
African War. And masses of aeroplanes would find no targets
for their bombs. On the whole, the idea of using bombing aircraft
to keep the peace did not appeal to me, either for efficiency or
cheapness.

I felt that no one could make a good security scheme without
knowing the political situation in detail.

In the few days left to me before we embarked for Suez I
proposed to see the sights of Baghdad, and to make the acquain-
tance of as many delegates who were going to Cairo as possible.

I must confess that I saw little of interest in the old City of
the Caliphs. It was so brown and dusty looking. There were no
beautiful gardens, though water was easily obtainable. It consisted of one long street running parallel to the Tigris throughout
the city's length. The practical-minded Germans had opened up
this street to a uniform breadth by doing away with many of the

old but picturesque alleys which ran down from the street to the river. They had left the great Mosque intact, and well open to view its beautiful green- and blue-tiled dome. It was amusing to see the pigeons, which were as numerous as they have always been in Trafalgar Square, perched precariously on its slippery surface, moving round regularly with the sun to catch all the shade they could in the heat of the day. One could almost tell the time by their position on the dome. In a corner off the main street stood the tomb of Marshal von der Goltz Pasha, the maker of the modern Turkish Army, who died in Baghdad. Like so many things in the East, it was already beginning to crumble away, thought the bold lettering of his name in Turkish characters could still be read. The body of the Marshal had long ago been taken away for burial in Germany. On the right bank of the river lay the vast deserted camps and establishments of the old Indian and British Expeditionary Forces, with two ugly pontoon bridges connecting the two camps. The shops were mean and dirty and the prices demanded by their owners very high. The General took me out and showed me the foundations of the gigantic cantonments, which someone had decided to build outside the limits of the City. It was to have contained two complete divisions and was modelled upon an Indian cantonment. I wondered what had been the plan which had brought such a monstrosity into existence. Luckily the plan was soon abandoned.

Two people I was particularly keen to meet—Miss Gertrude Bell and Jafar Pasha. From these two I thought I might get a good background to Mesopotamian affairs. Gertrude Bell was serving as Oriental Secretary to the High Commissioner. Jafar Pasha was in command of all the Arab forces, such as they were at that moment.

I first met Gertrude Bell when I sat next to her at a dinner in General Haldane's house. I had fully expected to find her a blue-stocking, and in a sense I did find her one. She had gained a distinguished Honours Degree at Oxford, but her mind had been broadened by practical knowledge acquired the hard way. At first I had found it difficult to understand how she had come to occupy such an important position as she did, but when I came to know her and her history I was no longer surprised. For twenty

N

years she had devoted her life to the liberation of the Arabs from their Turkish rulers. Speaking Arabic with great facility she had been able to gain their confidence to a high degree. She was also fluent in French and German. She was absolutely fearless. She had crossed from Syria to Baghdad quite alone in the days of Turkish rule, overcoming all the refusals and delays of the officials. If they shrugged their shoulders so did she. She could outdo them at waiting and, being more quick-witted, she always had her own way in the end. She was much better known in the Arab world than her chief, Sir Percy Cox, who had specialized mostly in work in the Persian Gulf. She knew a great deal about the Mesopotamian campaign, having served from 1916 onwards with the Headquarters of the Army. In a womanless Baghdad she dressed well, though naturally not in the latest fashion. Her fair sandy hair against her tanned face appeared as if it had been bleached by the sun.

In my talks with her I sometimes wondered if her enthusiasm for the Arab race did not somewhat blind her to the difficulties of the British Government, which had to deal with the world of Islam as a whole. She was a strong advocate of the setting up of an Arab Kingdom in Iraq, as I found Mesopotamia was now to be called. This was, she thought, the government most suited to the Arab brain. She was fully aware of the jealousies which existed between the ruling families in Arabia, but she had her own candidate for the new throne—the Emir Feisal. She thought the honour was due to him not only for his personal qualities, but for the work he had done in the war. She realized fully that he would have to be elected by the people whom he was to rule, and that he could not be forced upon them. But she had already prepared a scheme for presenting him to the people in the most favourable possible way.

Jafar Pasha and his brother-in-law Nuri-es-Said were two jovial soldiers to whom I took an immediate liking. Though both were Arabs, they had served as officers in the Turkish Army. Jafar Pasha had been through the Kriegschule in Berlin and was a highly educated soldier as well as a practical one. He spoke Turkish, French, German and English as well as his native Arabic. He had taken a most distinguished part in the attack against Egypt in the early part of the war, during which he was taken prisoner. Twice he nearly escaped, but in the second he broke his leg in jumping from a prison window which was twenty feet from the ground. When the Emir Feisal took part in the war on our side, Jafar became one of his most important subordinates. From Jafar I soon learnt that the negotiations for placing Feisal on the throne of Iraq were already far advanced, and appeared to be an open secret amongst the Iraqis. As Jafar put it to me, the people could discuss the matter between themselves and so get accustomed to the fact that they were going to have a king. Jafar was naturally keen to get the Iraqi forces formed at an early date. He wanted them raised by conscription. This law they understood, but the idea of volunteering was alien to their natures. He ridiculed the idea of us keeping a great British force in Iraq. 'Against whom are they going to fight?' he asked. 'Is it against us?' 'You are going to help us and not to fight us.' I thought more strongly than ever that the future British garrison in Iraq must be based on the fact that they were there to back up the Arab Army, not to watch it as if it were likely to be a potential enemy.

The High Commissioner, Sir Percy Cox, I found as inaccessible as ever. He held no conferences and did not discuss the affairs of Iraq with the soldiers. There would certainly be no combined plan to present to the Colonial Secretary. He did not discuss the situation in Persia with me, even when the news arrived that Reza Khan had led the Cossack Brigade over to Teheran after being released from Kazvin. Reports were that he had set up a new Government with himself as Prime Minister. I thought about my talks with him and the promises which I had exacted from him. I was most unlikely to have anything more to do with Persia, and our troops would soon be out of the country.

On the evening of 26 February we embarked in the Royal Indian Marine ship *Hardinge*. We were taking a full complement of British troops home to England. Amongst them was the 44th Battery, in which I had served throughout the South African War. I had left them fourteen years before and there was no one in the battery who had been with me. I was able to give the men a few talks upon what the battery had done. I also found 'F' Troop RHA on board, commanded by an old friend, Major W. L. Y.

Rogers, a famous rugger international. We were able to have a cheery Gunner table as far as Suez.

On 1 March we stopped to coal at the little port of Muscat. As we came in we were firing a twenty-one-gun salute to the Sultan, which was answered by some old guns in the fort which had been built by the Portuguese. The young British Political Officer came on board in full-dress white uniform to pay his respects to Sir Percy Cox. Rogers and I went ashore to see the sights. The sea at the entrance to the port was covered by some frightful spawn or weed which emitted a dreadful stench. It reminded me of old stories of the Sargasso Sea. The little town lay at the bottom of an extinct volcano and was closed in by a high wall. One could imagine what the temperature was like in midsummer. We wandered up into the old fort and examined the guns. One had been made by a gun-founder in Yorkshire named Sturges. Another was a long Portuguese gun which the Arabs told us was no longer fit to fire even a blank round. Most of the serviceable guns were made by J. Broome in the famous factory of Cossipore in India.

The rocks on the cliffs outside the harbour were disfigured with the names of ships painted in large white letters. I noticed many famous names, which I took to be those of the British gunboats serving in the Persian Gulf—*Hogue*, *Juno*, *Euryalus* and *Sapphire*.

At Aden we were joined by the Governor, Sir Thomas Scott, and the Governor of British Somaliland, Sir Geoffrey Archer. Sir Geoffrey had with him a sergeant of the King's African Rifles, in charge of two lion-cubs which were bound for the London Zoo. The arrival of the two delegates to the conference added fuel to our already exhausted conversation. We now discussed the amalgamation of the Somaliland Protectorate with the Aden Colony. Our RAF companions talked of planes flying backwards and forwards across the straits in a few minutes, with reinforcements in case of trouble.

On 11 March we reached Suez to hear the news that we were the last batch to come in. A special train was waiting with an excellent lunch in a restaurant-car, and by 3 pm we had arrived in Cairo. A host of large cars took us to the palatial Semiramis Hotel. I was provided with a bedroom, sitting-room and private bathroom. I was relieved to hear that I should not have to pay for them. I simply did not draw any allowances for the time I was there.

I had never attended a large conference before. The array of Middle East authorities was a formidable one. Sir Herbert Samuel, High Commissioner in Palestine, Sir Malcom Stevenson, Governor of Cyprus, and Sir Walter Congreve, C-in-C in Egypt, besides our party from the *Hardinge*. Colonel Lawrence, so-called of Arabia, was there as a member of the new department of the Colonial Office. We had attracted a goodly posse of journalists to report our meetings, and I saw a sprinkling of visitiors who were still staying at the hotel, notably Mrs Ronnie Greville and Mrs Rosita Forbes.

On the morning of the 12th we were addressed by Mr Churchill, smiling and businesslike. From the moment he entered the room he dominated it completely. He came straight to the point. There must be an abandonment of all prejudices in the effort to effect economies. There must be more co-ordination. It would be a shameful thing if we had to abandon all that for which we had fought so hard because we could not run our administration properly. Unless we reduced our outgoings we should have to do so. If we held on, history would relate that we had done well and better than any of our Allies. He gave us a wonderful feeling of power and efficiency. Every word he spoke sank deep into my brain. The Middle East was presented as one unit and not as a batch of separate states with different problems to be solved.

We from Iraq found ourselves faced with an ultimatum. Steps were to be taken immediately to reduce the garrison to twenty-two battalions, and the operation must be completed by the beginning of the next financial year in the beginning of the first week in April, less than a month away. There was a unit of Indian labour amounting to 15,000 men. This must be sent home to India in the first ships available. Both the High Commissioner and the C-in-C had come prepared to protest vigorously, should there be any cuts in the numbers which they had demanded. No protests were made by either and that afternoon the staffs sat down to telegraphing the first instructions to Baghdad. The shipping programme must be accelerated at once.

I heard for the first time of the hard bargain which the British Government had been forced to make with the Indian Government over the employment of Indian troops out of India. Each unit employed had to be paid for from the day it embarked for abroad until the day it returned to India, and then for a further six months after that. We then had to pay for a replacement unit in India for the one which had gone abroad. And in addition for a depot in India, from which the two units would be administered. We also had to undertake certain obligations towards the pensions of the men who had been wounded abroad, or of their dependants, if they had been killed. Under these hard conditions, the supposed great cheapness of Indian units had become somewhat illusory.

The day was concluded by another meeting, and there we soon realized the grasp of the situation which Mr Churchill and his new Middle East department had acquired. General Haldane described the procedure which had been ordered for units leaving Iraq. They were withdrawn to either Baghdad or Basra, where they handed in all their animals, and transport and any equipment which was to be left in the country. Mr Churchill at once asked what was being done with all the animals, and how many there were in the depots at the moment. The number was given to the Colonial Secretary, and they ran into thousands. Mr Churchill then asked whether fodder would have to be bought for these horses after the commencement of the next financial year. The answer to this was that a considerable amount would have to be bought. Without a minute's hesitation, out came the order, 'Have them all shot before the commencement of the financial year!' There came a moment of deathly silence and then the senior High Commissioner rose from his seat, obviously much moved as he turned to the Colonial Secretary with the words, 'Sir, in the name of all humanity I must protest against such ruthless cruelty to poor defenceless animals, which have served us well.' There was again a deathly silence in which no one spoke. I then stood up and told the conference that the War Office orders as to the disposal of surplus horses and mules were very strict. We were following these. We had thousands of animals to deal with and very few vets. We were ordered not to sell any animals, fit or unfit, in the countries of the Middle East where they would be cruelly treated. Every animal had to be examined by a vet. Those which had no more than another two years of service in them were to be destroyed at once. Those which had were to be shipped off to other places in the Empire. These explanations turned away the wrath of the Colonial Secretary and the incident was forgotten.

So far I had no personal interest in the Conference, but I went over all the details pertaining to Iraq in case I should be offered a new job there. It was not till the 14th that Mr Churchill broached the subject of my employment. I was summoned to have tea with him, and in his usual suave manner he asked me to take a job under him, adding as an enticement, 'If you do we shall have some important and interesting days out here.' It was a longish story, in many ways not at all to my liking. I was to take over the so-called Levies in Iraq, which consisted of Arabs, Kurds and Assyrians. Some of these existed already, but most of them would have to be increased in strength. They were to be raised to a strength which would allow the British garrison to be reduced to twelve battalions by the end of September, 1921. General Haldane would then go home and I should take over command of all the British troops in Iraq. My main task would then begin. I was to 'ready' things for the RAF officer to take over command as quickly as I could. I was to keep this plan secret until he gave it out to the conference.

Here was once more an odd-job, but Mr Churchill made its prospects seem very attractive. It would be creating something new and I would be gaining more experience. I should not be kept much more than a further year or eighteen months in Iraq. Surely, after being a Major-General of at least four years standing I might expect a permanent appointment. Once more I had to accept what was offered to me, because of the perpetual threat of half-pay. But I was far too eager to be sure of something, as I always was, and I did not sit down to think of what conditions I should exact before I tied myself to the job. I made no conditions as regards pay and rank, and above all I did not insist that, as far as flying risks were concerned, I should be treated exactly as the senior officers of the Royal Air Force were. I never asked anything about leave during my time in Iraq or afterwards. I was to suffer heavily for my thoughtlessness.

I was no longer a spectator at the conference, which was a distinct relief. My unimportant appointments always seemed to involve so much secrecy. I was the last person on earth who was likely to give anything away if I was told not to. The Air Ministry was going to take over the responsibility for law and order in Iraq. The Ministry, egged on by the Chief of the Air Staff, had long been asking for an opportunity to prove what aircraft could do in undeveloped countries towards keeping the peace. Now at last they were going to be given that chance. A scheme for the taking over of Iraq had been drawn up by Sir Geoffrey Salmond, the AOC in the Middle East. It was still far from being a detailed plan. It was put forward as a method of employing the mobility of the RAF and its offensive power in a country difficult of access to troops. It was argued that a great saving could be made in manpower, by using aircraft, and that would mean a great saving of money. The outline of the scheme was as follows,

'Throughout the country, Posts or Posts of Refuge, as they were variously called, were to be constructed. Five major ones at Mosul, Shergat, Baghdad, Hillah and Shaiba. Four minor ones at Kirkuk, Erdbil, Kifri and Khanikin. The major ones were to be able to hold out for a period of a month against anything which could be brought against them. The minor ones were to be able to hold out under similar conditions for a fortnight.

'Only Levies were to be used for mobile operations with aircraft. The Regular British troops were to be employed solely for the static defence of the Posts of Refuge.

'All Posts of Refuge were to be occupied permanently by their garrisons, and to be linked up with one another by an efficient system of wireless telegraphy.'

I studied the scheme for hours on the map and then had talks with Geoffrey Salmond. We were old friends and could argue with one another without losing our tempers. At first sight the RAF scheme seemed almost childish, and I could not imagine that any such plan could have been conceived by an officer who had been educated at the 'shop'. It seemed to be a return to the tactics of the Romans in Britain. However much the Army might be accused of not being able to handle aircraft, here was a paper which showed how senior officers in the RAF thought that troops should be employed in the field. The two Services had drifted very far apart in their ideas of combined tactics. It was certainly high time that a tactical doctrine was evolved and the troops trained in the use of it.

The situation as I saw it was very different from that on the North-West Frontier of India, where there were in fact two frontiers, with a species of no man's land in between. Here we were going to set up a new kindgom with a friendly king ruling it. He would wish to have his own regular troops and a police force of his own. With these two forces he would hope to keep law and order in his own land, and he would regard any garrision we left behind as something upon which he could rely in case of a crisis, something which would seldom be used against his own people and, when once his own kingdom had been established, something which he could get rid of. Such an idea as nine great Posts of Refuge dotted about the country, garrisoned by purely British forces, seemed to me to be fantastic. As the Iraq State grew in strength these posts would be regarded as menaces rather than helps.

What we needed from the Air Ministry was some sort of a charter, telling us, first, how much aggression Iraq might expect from outside her territory and, secondly, how much the offensive power of aircraft, bombing and machine-gunning from the air might be used against the subjects of the state. It seemed to me that the new king would wish to control pretty tightly the use of the aircraft stationed in his country. I suggested that the Air and War Ministries might draw up this charter jointly.

Finally, I queried the sole use of Levies in the field when working with aircraft. These Levies were not yet formed and they were certainly not trained for such work. Very few British officers were available for them, and any fresh ones who came out could not be efficient until they had learned a little of the language of their men. Close co-operation with aircraft must need efficient wireless communication between them and the ground. That could only be done by British troops. The British troops which were to be maintained in Iraq were to be employed in *static defence* of the Posts of Refuge. Arabia was no place for the employment of static defence troops. If we were going to employ eight battalions of British infantry for some considerable time, then they must be turned into motorized light infantry.

Of the rest of the problems before the conference, such as the reduction of troops in Palestine, the junction of Aden with British Somaliland in Africa, of Suez and Cyprus, we heard very little, so busy were we with our own affairs. Great economies were undoubtedly made in all the mandates, but little was achieved in the unification of direction in London. The Colonial Office, the India Office and the Foreign Office were very loth to give up their hunting-grounds in the Middle East. Mr Churchill's ideas of having one great Office such as a Middle East Office was never achieved.

We issued no progress reports to the Press, which was very indignant at being left out in the cold, and I never saw any White Paper which may possibly have been issued at a later date. There were a few demonstrations outside the Semiramis, made by students of the university and schoolboys, but they had no idea what they were complaining about and were very mild in character. A few flags with 'Go Home Churchill' painted on them were waved in processions, but the police were never called out.

I had learnt a little Arabic while a subaltern at Ambala in India, and I started on a course of one hour a day by myself with my old books in order to make my future work easier. I hadn't forgotten very much. I began to wonder whether I had done the right thing in taking on this new job in the East. I was terrified that I might be turned into an Eastern expert and debarred from going back to soldiering. I solaced myself with the certainty that I would have to lose my job as soon as the RAF had found their feet. They would work to get rid of me at the earliest possible date. A bare eighteen months more, and then surely there would be something permanent for me in the Army.

On 18 March, the delegates were issued with the final conclusions which had been reached on Iraq and its affairs. They were as follows:

1. Immediate reduction to twenty-three battalions.
2. Immediate formation of the following local forces.
   (a) Arab Army under Jafar Pasha.
   (b) Levies under British officers.
3. Reduction in September, 1921, to twelve battalions and six squadrons RAF.
4. Reduction during 1922–23 to either
   (a) A smaller army with six squadrons RAF.
   (b) Four battalions with eight squadrons RAF.

Mr Churchill had put through his economies in a masterly way, and with hardly even mild protests on the part of the Army authorities.

As usual, I was eager to get started with my new job, but the *Hardinge* was not due to sail till the 25th. Our final week was spent in a few discussions, many dinners and a good deal of sightseeing. I managed to get off a full account of the conference to Lord Rawlinson. His letters continued to come in to me regularly. In one he said that he thought that he would be the last British C-in-C in India. The day had gone when we could move Indian troops all over the world at will. It frightened me to think that our great Imperial Reserve would be gone, and I was saddened to think of the great training-ground, and pleasure-ground, which we should lose for the British army of the future. What a bombshell that would be for our military policy in the Empire. Where should we keep our Reserve, and where should we train it? What kind of an army should we have? Should I have anything to do with the making of the new army?

Three big dinners succeeded one another. The first was to Mr Churchill at the Semiramis, where Sir Herbert Samuel thanked him for the way in which he had led a difficult conference. A happy little speech, with an equally happy reply. I had known Mr Churchill in his young days, and I had vaguely realized that he had something in him which very few people had. Now I had seen him in full play dealing with great decisions. He was a great patriot and had a firm belief in the greatness of the British people. To a soldier it was delightful to hear a Minister of the Crown making decisions, based upon a wide military knowledge and a brilliant imagination. My opinion of him went up by leaps and bounds. I felt a pleasure in the knowledge that I should be working under him in my next job. The second dinner was at the Residency given to us by Lord Allenby. I had served under him as an RHA subaltern in England, and experienced his brusque and dictatorial manners. I had met him at Ypres as a humble GSO2 representing the VIth Corps, when he was the GOC of the Vth Corps, and had come to a meeting at the Menin Gate, where the boundary line between the two Corps had to be settled. I had seen him again in one of his most severe humours and had seen him give in to reason. And I can never forget a story told me by Sir Philip Chetwode, one of his Divisional Commanders in the great cavalry movement in the desert, which brought the final defeat of the Turks. Chetwode had ridden up to the right flank to see that the turning movement went on as long as the endurance of men and horses could take it. He had found two or three exhausted regiments making a halt. He had taken charge and driven them on for a matter of twenty miles. He then had halted when up came the Commander-in-Chief in a motor to see that everything possible was being done. Exhausted as they all were, the arrival of the 'Bull' took them on a further twenty miles, until the trap was closed in rear of the defeated Turks. There was what a determined leader could achieve by the strength of his personality alone. I heard the 'Bull' now making a speech as a civilian, a High Commissioner, and I must say that his patriotism and vigour did one good to see and to hear.

The final dinner was given to us by the Sultan of Egypt at the Abdine Palace. This was a most magnificent affair for two hundred guests. All the way up to the dining-hall the steps were lined on either side by gigantic lancers, some of the largest men I have ever seen in uniform. At the dinner table there were a hundred servants in scarlet and gold, and so good was the service that the long dinner of eight courses was over in little more than an hour. No sooner had one finished eating than one's plate was whisked away and a clean one put in its place. The Sultan Fuad, a short, stout man, was dressed in a black frock-coat with a fez and large gold chain round his neck. I understood that he spoke both French and Italian fluently, and I watched him carrying on a voluble conversation with the ladies on either side of him. He suffered from some nervous ailment which caused him to emit a short sharp bark every now and then, a sore trial to the two ladies with whom he talked. Apparently he had been shot in the throat in his younger days by a would-be assassin.

I was unfortunate in not having a chance to talk to Lawrence, who was serving at the time in the new department of the Middle East at the Colonial Office. He moved about in moody silence, speaking to no one. Perhaps he was shy of soldiers. Rumour had it that he did not think much of the general run of them.

My servant Kostia enjoyed himself vastly and I saw little of him. He was being monopolized by the lady's maid of one of the distinguished visitors in the hotel.

On our way home we reached Aden on 30 March. The Governor, Tommie Scott, took me out to see Sheikh Othman. He was anxious to get all the troops out of the old crater, where they lived cheek by jowl with all the cut-throats of the Red Sea, and in the most insanitary conditions. As with Hong Kong we had acquired a strip of Arabia so as to reduce the crowding in Aden itself. I was shown a battalion of Yemenis enlisted by us to police this strip. They were some of the finest local troops I have ever seen.

On board the ship the atmosphere was not wholly a happy one. The High Commissioner held no meetings and he seemed a man ill at ease. I had many conversations with Jafar Pasha and Gertrude Bell, both of whom were optimistic and pretty sure that all would be well under such a king as Feisal. I found that it was now no secret that he would soon arrive in Iraq. General Haldane seemed easier in his mind, though he had been offered no job at home. He seemed resigned at having to hand over to me in September. He agreed with me that my first job should be to take a month inspecting the country and visiting all the places where the Levies were now stationed. I was to do this by air and he signed a statement to that effect.

CHAPTER II

Air Crash

On 8 April, 1921, I left the *Hardinge* in the early hours of the morning to motor to Shaiba, where I was to begin my month's tour of Iraq. A start was to be made at 6.30 am for Baghdad, and after a change of plane there I proposed to fly on to Mosul that day. There was a chill in the air but it was a beautiful bright morning and I felt in great heart as I started on my new job. I reached the landing-ground about 6 am and there found one of the old DH.9A's waiting at the end of the runway. The two mechanics standing near the plane reported that there had been trouble with the tyres but that we ought to be able to get away by 7 am at the latest. The Squadron-Leader and the pilot came up a few minutes later. I made myself ready, tackling once more the ring over the back seat. As usual I could not strap myself in. The engine was started up and after a minute or two we taxied off to get into position. Both tyres collapsed at the same time. We limped back to the hangar. As the two mechanics had already replaced one set of tyres, everyone was becoming somewhat fussed. The situation did not improve when the Squadron-Leader greeted me with the words, 'My God, General! You are a bit of a Jonah!' I was getting very angry and even a good joke would have been out of place. We were losing more and more of the best of the day for flight. It seemed to take an age to get fresh wheels and tyres, and in the end it was fully 11 o'clock when we took the air. It showed to what a state the equipment of the RAF had sunk after long years of campaigning in the desert.

For an hour we flew steadily northwards, keeping at about 1,500 feet, with a full view of the railway-line below us. The wind had so far been light, though dead against us, but was just beginning to increase in strength. Straight ahead on the horizon I saw the sky going black, and we made less and less headway against the wind. I could now see clearly the advancing dust-storm. The pilot began to rise in an effort to get above it, but the air grew bumpier every second so he returned to about 1,000 feet. We could now only catch an occasional glimpse of the line as we struggled on. My goggles were ripped off my face, and after that I saw very little of what was going on. The dust was being driven hard into the skin of my face, and for a second or two I thought I should soon be covered with blood. The noise was terrific and I could not hear what the pilot was saying, until at last I saw that he was signalling that he was making a landing. He circled twice round what looked like an open piece of ground, being tossed up into the air each time he came into the wind. There came a lull and I though he was going to bring it off, but there came two terrific gusts of wind, followed by two bumps. The tail of the machine came up and I felt myself being catapulted out of my seat, my two thighs striking hard against the edge of the brass ring. I was conscious of no pain and I do not think that I was knocked out for more than a second or two. I found myself lying on my stomach and facing the machine at a distance of twenty yards from it. I must have landed on my head and made a complete somersault. Afterwards I discovered that my Cawn-pore topee was smashed in. I felt concussed but had no pain.

When I looked at the plane I saw that it was upside down with the pilot still in it. His flying helmet had come off and I noticed his longish hair hanging down towards the ground. I thought I could see or hear petrol or oil dripping down on to him and dimly realized that I ought to do something for him. I pulled myself up on my elbows and began to jerk myself forwards. I still had no pain of any kind, but I began to realize that there must be something seriously wrong with my right leg, for the toe of my shoe was facing up in the air. Both my legs felt numb. I reached the plane and tried to pull the pilot out. I even pulled his hair to try to wake him up. Then I remembered that he was strapped in. I loosened the quick-release and out he came. I faded out once or twice in my efforts to get him away from the plane, but succeeded in getting him clear. The pilot eventually came to and was virtually unhurt, though concussed.

I had the most frightful thirst but no pain. The next thing I can remember is that I had got back to the plane and was filling my topee from the radiator tap. I got a drink and then threw some in the pilot's face. After that my recollections are very dim.

Some time later a plane had come down near us with a doctor. People were trying to push something on my legs, which had swollen to enormous size. There was some talk of whether I should be taken to Basra or Baghdad. I felt like a tyre which had been blown up and I could not contain any more air.

When I woke again I found myself in bed with both my legs strapped up with weights hanging over the end of the bed. I now felt as if I had been run over by a steam-roller and was completely deflated. I still had no pain. It is curious that my first thoughts were as to whether I should ever be able to ride again. It never struck me that I might never walk again. The right leg was badly fractured and the other splintered in two places. I was stiff all over and drowsy, but they told me that I had been given nothing more than the anaesthetic to allow them to set the legs.

Thus ended my new job with the Levies and the RAF. It was a sad disappointment, but I realized that I was devilishly lucky to have escaped so well. I had fallen into the hands of a very able surgeon, Major McVicker of the RAMC and an Ulsterman. When he had done with me I could walk with a limp but had gone down over an inch in height on both legs. Within two years I was hunting again, though with very much shortened stirrup-leathers.

They told me in the hospital that when I first came round I had kicked up a devil of a fuss at the loss of a coin which I wore on a string round my neck. I had called it a thaler and they could not understand what I meant. By this time my servant Kostia had turned up and explained to them what all the trouble was about. The thaler was a silver coin about the size of an English florin. In my young days I had held a horse for a German officer in German south-west. He threw it at me with the arrogant action of such people, and I nearly threw it back. I kept it in case I might have a chance of making him swallow it one day. I had worn it for over nineteen years and now it was gone. It was never found and must have been taken by one of the Indian orderlies to add to his wife's rupee necklace. Many years later some unknown lady sent me a golden half-sovereign with the date 1921 on it, which I then wore in its place.

Such was my good progress that on 26 May, forty-eight days after my crash, I walked up the gangway of the *Hardinge* with the aid of crutches, once more on passage to England. I had been given a large deck-cabin, and all seemed set for a comfortable voyage at least as far as Suez, where I should find another ship. Brownhill and Kostia were coming home with me. On the 27th we cast off after the usual farewells given to a troopship going home. But before we crossed the bar of the Shatt-el-Arab there came two ominous bumps, and there we were stuck fast in the mud. All the 29th and 30th we were trying to get off, the ship quivering all over with the result of her efforts. It was no good. The next day the men and all their baggage were transhipped to barges and taken back to Basra. I remained in my deck-cabin with the day temperature at 125 degrees. Thank goodness there were no sand-flies on board.

Time passed very slowly and I came in for the only pain I had so far suffered, when the doctor came every day to break down the adhesions in my knees. It became a race between the two legs to see which would be first freed of the beastly things. Daily we went at it, leaving me sweating and exhausted but making good progress. On 2 June two large Anglo-Iranian tugs arrived and proffered their help, but the Indian Government refused to pay the big bill for the salvage they demanded. The Commander of the *Hardinge* told me that our mishap had already cost them over £3,000. With callipers on my legs I took a daily walk. Many people came down to see the ship and pay me a visit: Sir George Cory, who had succeeded me in North Persia. He was also one of the 'half-pay' officers and had enjoyed his little trip. One of the most interesting of my many visitors was Commander Brandon of HMS *Cyclamen*, then serving in the Persian Gulf. He was one of the two officers who were arrested for trespassing on forbidden ground in Germany. The other was a Marine officer. Both were sentenced to be imprisoned in a fortress for three years. He told me that the Admiralty had never forgiven them for their escapade.

O

There was no future for him, but he intended to remain in the Navy till he was retired for age. He told me that they had come away from their trip with no secret information worth a groat.

On 3 June, the King's Birthday, the ship was dressed overall and fired a salute. Grounded as she was on the mud, I wondered that they were not too ashamed to call attention to themselves. I remember that the heat that day reached a height of 130 degrees. I had spent ten days on the damned bar. On 5 June the troops came back again, and on the 6th we backed out under our own steam and recommenced our journey to Suez. At dawn on the 19th we berthed at the Suez dock. A medical officer came on board with the news that I had been given a passage in the Bibby liner *Yorkshire* which was due at Suez on the 22nd, leaving the same day for home. Meanwhile I was to disembark and occupy a room in a tin shed in the dock, which ranked as a quarantine hospital. Brownhill went along to reconnoitre the place and came back with the surprising report that there was no furniture in the place, no beds and no kitchen. They had not been able to get into the building as all the doors were locked. They encountered a clerk from one of the offices who told them that the place hadn't been in use for six months. I sent for an officer to come down from the Commandant's office, and he arrived in the shape of a very frightened young captain who could tell me nothing about where I was to go. It had been reported that I was suffering from some Eastern complaint. In the end I stayed quietly in the *Hardinge* till the *Yorkshire* came in. She did not berth and I was sent over to her in a launch. I managed to get out of the launch and up the gangway of the *Yorkshire*, watched by all the passengers with great interest.

At Port Said Geoffrey Salmond arrived to wish me well and to apologise for having tipped me out of one of his aeroplanes. We were both sad that there would be no more collaboration between us, to get the RAF settled into Iraq. I could not resist one last word of advice: not to spend millions on Posts of Refuge, in which no one would want to take refuge. I had done with the Middle East for some little time.

The voyage did me good and I was soon taking regular walks on deck. The food was so good on board that I had to cut my meals down in order not to grow fat. The doctor went on with the breaking down of the adhesions, and I could almost kneel down on both knees. I found myself fascinated by the long coast of Crete with its beautiful mountains. I thought of my Evzanoi orderlies and my Cretan Regiment which had greeted me with cries of 'Strategos'. The Straits of Messina with Etna all covered with snow. Stromboli in eruption, with all the people of the island in boats waiting to see what would happen. Doubtless they were well up in the eruptions of their own volcano.

At Marseilles we all three spent the day ashore. Lunch at Pascal's. Moules, langoustes avec salade, asperges and fraises. All the things that we had not eaten for so long. In the afternoon we drove along the Corniche and then lay basking in the sun on a little beach. How nice it was not to have to wear a topee. I slept like a log on the ship that night. Ordinarily I should have been all eager to go home by the Rapide across France, but this time I blessed the fact that we were going round Gibraltar. Going down the coast of Spain the mountains looked so inviting with their covering of snow. At Gibraltar there was a thick fog and we could see nothing of the Rock, which I had not yet seen but was to know so well in later years.

I had plenty to think about. By force of circumstances I had come to the end of seven years of active service, almost the same as I had been through in my first seven years service in the Army. Fourteen years out of a total service of twenty-one years I had been very happy through all the various jobs I had been given to do. I now had no fears than my physical health would not debar me from future service of the same kind. Another six months and I should be ready for anything. I had learnt my lesson. I would not ask for any job. I would await what Fate would deal out to me. Lord Rawlinson in India had assured me that he would ask for me the moment I was free, and I was sure that Mr Churchill would ask me when I could go back and take up the job he had given me.

I had not seen much of the Arab world, but I had talked for many hours with Jafar Pasha and Nuri-es-Said, the Arab soldiers who had served in the Turkish Army. From what I had heard from them, I was sure that the last thing to do to preserve the peace in a new kingdom like that of Iraq was to use bombs against Arabs. We should never get on with them if we did.

CHAPTER III

England

We berthed at Tilbury early on the morning of 8 July, exactly three months to a day from the date of my crash at Samawah. I remember that it was a beautiful summer's day. My wife had come down by train to meet me and we had breakfast together. There was an ambulance ready for me on the dockside, and my orders were to go straight up to Millbank Hospital. I managed to walk down the gangway with one stick, despite the calliper on my right leg. We had lots to say to each other but public places do not make intimate conversations very easy. We both drove up together in the ambulance, but there were two nurses inside to prevent us from saying what we wanted to say.

At the hospital I created something like a minor sensation. They had made preparations for a badly sick man on a stretcher, and there I was walking into the main door. In my room they had produced an enormous bed with water-mattresses, and two lusty RAMC orderlies to lift me about. They were so relieved that they gave me only a cursory examination, telling me that the Medical Board would overhaul me thoroughly the next day. After tea my wife went back to High Wycombe, where we had our little house, with the assurance that I should be back with her in two days at the most.

During the next two days I was subjected to an examination by several specialists. Every part of my body was X-rayed. All results were excellent. I had suffered no internal injuries. My spine was straight and undamaged. The callouses on both my legs were thickening up strongly. Both were shortened equally by an inch and a quarter, so that I should not have to walk with a limp. All I had to do was to go slow and to keep the weight off my legs as much as possible. Nothing would hinder me from riding again. It was a most heartening examination. I was complimented upon my magnificent physique.

On the 13th I came before a Medical Board, which recommended me for three months sick leave. At the end of that time I should be examined again. I was to attend at Millbank twice a week for massage and electrical treatment. Nothing could have been more kind or efficient than the treatment I received from the RAMC specialists. In the afternoon I left for High Wycombe. There I found a large batch of letters waiting for me, one of the first of which I opened being from the War Office. I was told that I had been placed on half-pay from 8 July inclusive. It made me laugh to see that because I disembarked before midday on that day, it was regarded as my first at home. I was also told that I would not be entitled to any further treatment at Millbank. Half-pay officers were not entitled to that. For a minute or two I sat looking at the letter in astonishment, and then my mind became invaded by a feeling of the deepest disgust. How could they treat me in this way, old soldier or young general as they might consider me? It was a fine ending to seven years' active service, after having accepted another appointment at the special request of the Colonial Secretary.

On the 15th I went up to London to pay my respects to the CIGS, Sir Henry Wilson, and Mr Churchill, the Colonial Secretary. Both congratulated me on my lucky escape from two crashes within little over a month. Both were full of enquiries as to when I should be fit for service once more. Mr Churchill was most anxious for an approximate date upon which I could take up the appointment he had given me in Cairo. I told them that a Military Board had given me three months sick leave, and that I should then be examined again and re-boarded. I also told them that I had received a letter from the Army Council, placing me on half-pay from 8 July, and thus debarring me from medical treatment at Millbank Hospital, which had been specially ordered for me. Both expressed deep surprise.

For the next month I became involved in a complicated and angry correspondence with the War Office which necessitated my making several journeys to London at my own expense. I put my case to them in the simplest language I could devise, but I was told that nothing could be done to alter the decision taken by the Army Council.

The arguments went something like this. The War Office said that I had passed out of their jurisdiction when I handed over the command of the North Persian force in Kazvin. I had come under the Colonial Office from that moment till I crashed at Samawah. The weak point of that was that neither were very sure who had paid me for that period. The Colonial Office said that I had not been given a new appointment in Cairo, but had gone back to Iraq to command the Levies under General Haldane. I did not come under the Colonial Office until General Haldane had gone home and I had taken over from him. The War Office said that the Levies had always been paid by the Colonial Office. Neither the War Office nor the Colonial Office would admit that I could possibly come under the conditions applicable to senior Air Force Officers in case of air crashes.

On 14 September I received a final letter from the Army Council telling me that nothing could be done for me.

I ruminated over this letter for two days, composing a reply which contained all the sarcasm of which I was capable. I concluded by a request that I might be allowed to retire from His Majesty's Army at the earliest possible date. I had been badly injured during the normal course of my duties, either under the War Office or the Colonial Office, whichever they decided I had been serving with at the time of my flying accident. Despite the reduced pension to which I should be entitled, owing to the short length of my total service of twenty-two years, I preferred to retire rather than to linger on upon half-pay so unjustly allotted to me.

I was still tinkering with my masterpiece of satire when I received a communication from the Military Secretary, dated 16 September, two days after the letter announcing the final rejection of my claims by the Army Council. I was now asked whether I would accept a nomination to the appointment of Commandant of the Staff College at Camberley.

My whole attitude to the future was altered in a moment. Quite unexpectedly I was being offered the greatest prize which could be awarded to an officer of my rank in the Army. I could no longer afford to be sarcastic towards an authority which was offering me such a future. My first act was to pick up my still unposted letter to the Army Council, which had taken me so long to compose in my anger at the way in which I had been treated. I walked over to the fire and dropped it on the top of the red hot coals. I watched it being consumed and reduced to ashes. A surprising turn of the wheel of fortune had come my way. What did another seven months of half-pay signify, annoying as they certainly would be, when compared with the certain prospect of the command of the Staff College for four years. I accepted with a very thankful heart.

By 30 September my appointment was announced in the paper. Many congratulations flowed in. My wife and I bought a new car. She settled down to thinking of the Government House we should be taking over, when she would be allowed to choose most of the furniture under the watchful eye of the Office of Works. Her long waiting at home, while I was rushing about the world in a sort of giddy procession, had been made up to her at last.

I began to get in touch with military affairs in England. I paid visits to Larkhill to see the latest gunnery developments. I was asked to lecture on Russia and North Persia at the Senior Officers' School. The news was out and I became much in demand. By the middle of November I had begun to play a little mild golf. I was sent a number of invitations to shoot. The days went happily and easily by. The date of my taking over was fixed for 1 May, in the middle of the spring holiday. In December I was once more passed fit for general service. I got hold of a quiet horse and began to learn to ride again, though with my two shortened legs I felt very clumsy in the saddle.

My luck was really in. On 3 January I received a letter from Admiral of the Fleet Sir Charles Madden, the Commander-in-Chief of the Atlantic Fleet, inviting me to come with him in his Flagship during his three months spring cruise. He told me that he thought it would be good for me to learn some more about the Navy, and especially of a fleet at sea, before I took over at Camberley. It was a great chance. The trip would set me up for good, and I should still have a month in hand when I came back to help my wife with her arrangements for taking over the Staff College House.

CHAPTER IV

Atlantic Fleet at Sea

Having accepted Sir Charles Madden's invitation to go to sea with the Fleet, I began to take stock of what I really knew of the Navy. It did not take me long to realize that my knowledge of it was small indeed. I had read a good deal of naval history, and as a student at the Staff College I had taken part in many combined exercises on paper. Towards the end of the South African War, a cruiser and a gunboat had helped to put ashore at Port Nolloth, close to the mouth of the Orange River, the mobile column with which I was serving. As a staff officer at Boulogne in 1914 I had seen the Expeditionary Force carried over to France without a mishap. I had also read the reports of the major naval engagements during the war, but like many another Army officer I had been too busy with trench-warfare to give them much thought. Of practical experience with the Fleet I had none. I had, in fact, taken the Navy very much for granted. The chance of seeing the Fleet in action was a great one and I looked forward eagerly to my cruise.

On 15 January, a Saturday, I motored over to Reading to catch the express to Weymouth, where I was to join the Fleet. I was met by the Flag-Lieutenant in a little 10 hp Wolseley, which the C-in-C took with him in the Flagship wherever he went. I was driven round to the club, where I met Sir Charles for the first time. He greeted me most warmly, putting me at once at my ease. He was a short, sturdy man of sixty with carefully trimmed naval beard, in which there was hardly a grey hair to be seen. He gave me an immediate impression of vigour and quiet confidence. I soon found that he was an encyclopaedia of naval history and always ready to explain things to me. To judge by the miniature admiral's flags which decorated his dinner table denoting the various commands he had held at sea, and the row of polished gun-tampions on the walls of his cabin coming from the ships he had commanded at sea, his experience of command must have been unique.

That night in the QE, as the Flagship was familiarly called, I met the Vice-Admiral and three of the Rear-Admirals. The former, Sir William Nicholson, was a real old salt and very outspoken in his conversation. He had lost a thumb off one of his hands and was known as 'Thumby Nick' to distinguish him from several other Nicholsons. The Commanders of the two Light Cruiser Squadrons were Sir James Fergusson and Wilmot Nicholson. I knew Wilmot well, his father, General Stuart Nicholson of the Royal Horse Artillery, being my godfather. The third Rear-Admiral was Cyril Fuller, the C-in-C's Chief of Staff.

The Geddes Report had just been published, and economy in the services had become the most pressing question of the moment. I found myself engaged in various discussions which were most refreshing, largely because of the manner in which Sir Charles encouraged his subordinates to express their opinions. The dinner table seemed to be a genial place for the discussion of service matters. I noted in my mind that in the Army we should have had such discussions round a formal office table, for in our messes so-called 'shop' was much discouraged, and at a general's dinner table there would certainly have been ladies present and the conversation more devoted to social affairs.

All the Admirals were very much impressed with the necessity for evolving a new pattern Fleet to meet modern conditions, and yet for preventing a too rigid economy from ruining their chance of doing so. Ships took a very long time to design and longer still to build. In a way I saw that their problems were easier than ours. They were engaged in improving what they had, for their great change from sail to steam had taken place years ago, whereas our great change from horse to engine had yet to come. They had ceased fighting to all intents and purposes, whereas we were still busily engaged in fighting in many parts of the troubled world. Machines for our new army were hardly

yet on the drawing board, and for the meantime we had to make
do with the horse.

On Sunday, after church, I was taken out in the little Wolseley.
Sailors ashore are great walkers and the C-in-C would have
preferred a long tramp, but I had to admit that my two broken
thighs were not yet fit for such an ordeal as he would have put
me through. So we drove up to the high ground behind the town,
from whence we could look down on the anchored battleships in
the bay. They made a proud picture with the sun shining down on
their spotless decks. Sir Charles explained to me that this would
be, perhaps, the last time to come for many years that we should
see so many ships in commission. I asked him what a Fleet would
be like in, say, twenty years time. He looked at me with a
twinkling eye saying, 'Who can tell? Only one thing is certain.
If we are to make a good Fleet, then we must be allowed to
work out our own salvation in our own way.'

I was quickly brought to realize how shortage of manpower
affected the Navy even more than it did us. We had long been
used to seeing skeleton units taking part in peace manoeuvres, with
flags representing at least half the men who were supposed to be
present. In the Navy, if there were severe shortages of men, it
soon became a necessity for more ships to be taken out of commission. But what was worse was that sea-time had to be curtailed
in all ranks, thus affecting the very bedrock upon which the
efficiency of a fleet depends. I was told that all the ships taking
part in the cruise were going to sea with a 15 per cent deficiency
in their normal complements. To go lower than this was not
deemed safe.

He then unburdened his soul to me upon the burning question
which was exercising all their minds. The Air Ministry had taken
over control of every machine which went into the air, and as
most of the air officers in the newly formed RAF had spent their
early service in the Army he felt sure that they knew little about
the Navy. As a consequence the Navy was being starved of what
it must have, owing to the new commitments, taken over by the
Air Ministry. For many years to come our trade would continue
to be carried in surface ships and fleets would be required to
protect them in war. So long as fleets were needed, aircraft must

accompany them to sea. In his opinion it was not possible for fleets to depend upon land-based aircraft for its reconnaissance and security services against attack from the air. If they were compelled to do so the range of action of a fleet might be drastically reduced. The Admiralty had made up its mind that it was possible to build suitable ships and suitable aircraft to land on their decks. Only thus could aircraft be made immediately ready to co-operate with the Fleet. The first of these ships would be with us on the present cruise, and he proposed to send me to serve in her for a time so that I could see what the Admiralty were aiming at.

He feared that the Air Ministry had already made up their minds that fleets were obsolete. It was so easy to pin-point aerodromes throughout our imperial possessions, and to draw from each a circle with a radius of the flying-range of the planes stationed there. They maintained that the day would come when the circumferences of these circles would meet. Then the sea could be controlled from the air by land-based aircraft. The Air Ministry passed lightly over the fact that all these dispersed aerodromes would have to be heavily defended at great expense, and that an enemy might easily isolate or capture one or several of them, thus destroying the structure erected for the use of land-based aircraft. Fogs, rain, storms and the darkness of the night, in fact all those conditions with which seamen have always had to compete, had been taken little into account. Aircraft were still much in the embryo, and they would be for a long time much more a sport of the elements than surface ships. Of what use were aircraft which could only stay a limited time over a naval battle? To him it was common sense that aircraft must be based on ships which could accompany the Fleet at all times. It was also common sense that these aircraft should be controlled by naval crews. The Navy was their user, and they should have a very complete say over the shape of these aircraft and the tactics they were to follow. No bureaucrat in an office should be allowed to prevent the Navy from working out their own salvation.

The Navy wished to get back their naval air service, and the Admiralty would fight till they did get it back.

I told the Admiral that we in the Army had been forced to

accept the Air Force theory that the Air Ministry was capable of building, supplying and training an Air Force for manoeuvring with an army in the field. But there were many officers who did not agree with the theory.

The cruise was to begin on Tuesday and the C-in-C held a conference in the *QE* of all flag officers and captains on the Monday. The scheme for the first exercise was a simple one. With a Battleship Squadron we were to escort a large convoy to Gibraltar. The enemy with a faster Battle Cruiser Squadron was to try to prevent us from doing so. We were to be three days and two nights under service conditions. For this manoeuvre orders had already been written. To me they were delightfully short and crisp. There was no need for those pages of administrative orders which would have been produced for, say, the operations of a corps in the army. I was beginning to understand why the Navy did not use such a large operational staff as we did.

As I looked round at the faces of the senior officers in front of me I was struck by their clear-cut lines, accentuated by the fact perhaps that they were clean-shaven. They were the faces of men of action, fit and hard both physically and mentally. They were the result of the severe weeding-out which takes place in the ranks of lieutenant-commander and commander. They were slightly older than I had expected to find them, this being accounted for by the fact that casualties amongst naval officers in the war had not been so severe as they were with us. But they were all men in their prime, and from what I had learned of the state of the Flag List they all had good prospects of future advancement at a reasonable age.

We weighed anchor very early on the morning of the 17th with a stiff breeze blowing from the west. Two ships of the convoy were late in taking up their stations, and were told of the fact in good round terms. 'Manoeuvre badly executed' was signalled to one of the battleships, which came to me as rather a shock. In the Army a general would never think of exposing one of his colonels to such a public reproof. I thought perhaps we might come to it when our signals improved.

The *Argus* took station immediately astern of the *QE*. She was a curious-looking craft with nothing showing above her deck but a tiny look-out station, which could be withdrawn below decks when her planes were working. She seemed to ride very high out of the water—sixty feet from the deck to the water line. She had been an Austrian Lloyd passenger ship built in England, which had been rushed into service at short notice. She was rolling badly and showed up the arrester wires on her deck, which were used to slow up the landing-speed of the planes when operating. Despite the weather she sent off and received back four planes during the morning.

The bridge of the QE struck me as a windy, cheerless place. The Admiral and his staff used it continuously during the exercise. I contrasted the discomfort they must have suffered with the comparative comfort which an Army C-in-C would have enjoyed. I was told that both Admiral Jellicoe and Admiral Beatty at the Battle of Jutland never left the bridges of their Flagships throughout the battle. I wondered at the restricted view which these bridges offered. Also, I noted that very little protection against aircraft attacking with machine-guns was to be seen.

Signalling in the Navy had reached a high pitch of perfection when compared with ours in the Army. For short distance work in the Fleet they used flags, besides lamps and semaphore. Every ship had its own wireless installation, and a very strict rule as to the employment of wireless had been laid down.

Just before a battle there must be no use of wireless, so that the enemy would not find the positions of the many units in the Fleet, but once the engagement had started there was no restriction upon its use. During the exercise we had an example showing the necessity for such restrictions. The enemy had placed two submarines at the entrance to Weymouth Bay, with orders to report when the convoy left its moorings. They duly made their report, to which the battle cruiser *Hood* replied. She thereby disclosed her position very accurately to our Fleet.

During the 18th and 19th the weather worsened quickly and *Argus* could send off no more planes. It showed how urgently necessary it was for the Navy to improve the new carriers and the planes which were to be carried in them. As we sailed on southwards I looked at the chart and wondered when we should come within range of the next British possession where planes might be based on land. Neither Gibraltar nor Malta had any landing grounds.

In the bad weather I took the opportunity of wandering about the innards of the *Queen Elizabeth*, and I found the atmosphere below very much like that we had experienced in deep dugouts on the French front. Everything was battened down, and the clearing of the air seemed very difficult. The naval ratings received better cooked rations than we did at the front, where we often never had a hot meal for days on end. The crew of a ship could always get hot coffee or cocoa at any hour of the day or night. I well remember a party of sailors who came to see what fighting was like in the Ypres Salient, day in and day out throughout the year. The idea was to show them how the other half of the fighting forces lived. Very soon they got themselves smothered in mud and infested with those horrible insects which made our lives a misery. Before they left they had to go to our very efficient hot baths in the cellars of the old buildings. There they had to take off their smart bluejacket's rig and put on newly cleaned and ironed suits of khaki, in which to rejoin their ships at least in comfort.

I created much amusement for the two snotties who escorted me to the control room in the depths of the ship. I had to divest myself of my coat and several sweaters before I could get through the tiny hatch they showed me leading to this space. The place was crammed with men using earphones, all very busy with intercommunication in the ship. I should not have liked to be down there during a fleet action. One could see nothing that was going on, but could imagine all the more what might happen.

Sir Charles had been a torpedo officer in his young days and was still a great believer in the weapon he used to work with. He cited to me the use the defeated German Fleet at Jutland might have made of them, as they withdrew through the narrow waters in the failing light. I was taken down into the torpedo flat, and was surprised to find that there was no power-loading there. The ratings in the flat had all been chosen for their good physique, just as our mountain gunners were so that they could load the guns on to their mules.

Curiously enough it had never entered my head that sailors could suffer from sea-sickness, but I saw a good few laid out during those first days of the cruise. Several of the officers acknowledged that they were regularly sick the first time they went to sea after a long period ashore. It was all taken as a matter of course, the cure being to carry on and think no more about it. Apart from one or two minor accidents the sick-rate of the QE was very low indeed, and I was impressed by the willingness of the ratings and their quickness in obeying orders. I liked to hear their cheery, 'Aye!, aye Sir!' as they doubled off to carry out an order.

I was much interested in the manoeuvres of the great battle cruiser *Hood*, which was the flagship of the squadron opposed to us. She was so much faster than the battleships, and the range at which she could fire her salvoes so much greater that she would have been a difficult customer to tackle in real war. She used to appear on one quarter of the convoy, and then, as soon as two battleships were detached to drive her off, away she went to appear again on another quarter to repeat her tactics. Without air reconnaissance the convoy would have been completely at her mercy. Carrier-borne planes were undoubtedly a necessity in a modern fleet.

After the exercise the big ships were concentrated in Vigo harbour, while the cruisers and destroyers went off to visit other Spanish ports. Our ships seem to have been always welcome in Spanish ports in those days, probably because of the money which was spent there by us. The staff was busily employed in getting in reports for the conference which was to be held in Gibraltar, but all officers and ratings were given a spell ashore to stretch their legs. Every open space near the jetties was converted into a football ground, with goal-posts and flags brought out by the Fleet. Within a few minutes all were fully occupied. Large crowds of Spaniards assembled in order to cheer the various matches. Football was evidently just beginning to become a national sport in Spain. Several trips to places inland were being arranged and to one of these I attached myself. It was being run for the benefit of any Catholics who were serving in the Fleet. Though not a Catholic, I was anxious to see the Cathedral of Santiago de Compostela which was still an important place of pilgrimage for Spaniards. The little train which took us there ran on a line constructed by British engineers and was still managed by a Scot, who met us on the station. The cathedral stands right on the top of the hill of Santiago, surrounded by the few houses which comprise the town. It was a lovely day and the Plaza was crowded with bands of pilgrims who had come in buses from the neighbouring villages. Most of the houses bore signs over their doors, worked in cockle-shells, to show that they offered hospitality to the visitors. The Portico de la Gloria, the entrance to the cathedral at which the pilgrims were greeted by the church authorities, was indeed a glorious flight of steps.

Services were going on in every corner of the building, and I saw confessional boxes standing round the aisles labelled for most European languages. The whole atmosphere of the place was marred by the horde of touts clamouring to be taken on as guides. They penetrated even into the pews where worshippers were kneeling in prayer, pestering them in loud and often angry tones. Outside at the foot of the portico was stationed a line of importunate beggars.

At dinner that night in the QE I met a great naval character, Admiral Sir Walter Cowan, commanding the Battle Cruiser Squadron. A veritable pocket admiral in stature, but full of the old spirit of the attack. Curiously enough I had met him before in the early days of the Boer War, though he had completely forgotten the incident which had brought us together. I was then an insignificant 2nd-Lieutenant and he was already a Commander in the Navy, serving as ADC to Lord Kitchener. The time was just at the moment when Lord Roberts was about to commence his march at Bloemfontein and Pretoria. A small Boer commando had invaded the Cape Colony, crossing the Orange River at Prieska and moving down towards the main railway at De Aar. They were opposed at first by about 300 men of the Warwickshire Regiment MI, supported by the 44th Battery in which I was serving, but after a sharp fight we were ordered to retire. A goodly number of young Boers from the Cape Colony had been persuaded to join this commando, and it was thought to be essential to drive it out of the Cape Province before the main advance took place. Lord Kitchener with a brigade of cavalry and a regiment of British infantry arrived to carry this out. During

16 *Above:* Hobbling to the boat from the hospital. Basra, 26 May, 1921.

17 *Left:* Kostia in his Black Watch uniform.

18 HMS *Argus*. This photograph gives a good idea of the difficulty of effecting a landing in any but good weather.

at Kyle Strome,
LAIRG, N.B.

Confidential

4th September,

My dear General Ironside,

The Secretary of State for War told me before we separated that you had received an offer from the War Office to take over the command of the Staff College. I should no in any case have allowed the commitments you had entered in over Mesopotamia to stand in the way of your professional advancement, as I regard your career as a matter of high importance to the Army. But since then I have received the report of your medical adviser to the effect that you are u for active duty for six months. This appears to me to be decisive. It would certainly not be worth while for you to go out to Mesopotamia on a six months' appointment to prepa the position for the Air Force. I had better in these circ stances invite General Haldane to stay on till the moment transfer, and I must abandon with much regret my hopes of being able to utilise your services.

Let me add that I hope very much that you will recover soon from the effects of your accident and will be able to take up your duties at the Staff College before the six months are out.

Yours sincerely,
Winston S. Churchill

19   Mr Churchill's letter to General Ironside.

the rush on Prieska I was on rearguard with my section of guns when a young man on a white Arab pony rode up and somewhat peremptorily ordered me to take a dismounted man on a limber. I could not quite place him, for he was dressed in khaki drill with a long string of medals on his jacket. He was clean-shaven and did not look like an army officer, though he had the badges of a Lt-Colonel on his shoulders. He told me at once who he was, adding that the dismounted man was Lord Kitchener's servant. When we moved on he trotted alongside me and chatted for a mile or two, telling me that he had just come from commanding a gunboat on the Nile. I envied him his active service and his row of medals.

He now invited me to join him for the voyage on to Gibraltar and I jumped at the chance. I spent a few delightful days in his great ship and got to know him well. I can picture him now as he stood on the bridge, pointing out to me her great length with the words, 'You know, I like to be mounted on something with a good rein.' As I got to know him I realized that he was never so happy as when on the back of a galloping horse. Had he not been a sailor he would have liked nothing better than to be a hussar. His cabin just abaft the bridge was hung with sporting prints of hunting and polo. He had been born in Gibraltar, where his father was then serving as a Captain in the Royal Welch Fusiliers. I found him deeply imbued with the old spirit of Nelson. Once when we were out for a walk ashore, he suddenly stopped and produced from his pocket a crumpled piece of paper, saying, 'I always carry this on me.' On it were written Nelson's words, 'That his Admirals and Captains, knowing his precise object to be that of a close and decisive action, would supply any deficiencies in signals. In case signals cannot be seen or clearly understood, no Captain can do wrong if he places his ship alongside that of an enemy.'

He was a fighting man of no mean order, and one of which the two Senior Services can well be proud. His story after he retired from the Navy in 1931 at the age of sixty shows this clearly. Nine years later when I was commanding the forces in Britain, I found him serving as a commander on the north-east coast of England. In 1940 he was serving with the Commandos,

P

and during 1941-42 he was in Tobruk, being taken prisoner when the place was rushed by Rommel's tanks. It is reported that he was in the front line when the defences were overrun. He emptied his revolver at an oncoming tank and then threw the useless weapon at it as it passed him. I do not like to think of his state of mind when he was taken by the Germans. I am glad to think that I met such a man during the years of his active-service life. He died quietly in his bed several years later.

During the voyage to Gibraltar the Fleet was exercised in various manoeuvres by the Commander-in-Chief. The speed at which events succeeded each other was to a soldier somewhat bewildering. With two fleets approaching each other at the rate of sixty miles an hour, only a very quick and active brain could have kept a clear picture before him. I should have liked to have been on the bridge of the QE to watch Sir Charles Madden's face. I was interested enough on the bridge of the *Hood*. The battle cruisers were never tied to the slower moving main fleet, and their power to direct their fire against any target ordered by the C-in-C was quite astonishing. I had a very good chance of seeing the naval signalling during an action. Wireless, lamp and flag were used with great effect. All officers dictated their signals to their yeomen of signals, and unlike our officers never wrote them. Most of their orders were rather what we would have called 'words of command' and their system of dictation was certainly the best thing for them. It was quick and accurate. These yeomen were absolutely trustworthy, and their spelling and handwriting extraordinarily good, comparing very favourably with those of many an army staff officer.

CHAPTER V

Gibraltar

We sighted the Rock early on the morning of the 27th. Even from a distance it appeared gigantic, rising as it seemed straight out of the sea. Fascinated, I stayed watching it loom larger and larger until we passed inside the mole. Our five great ships looked small and insignificant as they slipped quietly one after another into their berths. *Queen Elizabeth, Barham, Warspite, Hood* and *Repulse*. No fuss, no worry, no noise. It was almost as if they did not wish to wake the sleeping monster which towered above them.

I had never seen Gibraltar before and was eager to make a tour of the place. I had served under the Governor, Sir Horace Smith-Dorrien, in the early days of the 1914–18 War in France, and by a lucky chance I found that the Chief Engineer was a Colonel Bland, who had been our CRE in Roberts Heights near Pretoria when I was Brigade Major there.

On our first night in harbour the senior officers of the Fleet were invited to Government House for dinner and a dance afterwards. I was fascinated by the ceremony of the handing over of the Keys of the Fortress by the Garrison Sergeant-Major. To beat of drum they were marched round the seated guests and then placed in front of the Governor on a crimson silk cushion. They represented the emblem of our might as they lay there sparkling in the bright light of the dinner table. After the wine had gone round I had the honour of being called up with my glass to talk to the Governor. He told me of his feelings during the Retreat and of how well the men had fought at Mons and Le Cateau, bearing the whole weight of the German right-wing attack which Schlieffen had meant to be decisive. Before we left the table he called up the military secretary and ordered him to give me a pass which would take me wherever I wished to go.

I did not dance, having never learnt to do so, but spent the rest of the evening talking to Bland. The sailors were adepts and kept things going till late in the morning. The visit of the Atlantic Fleet was obviously one of the main events of the season.

I had been wondering how and where I should start my tour of the fortress and, the impulse being strong upon me to view the Rock from the land side before I looked at the defences, I prevailed upon Bland to motor me out to St Roque the next morning. We started off in plain clothes, passing through the Spanish Posts without question and without being asked for our passports. Perhaps they knew Colonel Bland well enough to let him pass. They must have been dealing with thousands of visitors and sightseers every season. For an hour or more we walked up and down the terrace of St Roque, all that remained of the ramparts of the little town, sitting down occasionally for a smoke and a talk upon what we saw. It was a wonderful sight which lay before us, the long knife-edged Rock rising abruptly at the end of the mile-long stretch of sandy isthmus which joined it to the mainland. This sandy expanse was divided almost equally into two parts, called the Spanish and British neutral zones respectively. In the middle, at the northern extremity of our neutral zone, we had built what was called an unclimbable fence. Behind this fence we had used our neutral zone as a sports ground for the garrison. A racecourse and numerous polo, football and cricket grounds, besides the kennels for the Calpe Hounds, with which we hunted foxes in Spain. The Spaniards had left their neutral ground untenanted.

Such was the clearness of the air that we had no need to use our binoculars to see the whole lay-out of the town, harbour and dockyard. In a shop in Gibraltar I bought some photographs which had been taken by a private plane flying almost directly over St Roque in Spanish territory, and represent the views at which we looked from the terrace. They showed how impossible it was to conceal from the eyes of potential enemies anything which was on the surface of the Rock.

We motored about for another hour in the country to the

north of St Roque and the little hill beyond it, called the Queen of Spain's chair. There were numberless hollows in the area, the bottoms of which were concealed from observation from all points of vantage on the Rock. From these hollows, mobile howitzers such as we had in France could have bombarded with impunity any part of the Rock and its belongings. Without observation from the air even the most modern artillery could have competed with them.

After taking lunch on the terrace in a little posada we motored back once more through the Spanish Posts, entering the gate of the fortress with a throng of Spanish workmen returning to work in British territory after their midday meal.

Little did I think that day, as I took my first look at the Rock of Gibraltar, that sixteen years later I should find myself Governor.

During the afternoon we visited the tunnel excavated by Sergeant Ince during the great siege. It ran inside the northern face of the Rock, climbing steeply until it reached the eastern edge. From the tunnel, numerous gun-embrasures had been cut, so that the Spanish works in what is now our neutral ground could be swept at short range. It was surprising how such a work could have been completed in such a short time with nothing but the picks and shovels of those days. It was of no use for modern defence. Even for the storage of food and material it would require entire reconstruction, owing to its narrow and exposed entrance, lack of breadth and steep inclines. In times of peace it had become the show-piece for the many visitors who wished to see the Rock. Its possibilities for storage or defence work had with the years become so fabulous that the tunnel became a positive nuisance. When I was Governor, to every request for permission to excavate in the Rock I was told that I must first exploit this tunnel. At last I compiled a list of the food and material I had been asked to store in it—thousands of tons of ammunition, oil, food, hospitals and refuges for the inhabitants. I sent twenty copies of the list, together with a large-scale plan of the tunnel, for distribution to all branches of the War Office which were likely to correspond about storage matters. That was the last I heard of the tunnel.

We then visited the water tanks which had been excavated

with modern tools under the direction of the municipality. They held some eleven million gallons of drinking water, and lay concealed in the very centre of the northern height of the Rock. The rain was collected in a concrete channel, skirting the height at 300 feet below its summit, and then delivered to the tanks by gravity. This scheme had paid a handsome dividend on the capital laid out, for not only did it provide the town with excellent drinking water, but was in great demand by all the local vessels plying in the Mediterranean. The work had been carried out by Spaniards, who came in from the mainland in the early hours of the morning to work until they had to leave in the evening when the gates of the fortress were locked. Watching these men at work with their electric drills and dynamite charges I came to the conclusion that the amount of work which could be done with local labour was unlimited, and done both cheaply and quickly. The only drawback to this was that one could not conceal any work that was being done from potential enemies. My mind went back to the mining companies of Engineers we had from the Canadian Corps on Vimy Ridge. What could I not have done with one company for only a year?

We spent the evening in going through the projects which were in progress, together with the mass which had been put forward by a succession of Governors and not accepted. There was no lack of imagination in some of the schemes put forward, but always the same dreary answer—'No money'. From what was going on, it was clear that the Admiralty were carrying out a steady programme for making Gibraltar into an efficient naval station, whereas the War Office had been hanging woefully behind in the matter of modern defences.

The reason for this backwardness on the part of the War Office was obvious. The fortress had just emerged from four and a half years war without mishap. Why should large sums be spent on defences if they were really not necessary? All governments are loth to pay out money for military bricks and mortar, for nothing in the world becomes obsolete so fast as a fortress. Two factors had contributed to the security of the Rock all through a long life under British sovereignty. The first was the strength and mobility of the British Fleet, and now this Fleet was stronger than ever after the disappearance of the German Fleet. The other was the isolated position of the Rock in regard to our enemies in Europe. If a circle is drawn with its centre at the Rock and with a radius of 1,000 miles, it will be seen that only three countries will be cut by its circumference—France, Portugal and Spain. The first two have been our friends and allies for a long spell of years.

As regards Spain, there can be no doubt that ever since its capture by us in 1704, all Spaniards have regarded our possession of the Rock as something which they cannot endure without great grief and pain. For years they tried to get the Rock back by force, but all to no purpose. There then followed many suggestions for exchanges, but few of these were succeeded by official negotiations. Ceuta, the opposing Pillar of Hercules on the African shore, was often put forward as a more suitable position for a naval base, and one less likely to offend the feelings of the Spanish people as Gibraltar did. But on a detailed investigation, two serious drawbacks came to light. Not only should we have to spend many millions of pounds upon building a new port and dockyard, but we should be exchanging a well-behaved population of 20,000 British subjects for one of 60,000, consisting of Spaniards and Arabs. All the writers who argued in favour of our giving up Gibraltar, in order to appease the Spanish Government, seemed to have forgotten that the Rock was a British possession by right of the Treaty of Utrecht (1713) and the Treaty of Versailles (1783), both of which had been freely negotiated between Spain and England. And there was a third and more important question to be considered in this question of relinquishing Gibraltar. What right had we to barter the birthright of these 20,000 British citizens?

Undoubtedly Spanish feelings on the subject of the Rock do rise and fall in intensity with the internal politics of the time. When I was there with the Fleet in 1922 I found that our relations with the Spanish Government were most cordial. We were allowed to hunt the country to the north of Gibraltar over a very wide area with the Royal Calpe Hounds for two days a week. There was also a small golf course near Campamento which was open to the garrision every day of the week. Passes to visit any part of Spain were liberally given, and there were no restrictions upon the amount of Spanish labour which we could employ. I found the same good relations existing when I took over the Governorship in 1938–39. The friendship over the Hunt had even been increased by the fact that the Mastership of the Hounds had become a dual one, the Governor acting together with a sporting Spanish marquis.

We next tackled the question of the numerous caves which existed in the Rock. Their military possibilities had become almost as fabulous as those of Sergeant Ince's tunnel, although they were not shown to casual visitors. In the Chief Engineer's office there were detailed accounts of the reconnaissances which had been made, dating from the Great Siege. Unfortunately none of these reconnaissances had been undertaken with any other idea than tracing where the caves went and examining them from an archaeological point of view. Colonel Bland told me that no demand had yet been made by the General Staff for shelter in the Rock, for either the people inside the fortress or for the storage of material and foodstuffs. I told him that a systematic examination of the caves should be made in the future. Nothing was done, however, for I found no papers on the subject when I became Governor in 1938.

I noted in my diary of 1922 that I thought that the War Office was going to gamble upon Spain not being drawn into any future fighting in Europe or other parts of the world.

There was no inclination to spend any money upon modernizing the fortress and I contrasted this attitude of *laissez aller* with the work which the Germans had put into fortifying the island of Heligoland after we had exchanged it with them.

The guns of the fortress could not be called modern and there was no anti-aircraft defence of any kind. I found a lamentable lack of co-operation between the Army and the Navy and very little notice was taken of the RAF at all. There was no doubt in my mind that it was futile to make Gibraltar into a modern fortress, but also under the political conditions that existed it was apparently not necessary. There was no necessity to let anyone else have it and what was there was sufficient to warn people away. I felt that no more money should be spent on military installations under the current situation, and politicians should be deterred by historical events from preparing a landing base for launching an expedition into Spain which could lead to an enormous commitment of infantry and a serious drain on the Empire. Any war would be won otherwise than at Gibraltar, and no Calais or Salonika should be contemplated.

A time-honoured rhyme written up on the side of one of the sentry boxes on the Rock reflected the feelings of peace time garrison duty.

> God and the soldier all men adore
> in time of trouble and no more.
> For when war is over
> and all things righted
> God is neglected
> and the old soldier slighted.

The final conference on what we had done up to our arrival at Gibraltar was most interesting. The thing which struck me most of all was the accuracy with which the sequence of events had been timed and recorded. There was never any argument upon when any particular order had been given. The C-in-C did not read any long and tedious papers; he knew what he wanted to say and said it concisely.

Sunday, 5 February, brought to an end a whole week of activities which revolved around the visit of the Fleet, and the social functions were not the least of the life of the Rock. The Navy were certainly energetic dancers and I found the late parties very tiring. I don't know how people manage to do their work as well, but I suppose they are necessary to make the world go round or people would have no regard for them.

On Monday morning I sailed with Rear-Admiral Wilmot Nicholson in the *Curacoa* for Pollensa Bay and exercises with the Mediterranean Fleet.

CHAPTER VI

The Mediterranean Fleet

The exercise to be carried out after leaving Gibraltar was to be the most important of the cruise, bringing together all the capital ships then in commission in the Navy with a total strength of 26,000 men. The idea was to test the power of aircraft in reconnaissance when carried with the Fleet. I was glad to have the opportunity of seeing the big ships operating from the viewpoint of the cruiser *Curacoa* in which my old friend Admiral Wilmot Nicholson was flying his flag. The Mediterranean Fleet based on Malta was to effect a junction with a weaker friendly fleet based upon Gibraltar. The Atlantic Fleet, based upon Pollensa Bay, Majorca, was to try and prevent this junction and to defeat the two hostile fleets in detail. It was exactly the sort of scheme we used to employ on land to produce what we called an encounter battle.

Considering the importance of the test being carried out the number of aircraft available in the two fleets was pitiably small. The Atlantic Fleet had *Argus* with only six of her Panthers fit for service, while the Mediterranean Fleet had the small carrier *Pegasus* with no facilities for deck landings. She carried flying boats and a few aircraft fitted with floats, which could land on the sea if the weather was good. The plans for this exercise made me recall my experiences recently in the Middle East with regard to the relations between the Army and the RAF. The war of 1914–18 had led to the creation of the RAF, but by government decree neither the Navy nor the Army were to be allowed to develop their own service aircraft for the future. This was to apply rigidly to the most intimate services, such as artillery observation, transportation of officers and other small duties. I had been considering for a long time how the Army would be affected. Soldiers have often been accused of being retrograde in thought, but this new theory would now prevent them from becoming air-minded. However, to my way of thinking there was a more dangerous side to this theory, which was that the RAF were contemplating a new form of warfare which would supersede all others. This was the bombing of everything on the ground which made modern war possible—factories, military establishments, naval dockyards and the like. They also talked of attacking the morale of enemy people. Fleets and armies were now things of the past. It appeared to me that the RAF were drifting apart from the two sister services and we were told that if air duties were necessary they would be carried out by RAF personnel. Already the Air Ministry were recruiting machine-gunners for service in Mesopotamia to supplement their force of armoured cars and tanks. They had also secured the services of commanders RN to run some of their gunboats and it was clear that they were having to create their own army and navy to replace that which had been withdrawn, thus defeating the real object of the change, which was to save personnel and money by policing the territory with aircraft only.

February 6 and 7 were occupied by the Atlantic Fleet getting into position at Pollensa Bay to be ready for the exercise which was to commence at midnight on 7th. As we steamed up the coast of Spain we were given a wonderful view of the mountains still covered with snow, and the Fleet carried out various manoeuvres on the way. Once again I was struck by the crowd of people on the bridge of the *Curacoa*. At one time I counted twenty-five, and movement by the Admiral and the Flag Captain was often difficult, though it was wonderful how the other officers and ratings stayed put so as not to impede them.

The encounter came off unexpectedly, as so often happens in similar schemes on land, and the Mediterranean Fleet was unable to join up with its friendly force, which ran into the tail of the Atlantic Fleet and was judged to have been put out of action. I saw little air reconnaissance although the day was beautiful. In fact *Argus* had been left with only three planes serviceable and *Pegasus* had to stop to get her flying boats hoisted aboard again.

After the exercise the two fleets formed up together and it was a very fine sight to see three divisions of battleships, preceded by the *Hood* and *Repulse*, with a great herd of destroyers led by the light cruiser *Curacoa*.

The main exercise to follow was the daylight destroyer attack on the Fleet and I had a most excellent view of the whole affair. The destroyers carried out their attack under a series of smoke screens covering their approach and withdrawal, and it was during one of these manoeuvres that I saw the destroyer closest to us heel over into a tight turn unexpectedly, and almost immediately afterwards a submarine surfaced on our bows with a strong list to starboard and a damaged conning tower. There was a lightning reaction from Rowley-Conwy, the Flag Captain of the *Curacoa*, who was a bit of a naval character and also reputed to be a fine seaman. He certainly proved himself to be so in the situation which now faced him. I was standing close to him on the bridge and I have never seen a man react more quickly than he did. The submarine was now close to us, still circling slowly like a blinded beast. His first order was the somewhat unconventional one of, 'Quit fooling', which announced that the exercise was over as far as his ship was concerned. A boat was lowered and within a few minutes three men were hacking away with axes at the badly damaged conning-tower and cutting with saws at some of the broken metal. We could plainly see the number on the conning-tower, *H.24* and also three large gashes in the outer hull just abaft of it. He took the *Curacoa* to windward and drifted slowly down towards the submarine and a steel cable was passed under her hull to support her.

Within ten minutes we saw the head of a submarine officer appear with a smile on his face, hailing us with the words that all was well. Several of the submarine's crew then emerged on her deck and none of them seemed to have been affected by what they had been through. To me it was all a fine example of discipline. No shouting or chattering. Instant obedience to orders. Within half an hour we were towing the damaged ship out of action.

Later at Pollensa I visited the *Maidstone*, the depot ship of these submarines. The commanders of these small 'H'-class ships were all young men glorifying in their first commands. I found they all had a firm belief in larger and more powerful ships, capable of remaining at sea for long periods. Theirs was a dangerous trade, but there appeared to be no lack of applicants for service in it.

During the night the destroyer attacks were continued, helped by the light of starshells. Of these there were several that failed to burn, and one of which struck the *Curacoa* but did no damage. Shortly after midnight the sea was dotted with little lights from the torpedoes which had finished their runs, and long after we had dropped anchor at Pollensa Bay the destroyers were still searching for them.

The great natural harbour of Pollensa held the two fleets and had room for many more besides. I was allowed to go up in a seaplane and take photographs of the assembled company. The immense length of the *Hood* and *Repulse* compared with the other ships stood out clearly.

For me there were two great historic events at Pollensa. A dinner in the *QE* for all the senior officers of the two fleets and an At Home for all officers of whom there must have been six or seven hundred present on the quarterdeck of the ship. I must have met the flower of the officers then serving in the Navy. There were many old friends, amongst whom there were some of my old CMB officers who had served on the Dwina in North Russia. I found it difficult to pick out those who impressed me most.

CHAPTER VII

HMS *Argus*

On 19 February I boarded the *Argus* for my long-awaited trip in the Navy's new carrier which was going to carry out exercises whilst on passage to Malta. I knew how anxious the Navy were to make a success of this experimental vessel of theirs and they stoutly refused to believe that any naval force which depended upon land-based aeroplanes for air support could do their work at sea. They wished to prove that they could and would take their mobile aerodromes with them. Unfortunately for the fairness of the trial, the Air Ministry refused to agree to the Navy having their own aircraft. They insisted that all flying personnel and all mechanics in the carrier must be of the RAF. The Navy disliked this. They meant to have their old air service back again, however long they had to fight for it.

I received a warm welcome from the skipper of the *Argus*, Captain Stirling, RN, a lean, sandy-haired Scot with a limp which was the result of a wound in China. He had been chosen for his considerable experience with the old Naval Air Service on the Belgian coast. I passed through the ship's main hangar as I boarded her to reach the Captain's quarters. She gave one the idea of spaciousness and it was obvious that the men on board were better lodged and looked after than those in a fighting ship. But as my stay on board lengthened she gave me another strong impression of a different kind. She carried men of two different breeds on board. They did not mix. They dressed differently and kept different hours. One did not see them hob-nobbing together. One breed were the sailors, the crew and the others were the passengers.

The machines which were being used on board were Panthers,

also very much experimental. The pilots were ordinary commissioned officers of the RAF, while the observers were ex-naval yeomen of signals, who had been given short-term commissions in the RAF and wore RAF uniform. These naval men were of course expert signallers, well able to keep in touch with the ship when in the air on reconnaissance. None of them were trained as pilots and there was no dual control if the pilot was injured.

The Captain lived by himself, but all the other officers of both services lived together in one mess. Here there was much good fellowship and a good deal too much drinking, which increased on the days when there was little flying owing to the weather. Pilots discussed the number of deck landings they had made. Taking off was easy, but landings on the carrier were much more dangerous than landings on an aerodrome, and I noticed the nerves and tempers of the flying personnel were getting frayed towards the end of the voyage. Stirling was very doubtful whether the RAF would be able to keep up a supply of the very best pilots together with the many other duties that they had assumed. I had already seen how the Royal Artillery had suffered in the war owing to the lack of trained observers.

The purpose of the exercise was for the cruiser *Dragon* to try and destroy the carrier, which had become temporarily separated from the fleet. One could see how easy it was for the *Argus* to become separated from the rest of the fleet when one realized that she had to keep her head to the wind whilst she was flying off or landing on aircraft. She could therefore be steaming for long periods of time in a completely different direction from the Fleet.

The day reconnaissances had begun at 5.30 am, and the five planes had returned by 7.00 am. It was only when the last two planes had returned that the *Dragon* had been accurately located. From that time onwards no reconnaissance plane was in the air to watch the cruiser's further movements.

The next operation was to get off three planes to carry out a bomb-attack against her. It took a matter of twenty-one minutes to get these three planes off in consort. The attack was duly carried out, and the cruiser was adjudged to have been seriously damaged and only able to steam at half-speed.

The tactics were quite new, but to my mind it seemed sheer folly for the Air Ministry to demand any control over naval weapons of war. It would take years to bring these carriers to perfection in their varied duties—reconnaissance against surface and submarine vessels, gun-spotting and attacks by torpedo, machine-gun and bomb. With dual control the improvement of the carriers would be slowed up. The theory held by the Air Ministry violated the principle that the user must have the final say in the making of the weapons he has to use.

On the 22nd the weather suddenly changed. It began to rain heavily, and visibility fell so low that all flying was abandoned. Our last precious day of training was lost.

We entered the Grand Harbour of Malta during the afternoon.

We were going to remain a month in Malta, and I had been considering how I should get as much information about the island as I could. I was lucky to find the Chief Administrative officer a Gunner, A. F. U. Green, and the CRE an old friend of South African days. The Governor, Lord Plumer, under whom I had served in subordinate positions in France, was away. When he came back and I presented myself to him, I found he was somewhat suspicious of what I was doing in Malta. He seemed to think that I had been given some sort of mission from the War Office, and it took me some time to convince him that I had suffered a bad aeroplane crash in Mesopotamia, and that I was on a voyage of convalescence at the invitation of Sir Charles Madden. I had jumped at the invitation, as I had been appointed Commandant of the Staff College and wished to see as much of the Navy as I could, before I joined on 1 May. He told me that I should find little of interest in the way of military fortification in the island. The garrison could accommodate five battalions of infantry, which had always been regarded as an Imperial reserve. But now conditions had changed. Battalions could be trained in Malta only up to a certain point, and they could not be made ready to go and fight in any part of the world without quite a lengthy training. Malta offered many advantages for musketry and work with the Navy, but for mobile warfare under modern conditions there were no advantages. He told me that there was no fortress in Malta, even such a one as existed in Gibraltar. He

20 Quarterdeck of the *Queen Elizabeth*.

21 Taking the submarine *H.24* in tow after it had been run down by a destroyer.

22 On bord the *Queen Elizabeth*. *Seated, centre:* Lord and Lady Plumer and Admiral Sir Charles Madden.

23 The fleet at Pollensa Bay, Majorca. *Argus* centre foreground.

gave me full permission to go where I wished, and hoped that I would come and see him before I left to tell him what I thought of it all.

Malta was, in fact, another naval station on our communications through the Mediterranean, with a magnificent land-locked harbour and a large dockyard with plenty of local labour. As day by day I wandered over the island I saw its stark military nakedness. For its security, like Gibraltar, it depended first upon the strength of the British Fleet. Again, it held an isolated position like Gibraltar, and had emerged from the Great War where Italy had been our ally, without mishap. Italy possessed a modern fleet, a sizeable air force and a large army, and was likely to prove a much more formidable enemy than Spain in the event of her being our enemy. The use of the naval station at Malta depended very much on the goodwill of Italy.

I decided to start with the air defence of the island first. At Cala Frana there was an RAF establishment for a squardon of flying boats, under Air-Commodore Sampson, who had been a naval officer in his younger days. He was very proud of his command, but told me quite frankly that his boats were in no way able to deal with modern land-based aircraft. They were slow, heavy and incapable of fighting in the air. Their chief use was in work with a fleet at sea or for transporting troops. He took me up to a small landing-ground which was being built above his station. It would be a year before it was fit to accommodate the fighter aircraft, which were essential for the defence of the island. I could see that the landing-ground was small, but there was room for constructing underground cover for the planes in the rocks which surrounded it.

I then ran across a curious line of defence, which had been constructed between the years 1860 and 1890. It consisted of several small forts joined by a high wall, which was intended to cut off the western and more uninhabited part of the island, if an enemy made a landing there. There was little deep cover in the forts and the wall was now nothing but a hindrance. There were good roads and with motor transport there would be no difficulty in moving troops quickly to any threatened point. What with the presence of the British Fleet, mobile light field-guns, mines and barbed wire, landings by any but the best troops accustomed to such operations were not likely to succeed.

A very modest beginning had been made with the AA defence of the island.

At that date, I did not conceive that it was possible to put up such a defence as the island did in the War of '39. That it was successful reflects a very great glory upon the commanders and men of the three services and upon the people of the island themselves.

The season in Malta was a gay one, all very new to me, for I had seen little of such life in my twenty-three years in the Army. For more than thirteen of those years I had been either on active service or in the rough regions of the world. Though there was a succession of parties, dinners and luncheons, the Navy worked hard. One squadron or another was out for days at a time on various operations, and in these I was asked to join. Yachting parties on cruises kept turning up, and many of the wives of the officers in the Atlantic Fleet came out overland to join in the festivities. I was asked to lecture to the garrison on North Russia, and to many naval gatherings on life in the Army. It was all very enjoyable. My broken legs were mending well and I could now walk for long periods without discomfort. I had quite recovered from any shock caused by my crash.

I was especially glad to find the Gordon Highlanders in Malta. A whole batch of young officers had joined since they were under me at Ismid, and the battalion was commanded by Colonel Ogston, with whom I had served on the Staff of the 6th Division in France. When I dined with them in mess, all their silver was paraded on the table and the pipers played throughout the evening, finishing with several sets of reels. The officers were wearing the new mess-kit, which I thought a very poor substitute for the old one. The jacket seemed to be a sort of tail-coat with half the tails cut off. The officers were all wearing trews and I never saw what it looked like with a kilt. I had an amusing bet with Ogston after dinner. I bet him half-a-crown that he must have an Ironside in the regiment, and he, thinking I meant an officer, told me that I was wrong. When we called in the Sergeant-Major he told me that I was correct. They had in the battalion a newly joined recruit from Buchan named William Ironside. He came from a farm named Bonnykelly. He was duly sent for and I had a talk with him.

The Gordons had an interesting connection with Malta. I found a little monument in the Malmaison gardens, erected by six sergeants of the 75th, Slater, Armstrong, Clarke, Pitman, Fitzgerald and Young in 1881. Two of them were killed shortly afterwards in the Egyptian campaign. It bore the following epigraph:

> Here lie the poor old 75th
> But under God's protection
> They'll rise again in kilt and hose
> A glorious resurrection
> For by the transformation power
> Of parliamentary laws
> We go to bed the 75th
> And rise the Ninety-twas.

Had I not been a Gunner I should have liked to be in the Ninety-twas.

The papers from England were full of all the difficulties we were having in Ireland, in India and with the Bolsheviks in Russia, but I must confess that in the life I was leading I could not feel more than distantly concerned, at least until 26 March when I left Malta for the return trip to England, again aboard the *Queen Elizabeth*.

CHAPTER VIII

Return Trip

I was very glad to get away from Malta after spending a little over a month aboard the QE moored in Grand Harbour. After a short stop at Syracuse the QE reached Gibraltar on 30 March. It was only a brief stay and she was on her way again the next day bound for Vigo, where I received an official letter confirming that I was to take up my appointment at the Staff College on 1 May. By that date I would have completed 11 months on half-pay. The ship left Vigo on 7 April for the last leg of the return journey, which would include air exercises in the channel, and I hoped that the good weather would hold out for these.

The C-in-C was interesting in what he said about torpedo plane attacks against the battleships. He said that in the past when exercising the Fleet he had always made it easy for the plane. Parliament and the Air Ministry were putting forward the most extravagant claims for the possibilities of air warfare and he could no longer sacrifice the reputation of the Fleet. He would now adopt the proper formation with screens of light craft to make it more difficult for the planes to attack the main fleet.

The ship reached Torquay on 9 April and I was not sorry to be back in England again with the thought of getting back to work once more. However, the trip was not quite over and the Fleet proceeded up the channel for the final exercise on 10 April with the First Lord of the Admiralty on board. In the exercise the Fleet was to be attacked by land-based torpedo-carrying aircraft organized by the RAF. I was impressed by the way the attack was delivered and pressed home. It certainly surprised the First Lord, who had never seen anything like it before, and the naval staff were very impressed. If the attack had been carried out in larger numbers it would have been even more decisive.

Unfortunately the senior staff of the RAF were unable to witness this success as the Air Marshal in charge of the operation failed to get to the scene of the attack owing to his pilot having missed the way. The Chief of the Air Force Staff College (Brooke-Popham) went out in a destroyer, was sick the whole time and so saw nothing. I was told afterwards that the Air Ministry was unable to obtain a report from their own people and this resulted in an amusing letter to me from Trenchard in which he said: '. . . that you were on a battleship that was attacked by aircraft off the Isle of Wight and I hear that you were impressed. Is it too much to ask you to give me your ideas about it from the point of view of a layman . . . just your impression on what you saw and what chance they had in your opinion of doing it without a great number of casualties. I won't use your report, but I am trying to get all the reports I can from people who are not experts, but have common sense. . . .' After all my years of fighting and commanding large air forces of aircraft I felt that I was least of all a layman!

On coming alongside South Railway Jetty at Portsmouth Harbour on 11 April there ended my trip with the Navy, and I reflected on the moment a year before when I was lying in the desert near Samawah with broken thighs and cursing my luck with the pilot of the crashed plane trying to prop me up. I had never felt any pain either then or later in hospital and was told that it would be a year before I was really fit again.

Had I not been smashed up I should still have been out in Mesopotamia and handing over to an Air Force officer about December. This was to my mind not a very high prospect and nothing to compare with going to command the Staff College. As it turned out I had experienced thirteen months of inaction and eleven months of half-pay, but the rest had probably been good for me and the last three months with the Navy did me exceedingly well both in health and experience. I had been fortunate in meeting Madden and through him to live with and experience the Fleet at work. He was certainly head and shoulders above any other Flag Officer I had met. On leaving the QE the guard and band turned out to give me a salute and all the officers were there to see me off. I was soon home at The Old Mill Cottage, finding all was well with my family.

Q

Epilogue

The Epilogue to this book was uncompleted when I went through my father's papers after his death, but there is no doubt that Camberley opened up a new phase in his career after something like eight years of continuous active military service, most of it spent fighting. It was the prelude to a long period of peacetime generalship, filled with further periods of half-pay and appointments which were better known for their retirement than their promotional prospects. He started to write as follows:

'The office of the Commandant of the Staff College at Camberley is a large and pleasant room, situated on the right of the main entrance into the building. In term-time visitors were not encouraged to bring their cars to this entrance during the morning, for fear of distracting the students in the front rooms. The office was a peaceful place in which to work...'

That was as far as he got.

He was told about the appointment by the CIGS on 12 August, 1921, the Glorious Twelfth indeed for him as he writes: 'Of all the things of which I had thought, that was the most unexpected. I really had no inkling that they could choose me for such a thing. I told him I was sure that I could make the show a human one. He said to me that I was one of the few people in the Army who had the chance of rising to the highest rank. I had plenty of experience in commanding but that the other side was necessary. Thinking the thing over professionally I could not have been offered a greater honour, especially when one thinks that my immediate predecessors have been Rawlinson, Henry Wilson, Robertson Kiggell and then Anderson. I am being offered the appointment at 10 to 15 years earlier in proportion to the time they got it. It will give one just the time necessary to digest all the stuff I have been accumulating during the war. It is a great responsibility to have the training of future generations of soldiers upon my shoulders. I have the feeling that I have not served my apprenticeship in vain. . . .

'I cannot complain about my luck, anyway. It has been thoroughly with me in not getting me wounded or sick just at the moment I was being put up in temporary rank. I shall now devote myself to the training of officers and men. Education and training; that must be my work in the future.'

Appendix

Instructions given by the Supreme Council to the Inter-Allied Mission under the Presidency of Major-General Sir Edmund Ironside, K.C.B., C.M.G., D.S.O., which is to supervise the Evacuation of Hungary by the Roumanian troops in accordance with the decision of the Supreme Council of the 26th February.

---

1. The present situation may be briefly summarised as follows (map 'A' attached):

The Roumanians have 3 Infantry and 2 Cavalry Divisions in the area to be evacuated East of the River Theiss.

The *total* strength of the *Hungarian* Army is not more than 25,000 men. (For approximate distribution on 23.1.20 see map 'B'.) About 3,000 men were despatched towards the River Theiss about February 9th to maintain order when the Roumanian troops evacuate. The Hungarian troops were not to cross the River without the authorisation of the Inter-Allied Military Mission (Headquarters at Budapest) which is supervising their movements.

2. An Inter-Allied Commission of military Experts is being formed to supervise the evacuation by the Roumanians and occupation by the Hungarians of the Trans-Theiss region of Hungary.

3. Under the authority of the Supreme Council you are appointed British Military expert on this Commission.

You will be assisted by French and Italian Representatives who are being appointed by their respective Governments without delay.

4. The object of the Commission is:

    (a) To fix a time limit within which the troops and Depots of the Roumanian Army should be withdrawn from Hungarian territory. This is to be done by fixing various stages of withdrawal.

    (b) To safeguard the interests of all the inhabitants of the territory to be evacuated by the Roumanians. You should in particular examine the situation of the Slovak population of Békéscsaba and report on what steps can be taken to safeguard their interest.

    (c) To carry out any such further duties in connection with the evacuation of Hungary as may be assigned to them by the Supreme Council.

5. The Roumanian Government state that action as regards evacuation has been delayed for the following reasons:

    (a) Difficulty in clearing food and clothing Depots formed in the occupied territory—the clearance of the depots has been commenced.

    (b) Transport difficulties, wintry weather and lack of fuel.

    (c) Want of accommodation for the troops.

    (d) Need for evacuating Roumanian and Czecho-Slovak Nationals.

    (e) Necessity for holding on to certain strategic points on account of the alleged hostile intentions of the Hungarians.

6. The Hungarian Government profess anxiety as to the probable treatment by the Roumanians of Hungarian Nationals during the evacuation, and are apprehensive lest anti-Jew riots should break out, Particularly in DEBREZCEN, because the Jews were on good terms with the Roumanians who are alleged to have behaved harshly towards the bulk of the population.

7. It is considered that, in the first instance, you should get into touch with the Roumanian General Staff and Army Headquarters at Bucarest and also with Admiral Horthy's Headquarters at Budapest, regarding conditions generally in the territory to be evacuated.

At Bucharest, Mr. Rattigan, Chargé d'Affaires, and Colonel Duncan, Military Attaché, and at Budapest, Mr. Hohler, Chargé d'Affaires and Brigadier General Gorton, Inter-Allied Military Mission, will be able to assist you. Subsequently it will be necessary to establish your Headquarters in the territory to be evacuated, in order that you may be free from outside influence and able to take an impartial view of conditions.

8. Periodical reports should be furnished to the Foreign Office to include matters of general interest, but describing in particular progress made in their withdrawal by the Roumanians. A copy of such reports should be sent direct to the War Office.

INDEX